Cognition and Sex Difference

Cognition and Sex Differences

Colin Hamilton

First published 2008 by
PALGRAVE MACMILLAN
Houndmills, Basingstoke, Hampshire RG21 6XS and
175 Fifth Avenue, New York, N.Y. 10010
Companies and representatives throughout the world

PALGRAVE MACMILLAN is the global academic imprint of the Palgrave Macmillan division of St. Martin's Press, LLC and of Palgrave Macmillan Ltd. Macmillan® is a registered trademark in the United States, United Kingdom and other countries. Palgrave is a registered trademark in the European Union and other countries.

ISBN-13: 978–1–4039–0017–3   hardback
ISBN-10: 1–4039–0017–5   hardback
ISBN-13: 978–1–4039–0018–0   paperback
ISBN-10: 1–4039–0018–3   paperback

This book is printed on paper suitable for recycling and made from fully managed and sustained forest sources. Logging, pulping and manufacturing processes are expected to conform to the environmental regulations of the country of origin.

Library of Congress Cataloging-in-Publication Data
    Hamilton, Colin.
    Cognition and sex differences/Colin Hamilton.
       p.cm.
    Includes index.
    ISBN 1-4039-0017-5 (alk. paper)
    1. Cognition 2. Sex differences (Psychology) I. Title.
    BF311.H3133 2007
    155.3'3—dc22   2007040779

A catalog record for this book is available from the Library of Congress.

10 9 8 7 6 5 4 3 2 1
17 16 15 14 13 12 11 10 09 08

Printed and bound in China

Contents

List of Figures

List of Tables

Part I
Introduction

1 Rationale, Issues and Overview

Introduction

The aim of this introductory chapter is to discuss the major rationales of this book, to identify some of the most relevant issues in the research discussed by the text and to make explicit the organizational framework of the book.

The conventional individual-differences approach considers task perform-ance as the focus of the research, employing statistical tools such as factor analysis and meta-analysis. The next section of this chapter makes an argu-ment for a *process-oriented* approach where the aim of the research is to identify and understand the individual differences in the underlying cognitive processes demanded by a particular task. The organization of this textbook adopts this perspective. The chapters in Part II, where the first major empirical findings are discussed, each begin with a brief outline of the cognitive processes discussed in that particular chapter. These chapters thus are cognitively driven, and explicitly attempt to place individual differences within a cognition framework.

In the subsequent components of this chapter, the issues relating to the use of the terms *sex* and *gender* will be discussed. While many social scien-tists would employ these terms synonymously, it is argued that sex and gen-der should not be considered as equivalent constructs in the psychological literature. Thus research will be discussed where gender, as (predominantly) a socially constructed process, may vary within the sexes. Consequently, the notion of gender as a within-sex variable emphasizes individual differences beyond those associated with any differences between men and women. The chapter is developed with a discussion of two issues highly pertinent to the understanding of individual-differences research. The socio-political context in which individual-differences research is carried out has led to some psychologists suggesting that such research should not be carried out. This component of the chapter identifies some of the issues associated with this debate. In addition, some of the methodological issues associated with individual-differences research will be considered, for example the inferen-tial constraints associated with non-experimental research.

The final element of the chapter is a brief account of the organizational framework of the book. Part II of the book considers the individual differences associated with men and women in cognitive processing, for example perception, attention, imagery and memory. Part III emphasizes individual differences associated with within-sex differences, for example gender characteristics, hormonal influences and lifespan processes. Finally Part IV identifies the major theoretical approaches within the field – evolutionary, socio-cultural and, interactionist – before ending with a chapter which puts forward a synthesis of the theoretical accounts and suggests possible ways for the research.

Task Performance Versus Process Measurement

The conventional psychometric approach to individual differences emphasizes the relationship between performances across a number of tasks (see Deary 2001). Analysis of this form of data can be with factor analysis or with meta-analysis where individual differences in task performance across a number of research studies are summarized in a quantitative manner (see Rosenthal 1991). Examples of meta-analytic publications investigating sex differences in visuo-spatial cognition are Linn and Petersen (1985) and Voyer *et al.* (1995). Voyer *et al.* considered sex differences in three different spatial abilities: *mental rotation, spatial perception* and *spatial visualization*. The cognitive processes contributing to these tasks will be discussed in detail throughout Parts II and III.

One feature of the traditional approach is the use of factor analysis to identify cognitive tasks which share common cognitive resources. Table 1.1 gives a simplified schematic representation. The table identifies a set of verbal (V) and spatial (S) tasks and the correlation pattern which exists between the task performances.

Table 1.1 indicates that there appears to be only a relatively small correlation between all of the tasks; should this relationship be significant then this would be an indication of what is called 'little g', a general measure of intelligence. However, there appears to be a stronger correlation within the verbal tasks, indicated by the dotted circle pattern, and within the spatial tasks, indicated by the dashed circle pattern. This suggests the presence of two main factors. This pattern, evidenced in much of the earlier psychometric literature (Kline 1991), would suggest that intellectual ability is composed of verbal and spatial factors. A closer look at the pattern indicates that within the verbal and the spatial tasks there appear to be differences in the strength of the relationship. The correlation matrix suggests that the two verbal tasks, V1 and V3, are strongly related with one another but not so strongly with the V2 task. The S1 and S2 Tasks also show a strong correlation with one another but not so strongly with S3.

This finer pattern indicates that within the verbal and the spatial domain there are distinct forms of verbal and spatial abilities. This has been the pattern

Table 1.1 A schematic representation of the factor analysis process

Task labels	V1	S1	S2	V2	S3	V3
V1	–	+0.28	+.030	+0.52	+0.21	+0.78
S1		–	+0.75	+0.19	+0.43	+0.20
S2			–	+0.21	+0.48	+0.22
V2				–	+0.33	+0.51
S3					–	+0.18
V3						–

found in recent meta-analytic studies (McGee 1979; Linn and Petersen 1985; Voyer *et al.* 1995). Caplan and Caplan (1997b) identified close to 40 different measures of verbal ability discussed in the literature. The findings suggesting that verbal and spatial abilities are diverse and complex have led to the suggestion that a substantial number of individual-differences studies have employed tasks with dubious or unknown construct validity (Caplan and Caplan 1997b).

In contrast, much research has focused upon the underlying cognitive processes; thus Pezaris and Casey (1991) looked at the impact of concurrent verbal and spatial interference upon mental rotation task performance in young women. Their interest lay not in task performance *per se*, but in the strategies that the young women employed in the task. This is an example of individual-differences research which is 'process-oriented' (Halpern and Wright 1996). Another example of this approach to be discussed in Chapter 3 ('Attention and Memory') is the research by Loring-Meier and Halpern (1999), which looked at the performance of women and men in specific visuo-spatial imagery and working memory processes.

However, a brief historical consideration of many of the studies that have looked at men and women's cognitive performance does suggest that the 'process-oriented' approach is difficult to apply. The major reason for this is likely to arise from the complexity of the tasks traditionally given to the participants in the research. Without a fine task analysis and manipulation it may be possible to identify a difference in performance of men and women in a task but not know where in the cognitive demands these similarities or differences are occurring. An illustration of this difficulty can be derived from a consideration of an early sex-differences study on spatial memory.

Silverman and Eals (1994) discussed a 'spatial memory' task in which the women in the research achieved a higher performance level than the men.

The task involved the participants scanning an array of a large number of common objects for a fixed period of time; subsequently, a new display either showed the original display with some new objects, or the original display with some of the objects having exchanged position (see Chapter 3, Figure 3.6 for a more detailed view of this procedure). The participant's task was to either identify the new objects or identify the exchanged objects. What are the cognitive processes involved in this task procedure?

In the initial phase various cognitive processes appear to be at work: visual attention to the array, a visuospatial working memory representation of the objects and their location, a verbal working memory representation of the nameable objects. Subsequently (or concurrently), long-term memory representations of these visuospatial and verbal features will be constructed and finally there is retrieval from long-term memory of these features. Thus precisely which cognitive process or processes contribute to the findings of higher memory performance in women?

According to Eals and Silverman and others (Cherney and Ryalls 1999; Kimura 1999) the advantage for women is one of spatial memory, though these authors do not dissociate working memory processes from spatial long-term memory processes. Other authors with a slightly different task procedure (Postma and De Haan 1996) emphasize spatial working memory processes. James and Kimura (1997) attribute the advantage for women, in part, to their efficiency in the verbal representation of the objects in the array. Yet more authors (McGivern *et al.* 1997) attribute the difference in performance to an advantage in women's attention early in the task procedure. The diversity of these interpretations may be a direct consequence of the diverse cognitive demands of the task. In order to determine whether it is attention, working memory or long-term memory processes underpinning the observed differences in performance a research procedure with task analysis stages is required.

A final issue related to this approach lies in the conventional emphasis upon *differences* in task performance between women and men. However, when the emphasis is process-oriented, differences in task performance are not the only informative outcome or even the desirable one. A study by Hamilton (1995) employed a sample of women and men who undertook two visuospatial tasks: mental rotation and embedded figures (see the discussions of cognitive processes in perception and imagery task performance in Chapters 2 and 4). The results suggested a significant difference in performance in the former task but not in the latter. This dissociation of performance supports the suggestion that there is unlikely to be a generic spatial ability difference between men and women (Voyer *et al.* 1995). The presence *and* absence of individual differences in these two tasks focuses subsequent research attention on a consideration of the individual differences associated with the particular cognitive processes employed in these tasks. Thus the dynamic spatial processes that are important for mental rotation task performance appear to elicit individual differences associated with the women and men in the sample while the differing cognitive processes underlying embedded figures do not result in such differences.

In some research contexts where one is investigating individual differences associated with men and women an absence of difference in performance may actually be preferable. Imagine the case where in a particular reasoning task the findings suggest that women display a higher level of performance than the sample of men. The researcher's principal aim is to identify whether men and women differ in their use of some verbal strategy when carrying out the task. The data indicate that indeed there is a sex difference in verbal strategy use, with women using the strategy more frequently. Does this finding indicate a genuine difference in strategy use between men and women? In fact such an interpretation may be confounded by the performance difference in the study. In order to be more confident that it is a genuine difference between the women and the men in strategy use, it would be more appropriate to make the comparison when performance level is equivalent.

Individual Differences Associated with Sex and with Gender

A further issue to consider at this point is the labelling of women and men with the terms 'gender' or 'sex'. The conventional approach is to associate the label 'sex' with the biological distinctions between men and women, based upon the differences in anatomy, physiology and so forth. Gender is typically perceived as a social construction derived from the characteristics a particular culture stereotypically associates with the two sexes (Unger 1979). The usage of the terms is contrasted in two textbook publications in the area. In Halpern (1992), the emphasis is upon 'sex differences', the author justifying her use of the label early in the volume:

> I have decided to use the term sex to refer to both biological and psychosocial aspects of the differences between men and women because these two aspects of human existence are so closely coupled in our society. (p. 18)

Caplan *et al.* (1997) adopt the alternative label 'gender differences', and posit a different justification:

> In most psychological research (but not all) it is appropriate to talk of 'gender differences' rather than 'sex differences,' because the participants are categorized on the basis of their outward appearance and behavior, not on the basis of biological characteristics. (p. 7)

In the social sciences, and in the UK media, 'gender' is the label most frequently employed (see Pryzgoda and Chrisler 2000 for the presence of ambivalent lay perceptions of the term 'gender'). However, in particular psychological research contexts 'gender' cannot be treated as a more appropriate label for 'sex'. This is in the context where inventories or questionnaire measures are employed to identify gender-characteristic possession, for example with the use of the Bem Sex Role Inventory (BSRI; Bem 1974). Table 1.2 drawn from Hamilton (1995) indicates the association between the gender characteristics and the sex of the participants in this study.

Statistically, there may be an association between sex and gender as Halpern (1992) suggests above; however, it also clear from Table 1.2 that most women and men do not appear to perceive themselves as possessing the congruent gender characteristics. Thus while a statistical association may exist, gender-characteristic possession is clearly not the same as biological sex. These results suggest that 'sex' and 'gender' should not always be considered as synonyms for one another. In this book, gender (trait) measurement forms the focus of Chapter 6, the first chapter in Part III, which attempts to account for individual differences within men and within women. It is not appropriate to use 'gender' when it refers to men or women during Part II and then in Part III employ the term to refer to psychological constructs such as masculinity or femininity within either sex. Accordingly, in this book 'gender' will subsequently be used consistently to identify the psychological characteristics measured by tools such as the BSRI. 'Sex' will be employed when referring to women and men.

This use of 'sex' could be construed as implying a biological or *essentialist* characteristic in the text discussion (Hare-Mustin and Marecek 1994). However, the theoretical discussions in Chapters 11 and 12 emphasize the intimate interaction between life experiences and *experience-dependent* brain processes. This focus emphasizes the potentially dynamic process of neural plasticity. Within this context there should therefore be no motivation to consider the use of any label as implying an essentialist approach. By perceiving gender as a within-sex construct the text emphasis is in the opposite direction, that is both women and men possess the potential to be variable in their adoption and expression of gender characteristics.

The initial focus in this book will be on the consideration of individual differences, associated with sex differences, in cognition. However, this emphasis

Table 1.2   The association between the gender trait characteristics (BSRI measure) and the sex of participant

Gender Sex	Undifferentiated	Androgynous	Masculine	Feminine
Women	28 22.5%	24 19%	28 22.5%	45 36%
Men	10 18.5%	17 31.5%	19 35%	8 15%

will be supplemented by a framing of the research within a broader individual-differences context where within-sex variability will be considered. Gender, the possession of stereotypically masculine and feminine characteristics, will be the first major factor to be discussed as a source of within-sex variation. The advantages associated with the inclusion of a within-sex account of individual differences are briefly discussed below.

Between-Sex and Within-Sex Approaches in Cognition

The conventional approach to individual-differences research as identified above is to consider performance at the task level. However, one of the major themes of this textbook will be the focus upon the underlying cognitive processes. The second major emphasis of the textbook is the embedding of between-sex differences within a broader context where individual differences associated with within-sex processes are given equal consideration in the discussion. This rationale is illustrated by a consideration of Figures 1.1 and 1.2.

Figure 1.1 displays the performance of a sample of 929 participants undertaking a cognitive task, a mental rotation task (MRT); the figure shows the mean scores and standard errors for 593 women and 336 men. Hamilton (1995) considers a sample of these data with this procedure in more detail.

The representation of the findings in this manner would indeed support the suggestion that men and women are quite distinct and that in addition there is little variability within men and within women in their task performance. As discussed earlier in the text, MRT performance does tend to reveal a large significant advantage for men (Voyer *et al.* 1995). However, the same data could be represented another way, as shown below in Figure 1.2. This representation of the data shows the idealized versions of the performance distributions of the women and men.

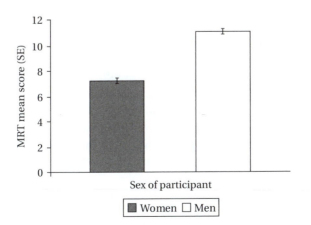

Figure 1.1   Mean MRT achievement in women and men

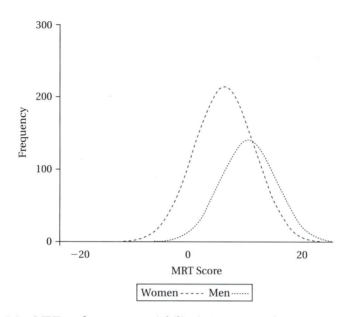

Figure 1.2   MRT performance variability in women and men

   The impression given by this data representation is that there is extensive
overlap in MRT performance between women and men. The distributions
also suggest extensive variability both between men and between women.
Figure 1.2 indicates that while sex appears to be an important variable in
explaining variance in task performance, there are also other variables,
within-sex factors, which account for the individual differences present in
MRT performance. Factors such as age, gender, hormonal balance, handedness, personality, social cognitions and so on contribute to within-sex factors. Thus a representation such as this emphasizes, in part, the similarities
between women and men (Hyde 2005)

The Context of Individual-Differences Research

Research is rarely carried out in a vacuum; it is placed within a theoretical
and/or empirical context. Research areas that focus upon individual differences
whether it is within women and men or within different ethnic groups have
elicited considerable concerns over the implicit agenda underlying the research.
The extent of the criticism of this research can be identified in the comments
of the following researchers. Hare-Mustin and Marecek (1994) suggested that:

> whatever the intentions of individual researchers, research cannot be neu-
> tral, value free or apolitical … assertions about sex difference have been
> used to argue women's inferiority, to limit their spheres of action, and to
> restrict their autonomy and freedom of movement. (p. 532)

Caplan and Caplan (1997a) stated:

> We hope that this chapter has illustrated the truly shoddy nature of the research that has been used to justify keeping women out of powerful, influential and often well-paid positions on the grounds that they lack the intellectual capacity to carry out the duties that these positions require. (p. 76)

For these psychologists the most important issues are related not to any individual differences in cognition, but rather to how the research has been employed to underpin and sustain a gendered society (Crawford and Chaffin 1997). This is part of the discussion over whether psychologists should study differences in cognition between women and men (Kitzinger 1994). For a more detailed consideration of this debate the reader is referred to a special issue of *Feminism and Psychology* (volume 4, number 4 1994), where psychologists debate the issue.

One of the major aims of this book is to place the study of men and women's cognition within the broader range of individual differences. While Part II of the book considers the similarities and differences between women and men, Part III considers individual differences between men and between women. The suggestion will be made that many of the factors proposed to underlie differences between men and women may also account for the individual differences within women or men. Figure 1.2 above sets this theme for the book, where common factors such as gender role, task expectation, hormones, handedness and so on may account for a variety of individual differences, regardless of the sex of the participant.

Difficulties with Non-Experimental Research Designs

In the field of individual differences, whether comparing young versus old, women versus men, visually impaired versus sighted, the groups being contrasted make up what is known as 'existing groups'. According to Neale and Liebert (1986) such a research design can never be a 'true experiment'. These authors suggest that the true experiment is 'one in which casual inference is made on the basis of random assignment, manipulation of relevant variables, and direct control over irrelevant variables' (p. 134). The three elements of this quote provide difficulties for research which aims to understand why men and women may differ in cognitive ability. A fictional example of a *true* experiment can provide the contrast with an individual-differences-based research design.

A researcher may be interested in the impact of a training programme upon the ability to perform a problem-solving task in physics, an ability which may be presumed to demand visuospatial processing. The researcher draws her sample from a population of Advanced Level science students in

England (typically 17- to 19-year-olds) and then randomly allocates, say by the toss of a coin, the students into one of two experimental conditions or levels. In the first experimental condition, students are exposed to a teaching technique aimed at developing visuospatial representation skills, while in the second they receive the normal teaching strategy associated with the physics topic.

Let us assume that the research finds a difference in problem-solving performance between the students in the two conditions. What would this researcher conclude? She would probably like to conclude that it was the experimental manipulation, practice versus no practice at visuospatial representation, which contributed to the problem-solving performance difference. However, we could readily imagine that numerous factors could impact upon the problem-solving performance, for example general intelligence, experience of relevant or related courses such as mathematics, or other science courses, enjoyment of the course and so forth. How confident can the researcher be that any of these factors have not contributed to the difference between the students in the two groups?

It is possible that the majority of the more intelligent students were placed into the condition where students' exam performance was greater; potentially students with the most relevant course experience could have been allocated to this condition. Therefore, when allocation to one or other condition is made, there is always the potential for participants possessing a relevant characteristic (to problem-solving performance) to be allocated disproportionately to one condition. The key to overcoming this concern is in the nature of the allocation to the experimental conditions; random allocation with a large sample should ensure that any relevant participant characteristic is as likely to be allocated to one condition as it is to the other condition. Thus random allocation is a way of ensuring control over these extraneous variables and allowing the researcher to make causal inferences from the findings; as such it is one of the most powerful tools the researcher possesses.

Now consider the situation when women and men are being compared in a physics problem-solving context. This 'existing groups' design means that the variable of interest, being a woman or man, is not under the manipulation of the researcher, the characteristic being one brought by the participants to the research. Random allocation to one of the conditions has therefore also been denied in this design. However, the numerous characteristics which affect problem-solving are still present in the women and men in the sample. Therefore, it is possible that these extraneous variables may not be distributed equally between the men and the women. Consequently, any observed difference in performance between the women and the men could be due to any (one or more) of these characteristics being disproportionately represented in the men or in the women. In this design context the researcher can still comment upon whether there is a difference in problem-solving but can no longer go on to infer *why* the difference occurred; a causal inference is now precluded.

The researcher may consider that the most appropriate methodology to employ would be a matched-subjects design, with a *precision control* matching procedure employed (Christensen 1988). This procedure would mean that for every woman in the sample, a man would be sampled who would be similar to the woman with respect to general intelligence, experience of relevant or related courses such as mathematics, and so on. Thus the hope would be that these extraneous variables would be held constant across the sample of women and men. Now the researcher would have better control over these extraneous variables and would be more confident in ruling them out as factors contributing to a difference in observed problem-solving.

However, were a difference in performance still to occur then the researcher might still be unable to identify whether unknown extraneous factor(s) contributed to the difference. For example, 30 years ago it would not have been considered relevant to hold constant between groups the measurement of finger digit ratio (a measure of the relative lengths of the second and the fourth digit of the hand). However, recent research (Manning *et al.* 1998) has suggested that digit ratio may be a behavioural marker of prenatal levels of testosterone. Thus today we could control for this variable in order to remove its impact upon the relevant cognitive measure. Thirty years ago this would have been an unknown relevant characteristic. It implies that in a matched design there is a possibility that an unknown but pertinent variable is not matched and casual inference remains flawed. The advantage of being able to randomly assign participants in a *true* experiment is that any unknown characteristic (as digit ratio has been in the past) would be equally distributed across experimental conditions and therefore would no longer be likely to act as a confounding variable.

It is evident in this discussion that in a research context where randomization cannot occur, the nature of the sampling of the samples of women and men may be even more critical than normal for the interpretation of the findings. Any biases in the sampling of the women and the men would further confound the study, yet there is extensive psychological research, which makes use of opportunity or convenience sampling within an undergraduate population of psychology students. With the use of a data set the author (for example Hamilton 1995) has developed it is possible to illustrate the impact of sampling bias arising from opportunity sampling. (Note that this data set is itself predominantly from an undergraduate population.) The data set is composed of 541 women and 344 men who carried out a mental rotation task (MRT). An educational measure is also included in the table, namely the number of GCSE passes obtained by the participants (in England, students typically take this exam at 16 years of age).

Table 1.3a indicates the mental rotation task (MRT) performance of women and men in the full data set. The MRT task is based on the procedure

Table 1.3 The impact upon individual differences as a result of random and opportunity sampling from a larger dataset

Table 1.3 a

		Full dataset MRT	GCSE number
Women	Mean	7.09	8.13
	S.D.	5.01	2.36
Men	Mean	11.05	8.11
	S.D.	4.55	2.07
Effect size *d*		*+0.76*	*−0.009*

Table 1.3b

		Random sample1		Random sample 2	
		MRT	GCSE number	MRT	GCSE number
Women	Mean	7.80	8.16	8.26	8.57
	S.D.	3.65	1.95	4.77	2.32
Men	Mean	11.10	7.96	11.54	8.31
	S.D.	4.10	1.90	3.96	2.21
Effect size *d*		*+0.78*	*−0.11*	*+0.72*	*−0.11*

Table 1.3c

		Opportunity sample 1		Opportunity sample 2	
		MRT	GCSE number	MRT	GCSE number
Women	Mean	7.50	9.72	5.62	5.9
	S.D.	4.98	0.71	6.27	1.92
Men	Mean	9.74	6.48	11.48	7.82
	S.D.	5.23	1.75	4.69	1.12
Effect size *d*		*+0.43*	*−1.54*	*+0.94*	*+1.55*

employed by Shepard and Metzler (1971) which requires participants to mentally rotate a pair of block shapes in order to determine if the block shapes are the same or mirror images (see Chapter 4, Figure 4.5 for a detailed description of this stimulus). The mean difference indicates an advantage for men, the effect size, d, is a measure of mean difference between men and women in relation to the overall distribution of their scores. The effect size is $+0.76$, a typical reported effect size for this particular task. Note also that academic achievement as measured by the number of General Certificate of Secondary Education (GCSE) passes indicates that there is little difference in overall GCSE achievement between the men and the women in the data set. Table 1.3b indicates two random samples (courtesy of SPSS), $N = 50$, from the data set. (Notice that random sample means will not necessarily be the same as the data set mean but will show a sampling distribution centred upon the data set mean.) These random samples show effect sizes similar to the full data set effect size. However, Table 1.3c illustrates extreme outcomes that could occur with opportunity sampling ($N = 50$). In the first opportunity or convenience sample, where women with relatively high GCSE achievement are sampled, and men with relatively lower achievement are sampled, the effect size falls to $d = +0.43$. Where the sample bias is reversed in the second opportunity sample, the effect size increases to $d = +0.94$.

Despite the observation that the vast proportion of the data set appears to be a selective sample drawn from an undergraduate population, the table indicates that, within this 'population', convenience sampling could give rise to fundamental differences in the characteristics of the men and the women in the study. The presumption of a matched (for educational achievement) design because the sample is made up of undergraduates may be premature and research needs to ensure that educational achievement is genuinely matched.

Organization of the Book

Part II: Sex Differences Research Findings

This part considers the research evidence for sex differences across a range of cognitive processes. Each discussion in the chapters will be prefaced with a brief outline of the cognitive processes, thus framing the individual-differences research.

Chapter 2 will consider the evidence for sex differences in low-level vision, perception, and sensory processes. The emphasis will be on visuospatial cognition. The chapter will begin with a description of the *dorsal* and *ventral* pathways in primates and humans. This discussion will form the basis for an emphasis upon the visual properties and the spatial properties of the visual stimulus. This research acts as a platform for the discussion of attention and imagery studies which forms the content of the subsequent chapters. The next chapter, Chapter 3, focuses upon attention, working memory and long-term memory.

Detailed research into individual differences associated with working memory processes is relatively sparse (with some notable exceptions: see Cornoldi and Vecchi 2003). However, Chapter 4 suggests that many of the imagery tasks carried out in the research literature may make demands upon visuo-spatial working memory. Consequently, it may therefore be the case that individual differences in VSWM functioning (slave processes and/or executive process) could account for some of the variability between the sexes in imagery task performance. This emphasis reflects the process-oriented theme in the book. Chapter 3 also emphasizes specific memory paradigms which draw upon (ostensibly) non-verbal working memory and long-term memory, namely object location memory and geographical/navigational memory.

One of the emerging issues in the literature to be discussed in this chapter will be the intrusion (or cognitive penetrability) by verbal processes and representation into the performance of commonly employed tasks which traditionally have been presumed to be visuospatial in nature. Not only do issues such as this have relevance for the sex differences literature but these sex differences findings have implications for the nature and interaction of cognitive processes in imagery and memory.

The final chapter of Part II, Chapter 5, considers the evidence for sex differences in performance within an educational context. Mathematics achievement by girls and boys will specifically be considered. The chapter will begin with a discussion of the nature of mathematical competencies and go on to consider the relationship between certain spatial abilities and mathematics achievements. The consideration of the cognitive processes, particularly working memory and long-term memory processes, will be developed with reference to recent psychological research. While the extensive findings from North America will be discussed, the chapter will also consider the findings of school achievement patterns in the UK where an increasing female advantage in GCSE achievement has been observed. This chapter places individual differences within the broadest context, where social cognition, socio-cultural and personality processes may also impact upon academic achievement.

Part III: Within-Sex Differences Research Findings

The aim of this part is to take the discussion of individual differences beyond the conventional sex differences literature and consider cognitive process variability within the sexes. Thus factors such as gender, hormonal influences, handedness and cerebral lateralization, and lifespan development will be discussed in order to consider their contribution to within-sex variability.

The gender chapter, Chapter 6, will begin with a reminder of why it may be advisable to view sex and gender as distinct concepts, with the former informing research findings into sex differences and the latter affording the initial view, in this text, of factors affecting within-sex variability. The research linking gender characteristics and cognitive task performance will be reviewed and then interpreted within both the socio-cultural and evolutionary perspectives. The content of the chapter will also focus on the methodological issues associated with the assessment of gender as a psychological construct.

Chapter 7 will consider the role of hormones in cognitive task performance. The concepts or *organizational* and *activational* hormonal effects will be discussed. While these have been examined previously in the context of sex differences, an extensive literature exists which implies that the cognitive impact of hormonal processes varies substantively within the sexes. Thus research has looked extensively at the cyclical influence of menstruation upon visuospatial and verbal processing in female participants. Affects of seasonal and daily hormonal variation will also be considered. This research also extends into the impact ageing has upon the central nervous system (CNS). Methodological issues associated with hormonal research will also be discussed.

The final chapter of this part considers individual differences associated with lifespan development. Variability in cognitive processing efficacy is strongly associated with development. Theoretical accounts of the changes in cognition associated with ageing will be discussed, along with the literature relating to child development and adult ageing. In the latter context, a consideration of the importance of hormonal differences between women and men will be included. This is the suggestion that the hormonal influences women experience act as a neuroprotective factor and result in a less steep cognitive decline in older age.

Part IV: Theoretical Frameworks

Having discussed in detail the individual differences associated with between-sex and within-sex factors it is now possible to consider the various theoretical frameworks which have been employed in order to explain sex differences in human cognition.

Chapter 9 focuses upon the evolutionary approach and is the first theoretical perspective discussed in this part. This approach has at its centre the process of natural selection which assumes that behaviour between individuals will vary and that those behaviours which lead to efficient adaptation to a particular environment will be selected over time (assuming that they have a genetic component underlying their emergence). Variability in behaviour can arise from females and males carrying out distinct tasks. Thus, in prehistory, if males carried out mating practices demanding travel over large distances, then selection would have favoured males with good geographic skills. Alternatively, if females carried out tasks which demanded the location and identification of plants and fruits, selection would favour females with good object memory and location skills. One possible outcome of such processes is that the brain would, *over many generations*, become hard-wired for specific and discrete skills in the two sexes. Arguments such as these will be employed in Chapter 3, in the sections discussing sex differences in working memory and long-term memory.

The subsequent chapter, Chapter 10, considers more recent environmental pressures on human behaviour by considering the socio-cultural environment in which girls and boys develop. If children develop within a culture where clearly demarcated roles are forced upon them in the process of sex-role stereotyping, then at least two major outcomes may be anticipated:

• The child will have a relatively limited range of experiences/opportunities and this may limit in turn which cognitive processes they effectively develop.

• The child will develop gender-stereotypic views and expectancies of tasks and abilities carried out in that culture and this may limit their ability to go on and complete these tasks successfully.

However, the chapter discussion on gender would suggest that in gender-schematic individuals both of these processes may additionally lead to variability within women and men in cognitive processing (see the section in Chapter 6, entitled 'Individual Differences Associated with Gender').

The third chapter in this part, Chapter 11, 'An Interactionist Approach', integrates the two approaches above and considers that cognitive development, underpinned by CNS development, is a *product* of biological genotype influences and environmental interactions. The framework adopted from Greenough *et al.* (1987) considers CNS development which is *experience-expectant*, that is particular environmental experiences can be predicted to occur for all members of the species and thus the neural apparatus required to process the events can be pre-wired in the brain. However, a second set of developmental processes, experience-dependent processes, are CNS processes which can develop only with the occurrence of events which are more idiosyncratic to the child. Within such a framework, the mature CNS processes, and thus adult cognition, have to be viewed within a constructivist framework where genotype and environmental experience inevitably interact. This chapter will also consider more specific interactionist theories.

The final chapter in the book, Chapter 12, attempts to synthesize the various theoretical perspectives and research findings. The content will consider the common ground between the theoretical approaches as well establishing where outstanding differences still remain. The research findings will be discussed within these frameworks but in addition the outstanding methodological issues associated with the literature will be reiterated. The synthesis will conclude by identifying a set of issues/questions which need to be addressed by future research in the field and which encourage the reader to consider for themselves the research procedures required to be undertaken in order to address such issues.

Part II
Sex Differences
Research Findings

2 Sex Differences in Sensory and Perceptual Processes

Aim and Overview

This chapter will consider the individual differences associated with women and men in tasks which predominantly make demands upon sensory and perceptual processes. The primary component of the next two sections of the chapter will be a discussion of general processes in vision and audition. The aim of these sections is to provide basic neural and cognitive frameworks within which the individual difference research may be interpreted.

The visual perception section begins with a consideration of visual processes; in particular the major visual pathways will be considered, beginning with the retina but also with an emphasis upon the notion of parallel pathways from the retina through to the cortex. The discussion will briefly discuss magnocellular and parvocellular structures and processes in the retina and lateral geniculate nucleus in the thalamus; there will also be a discussion of the notion of ventral and dorsal pathways in the cortex. The subsequent empirical component of the chapter will consider in detail the individual-differences research associated with visual and perceptual performance in women and men. The section will begin with a discussion of sex differences in sensory processes and finish with a discussion of recent studies of face perception.

The auditory perception section will look at the auditory sensory pathways, noting similarities between auditory and visual processing, for example the presence of segregated cortical pathways in both systems. Only sex difference research which considers sensory and low-level auditory perception will be discussed. Phonological processing and other verbal research will be discussed in Chapter 3, 'Attention and Memory', in the sections dealing with working memory, semantic memory and episodic long-term memory. The last empirical section of the chapter will consider sex difference findings in other sensory processes.

Visual Perception

Cognitive Processes

An understanding of visual perception is facilitated by a consideration of the anatomy of the eye and the visual pathways. When light passes through the pupil and enters the eye it impinges upon the retinal surface at the back of the eye. The retina is a complex structure with several layers containing different structures: the photoreceptors (rods and cones), horizontal cells, bipolar cells, amacrine cells and ganglion cells. Despite being at the very back of the eye, the rods and cones are actually the first structures to respond directly to light. Ultimately, the information from all of these retinal structures are passed on to the ganglion cells, which then generate action potentials to be passed along the optic or visual pathways.

An important observation is the relatively large number of photoreceptors relative to the number of ganglion cells. In each retina there are over 120 million photoreceptors but less than 2 million ganglion cells. This process of convergence is critical for an understanding of a crucial concept in visual science: the notion of a receptive field (RF). A neuron's receptive field is essentially the extent of photoreceptors on the retinal surface which when active will influence that particular neuron. On average, over 60 photoreceptors must converge upon a single retinal ganglion neuron; however, there is great variability in the ratio of convergence. In the foveal region of the retina, relatively very few photoreceptors converge upon a ganglion cell; however in the peripheral retina many more photoreceptors converge upon one ganglion cell. Thus, across the retina, neurons have different RF sizes. In fact within any region of the retina RF size may differ depending upon the type of ganglion cell. Two major types of ganglion cell are the M and P types shown in Figure 2.1.

The M ganglion cell type has a relatively larger cell body, and collects information through its dendrites across a relatively larger area of the retina than the P cell. Therefore, in any given retinal area, the M cells have larger RFs than the P cells. These cell types appear to differ in a variety of way, with different preferences for the patterns of light falling on their RFs. M cells appear to prefer stimuli with coarser detail (low-spatial-frequency information; see below), stimuli that move across the RF rapidly and are sensitive to low-contrast stimuli. P cells will respond to finer spatial detail (high-spatial-frequency information), prefer slower moving stimuli, and because of the arrangement of cones within the RF can indicate information about the colour or wavelength of the light falling on their RF. Figure 2.2 illustrates the spatial frequency and the contrast characteristics of grating stimuli.

At a typical reading distance (0.6 metres), the low-spatial-frequency grating is about 0.6 cycles per degree (about 0.6 c/deg), while the other grating pattern is about 4 c/deg. The highest spatial frequency detectable, typically about 50 to 60 c/deg in adult humans, known as *grating acuity*. This type of

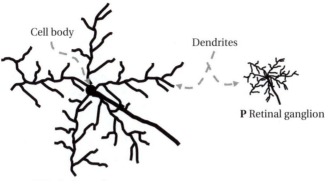

Cell body

Dendrites

P Retinal ganglion

M Retinal ganglion

Figure 2.1   Retinal ganglion cell types

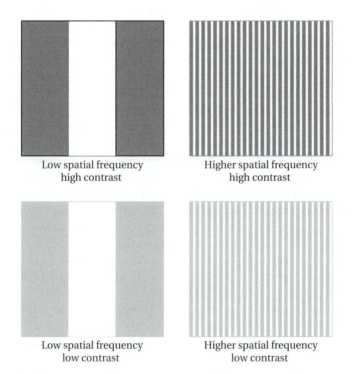

Low spatial frequency
high contrast

Higher spatial frequency
high contrast

Low spatial frequency
low contrast

Higher spatial frequency
low contrast

Figure 2.2   Grating stimuli varying in spatial frequency and contrast

evidence suggests that already in the retina, different neurons are extracting different information about the visual world, and this differential processing forms the conceptual platform for the subsequent parallel processing in the visual pathways. The information from the ganglion cells is transmitted to several parts of the brain, the major pathways in humans being through the lateral geniculate nucleus (LGN) to the visual cortex, initially striate cortex (sometimes called area 17, or V1).

The anatomical organization of the LGN further suggests that parallel processing occurs early in the major visual pathway. Different layers in the LGN contain large-bodied M cells and P cells; this separation is maintained in the projection to striate cortex, where the M and P pathways synapse in different sublayers of V1. There is evidence to suggest that this separation is maintained sufficiently to form the basis of two major cortical pathways: a *ventral* pathway, which extracts object identity information (orientation, shape, colour and so on) from the striate and prestriate cortical areas and passes this on to the temporal lobe, and a *dorsal* pathway which extracts motion information about the visual world and passes this on to the parietal cortex. Bruce *et al.* (1996; 2003) suggest that while these 'what and where' pathways have extensive support for their existence, it is also clear that from the striate cortex onwards through the prestriate cortex areas there are extensive interactions between the systems. Thus the pathways may be parallel but one should not presume they are fully independent. Research in the past decade has led to a revision of how the functional characteristics of the pathways are considered.

The work of Milner and his colleagues (summarized in Milner and Goodale 1995) suggests that the ventral pathway be considered a pathway necessary for conscious visual awareness of the visual world. In their view, the dorsal pathway extracts visual information in order to allow control of actions by the viewer. Thus their perspective considers that one important function of vision is to allow animals to successfully interact with their environment. This ecological approach has important implications for theories of sex differences in perception which are derived from explanations based on hunter/gatherer roles in early hominid history. One would presume that hunters, interacting with rapid and dynamic animals, would require highly competent action-based perceptual systems, that is dorsal systems. Alternatively, if early hominid male competition arose in mate selection then the dorsal system would also be important in effective fighting behaviour.

In the last two decades 'higher-level' perceptual processes have been extensively investigated. One such process relates to the spatial scale involved in the perception, the notion of *local* and *global* processes. A second emphasizes

Local/Global stimulus   Categorical/Coordinate stimulus

Figure 2.3   Image illustrating local/global and categorical/coordinate stimuli

the nature of the spatial representation of the stimulus: *categorical* or *coordinate* spatial relation processes. Typical stimuli employed in this research are shown in Figure 2.3.

With the stimulus on the left side of the figure, local perception would focus attention on the small letters, the F-shaped letters, and global perception would direct perception to the overall shape, a coarser spatial scale, to identify the L-shape. In the right-hand stimulus, categorical spatial relation processes would determine whether the square was above or below the line. Coordinate spatial processes would determine precisely how far the square was away from the line, that is provide fine metric information about the stimulus array.

Sex Differences in Visual Perception

Sensory Processes

There have been at least two major reviews of perceptual differences in women and men in the past 30 years. Baker (1987) reviewed the research across a range of sensory modalities and across levels of processes within modalities. This text also draws upon an earlier extensive review by Velle (1987). One task in which sex differences appear to occur is in visual acuity procedures.

Visual acuity may be measured in numerous ways, as shown in Figure 2.4. These acuity measures are dependent (in part) upon retinal receptive fields being small enough to discriminate between black-and-white high-contrast differences in letters (standard Snellen measures), C or grating stimuli. Presumably, these small RFs would provide information for the ventral, object identity, pathway. However, the ability to resolve very fine detail also suggests that coordinate spatial processes are recruited. Both Baker and Velle suggest that visual acuity is greater in men than women (see Solberg and Brown 2002, below, for a qualification of this conclusion). Therefore, one might presume that in men finer visuospatial information is available to the ventral system. These authors identify sex differences in another measurement of acuity, dynamic visual acuity, where there is relative motion between the observer and the stimulus being viewed.

Any advantage for men may well be age-dependent, with a significant advantage only present at 5 years of age (Ishigaki and Miyao 1994). This measure of acuity demands the extrapolation of spatial information from a moving object; it thus demands 'form from motion'. Success in this task is likely to involve crosstalk between the ventral and dorsal systems. For instance, in an object-catching task, the ventral system would provide fine details on the shape of the object in order to determine grasp mechanics while the dorsal system would be demanded in the guidance of the general action underlying the interception.

Some evolutionary psychologists have suggested an evolutionary cultural context where men were the traditional hunters (see Chapter 9 and the section

a. the conventional Snellen letter chart, where the viewer has to read down the set of letters, until they are so small the letter cannot be discerned.

b. Landolt (C) ring, where viewers have to identify where a gap appears in the ring; the rings become increasingly smaller until the gap location is not recognized.

c. grating acuity, where the bar width is reduced, that is with higher spatial frequencies, until the viewer can no longer resolve the bars.

d. vernier acuity, where lines are offset and the viewer has to identify the offset lines. The extent of offset is reduced until the viewer can no longer resolve the offset.

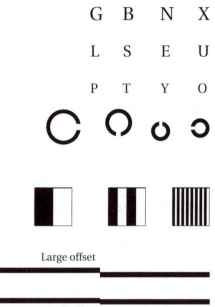

Figure 2.4   Standard visual acuity procedures

'Evolutionary Psychology'). If this account is accurate then it would be logical to presume that over many generations men would develop relatively efficient dorsal system processing. The measures of dynamic visual acuity would support this presumption. Research on a measure of movement sensitivity, the detection of flickering gratings, showed a male advantage and again would suggest a dorsal system advantage for men. However, not all of the research is consistent with this interpretation. Brabyn and McGuinness (1979) found a low spatial frequency advantage for women, which would imply an M system advantage for women. Recent spatial frequency grating research by Solberg and Brown 2002 failed to replicate this advantage for women, finding no differences between the sexes at the lowest and highest spatial frequencies. The latter study therefore failed to replicate differences in (static) grating acuity between women and men.

A major sex difference in ventral subfunction is evidenced in the rates of colour blindness between men and women, according to Velle (1987); the incidence of colour blindness is 8 per cent in men and 0.5 per cent in women. The locus of this deficit lies in anomalies in the photoreceptor layer in the retina and is presumed to be a result of X–X-linked genes. Alexander (2003) has attempted to relate evolutionary accounts of photoreceptor properties and visual pathway development with early toy selection and with the P and M channels. Alexander considers the evolutionary theories deriving from ancient hunter/gatherer roles (suggested by Silverman and Eals 1992; see Chapter 3 and later discussion in Chapter 9). Recent research by Regan *et al.* (2001) has also suggested that primate colour vision has evolved within a context of fruit-gathering. Thus Alexander suggests that the ability to detect yellow fruit and edible red leaves against a backdrop of green foliage gives food gatherers an advantage. In the object location and memory task procedures to be discussed in Chapter 3, early research suggested that women were more efficient in these task procedures (Silverman and Eals 1992).

More recently, research has suggested that red objects on green backgrounds were more effectively recalled than stimuli with green objects on red backgrounds (Hellige and Cumberland 2001). This research explicitly links colour-processing with object location and memory performance. Neuroimaging research by Cowan *et al.* (2000) also suggests that colour-processing is different in men and women. However, in this study the difference in cortical response between the sexes was with blue light stimulation rather than with light of a red wavelength; men showed more sensitive responses to the blue wavelength. Therefore there was a different wavelength emphasis from Alexander's review. It may be that these differences in colour sensitivity in men and women account for the colour preferences found in questionnaire research. Ellis and Ficek (2001) found in their questionnaire study that men had a greater preference for shades of blue.

Sensory-Motor Processes

The Alexander paper raises some interesting and important issues relating to perceptual processing in women and men. The paper for instance suggests that there is developmental evidence to indicate that boys are more effective in tasks demanding the dorsal system. In this context it is surprising that more is not made in the paper of the action-based characteristics of the dorsal pathway. The Milner and Goodale (1995) perspective provides an opportunity to link potential perceptual (motor) skills derived from the hunting and capture of animals to the current research, which identifies sex differences in 'spatiotemporal' ability (Halpern 2000).

The perceptual competencies involved in judging the approach of a dynamic object (for example a hunted animal or male rival) and constructing the appropriate visuomotor action to intercept the animal (catch or throw spear) or deflect a blow appear incredibly complex. Humans and other animals may make use of the approaching object's increasing retinal image size (one use of the derivative of this information, *tau*, is discussed by Bruce *et al.* 1996) and possibly binocular information from the two eyes such as vergence cues. In response to this visual information, the dorsal system must make use of these dynamics in order to activate the relevant visuomotor action.

An insight into the typical procedures in the research is given by the work of Watson and Kimura (1989, 1991). They employed an interception task where a ball was projected to one or other side of the participant at a rate of 62.5

metres per second from a distance of 4.5 metres. The participant's task was to merely touch the object rather than catch it; even this 'less demanding' effort would require an action to have occurred within 70 ms! In addition, a throwing task was used involved throwing a 25-g dart at a target 3 m away. The authors also employed a range of paper-based spatial tasks, and assessed the participants' sporting experience. The largest difference between the men and the women was in their performance on the throwing and intercept tasks, with men performing more effectively. The sporting experience of the women was related to their visuomotor task performance, and overall this pattern was observed for the total sample. However, the advantage for males in these spatiotemporal procedures remained after sporting experience (and height and weight) were partialled out. Watson and Kimura (1991) interpreted their results within the context of ancient hunting roles. It is interesting to note that the study also observed little relationship between the competencies in the pen-and-paper spatial tasks and in the visuomotor tasks.

More recent research by Peters (1997) has attempted to disentangle the motor and the perceptual processes within spatiotemporal task procedures. The visuomotor task involved throwing a bag at a moving target so as to intercept the target at a predetermined location. The perceptual task analogy was the pressing of a button when the moving target reached the predetermined location. There were thus two anticipation tasks: one with a visuomotor component and the other with the visual component predominating. Peters found an overall sex difference in both tasks, with men producing smaller timing errors and higher accuracy. However, the pattern of performance between women and men differed in the two procedures. In the throwing task, the largest difference in performance was when the moving target was at its fastest, 5 m/s, though in the button-pressing task the largest difference occurred at the slowest speed, 2 m/s. This pattern led Peters to conclude that 'the spatial-perceptual aspects of the intercept task are not comparable for the button press intercept task and the throwing tasks' (p. 295).

The throwing intercept task appears to make full demands upon an action-based dorsal visual system, from visual information pickup right through to the motor action: an action-based process which Peters suggests is part of a hardwired specialized throwing neural system. Once the response becomes button-pressing, another system contributes, perhaps making less demand upon the dorsal visual pathway. However, one would again presume that there would need to be recruitment of coordinate spatial processes in order to be accurate at the task.

Research by Millslagle (2000) also decouples visual and visuomotor components in anticipation tasks. He employed a dynamic visual acuity task in conjunction with a button press anticipation task and found no correlation in performance between the two tasks in a sample of women. Interestingly, while sporting experience of the participants was related to the dynamic visual acuity task, this experience was not related to the button-pressing anticipation task. Thus the research above highlights several tasks appearing to demand the use of dynamic visuospatial information, but the results suggest that three different processes may well be at work.

One source, which could contribute to individual differences in many of the task procedures discussed above, is the presence of sex differences in motor skills. Many researchers such as Kimura (1999) make a distinction between gross and fine motor skills: the former would be involved in activities such as throwing or intercepting, the latter in tasks such as needlework or model making. Kimura has emphasized the appearance of sex differences in activities which demand 'throwing accuracy or targeting', a difference favouring men (Westergaard *et al.* 2000). She links this competency with the observation that in most hunter-gatherer societies it is men who are active in hunting. This evolutionary frame is supported by the observation that the motor cortices may differ between men and women (Amunts *et al.* 2000).

Interestingly, a sex difference in neuroanatomy may exist even after extensive motor experience (Hutchinson *et al.* 2003). Kimura also suggested that a sex difference in fine motor skills, favouring women, might also exist. An example of procedure demanding fine motor skills is the Perdue pegboard task where participants have to pick up small pegs and place them in order along the pegboard (see also Chipman *et al.* 2002; Epting and Overman 1998). It should be noted that not all research findings concur with these observations. For example Peters and Campagnaro (1996) varied the task demands within a peg-moving task and concluded that the sex difference in such tasks was due to the difficulty of picking up the pegs with large hands, as the sex difference disappeared when tweezers were employed.

Visual Illusions

Research focusing upon visual illusions has also revealed apparent sex differences. Visual illusions occur where the perceptual experience does not accurately reflect the sensory stimuli present.

Consider the Poggendorff example shown below in Figure 2.5. The typical stimulus shows an oblique line running behind a rectangular shape. The

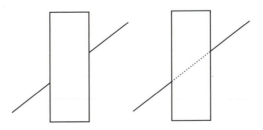

Figure 2.5   The Poggendorff illusion

oblique line is actually straight (see right hand figure) but the right-hand side of the line appears higher than it should be were it a genuinely straight line.

The identical stimulus on the right figure stimulus includes a continuous line demonstrating that the line on the left of the figure is indeed straight despite its appearance.

McGuinness (1985) reviewed research findings indicating that there are sex differences in perceptual tasks where there are intersecting lines forming acute angles, such as the Poggendorff (Heywood and Chessell 1977; Porac *et al.* 1979). Typically, the findings suggested that men were more susceptible to the illusions. Declerck and De Brabander (2002) provided contrasting evidence for sex differences in performance in the Poggendorff illusion. They observed that the illusory error in the task was greater for women. A recent paper (Ling *et al.* 2006) has employed a process-oriented or functional approach to further investigate the locus of the error in the Poggendorff task. The authors decomposed the stimulus into two displays, the full display with the inducing rectangle present and a display without the inducing presence of the rectangle. In the latter stimulus context the authors were interested in identifying whether the observed sex difference identified by Declerck and De Brabander could arise from the task of aligning the oblique lines. Thus coordinate spatial relations demand in this component of the task could have contributed to the observed sex difference. Their results suggested that while coordinate relations spatial judgements contributed to the overall error in the task, the sex difference in task performance emerged only when the inducing rectangle was present.

Miller (2001) however found that in a task employing the Ponzo illusion women were more susceptible to the illusion. The stimuli employed in the study are shown in Figure 2.6. The participant's task is to judge the relative length of the upper and lower horizontal lines in each of the three diagrams.

The central stimulus, B, indicates that the two horizontal lines are equivalent (in fact all six horizontal lines are equal in length). However, the upper line in 2.6A, and particularly in 2.6C, appears relatively longer. Miller found that women were more susceptible to this illusion. This is despite the presence of numerous acute angles created by intersecting lines (McGuinness 1985). One common explanation for this illusion is that the converging lines

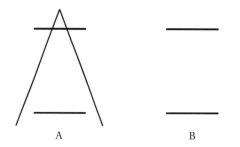
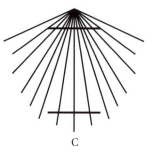

A   B   C

Figure 2.6   Variants of the Ponzo illusion

behind horizontal lines provide a source of depth information, which leads to inappropriate constancy scaling. This is a cognitively complex explanation, which indicates that the perception of a stimulus may be greatly influenced by the context in which it is presented.

This suggestion that women may differ in their use of 2-D 'depth' cues and actual 3-D depth cues is also suggested by research (Deregowski *et al.* 1997; McWilliams *et al.* 1997). However, Miller (2001) argued that female participants were less likely to disembed the line from the background and suggested that the female participants' performance was constrained by their *field dependence*. The study found that *field dependence/independence* was related to the Ponzo task performance, but only in the female participants. Interestingly, Miller also observed that the visual error in the female participants was related to the ratio of women to men concurrently participating in the procedure (though this pattern of results could have been due to methodological issues within the study). Research has also suggested that the neural architecture underlying susceptibility to illusions may vary between women and men (Grabowska *et al.* 1999).

Field Independence and Dependence

The concept of field dependence/independence (Witkin *et al.* 1971) is one of the processes contributing to *spatial visualization* (Voyer *et al.* 1995). One perceptual task commonly employed to assess field dependence/independence is the Embedded Figures Task (EFT). This task was employed in the Miller (2001) study. In this task the participant has to locate the simple shape in the more complex shape (shown in Figure 2.7).

In the Voyer *et al.* meta-analysis, spatial visualization displayed a relatively small effect size associated with the sex of the participant. The EFT only displayed significant sex differences when the participants were over 18 years old. Thus Hamilton (1995) found no sex differences in EFT procedure, but in the same participants found a difference in mental rotation performance.

The task demands in the EFT appear relatively simple; however consideration of one of its components suggests a role for imagery and short-term visual memory. In the EFT procedure, the participant must view the simple shape then construct an image of the shape and then maintain the simple shape

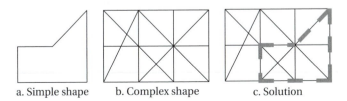

a. Simple shape   b. Complex shape   c. Solution

Figure 2.7   Embedded figures task stimuli

image when viewing the complex shape. If there is a sex difference in EFT task performance where does the cognitive difference lie? The difference could lie in the ability to generate the image, and/or maintain the image, and/or match the image with elements of the complex figure. Voyer *et al.* were particularly critical of this category of spatial abilities; they suggested that 'the spatial visualisation grouping appears to be a catchall category for tests that do not fit the definition of mental rotation or spatial perception tasks' (p. 252).

Their meta-analysis indicated that the group of tasks typically included in the spatial visualization did indeed show extensive heterogeneity, suggesting that more than a single spatial process was indicated by the data (however, the mental rotation category appeared to indicate as great a problem with heterogeneity – see Chapter 4). This current heterogeneity could arise from different studies employing slightly different procedures, for example individual versus group testing, different scoring techniques and so on. The variability could also arise from the fact that different tasks within the category could make demands not only upon some common cognitive processes but in addition upon some discrete cognitive processes. A process-oriented approach would attempt to consider each of the potential cognitive processes in turn. Indeed the work of Loring-Meier and Halpern (1999) in a related research area will be discussed in Chapter 4.

The Voyer *et al.* meta-analysis also considered sex differences in spatial perception tasks: the two dominant tasks in this category are the rod-and-frame task and the water-level task. These tasks are shown in Figure 2.8. In the rod-and-frame procedure the participant may have to rotate a central line until it appears truly vertical. The line stimulus may be flanked by a frame which does not possess vertical and horizontal edges ($d = 0.48$, favouring men; Voyer *et al.* 1995). In the water-level task the participant has to draw a line indicating the water-level mark within a jug which is tilted. Regardless of the angle of the jug, the water-level should be horizontal ($d = 0.42$, favouring men; Voyer *et al.* 1995). The water-level task (see Figure 2.8) is derived from the early work of Piaget (1967). Pulos (1997) suggests that 40 per cent of college

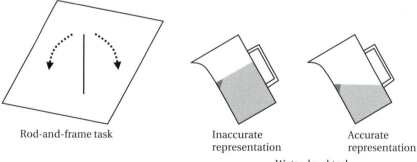

Rod-and-frame task   Inaccurate   Accurate
                                      representation   representation
                                           Water-level task

Figure 2.8   Spatial perception tasks

students and 60 per cent of non-college adults show some inaccuracy in the task. It is difficult at a first glance to imagine that differences in the experience of pouring containers could account for sex differences in line judgement, given the extensive experience most adults have in pouring liquids.

However, two more recent studies have attempted to establish whether occupational experience could actually be related to task performance. These studies are interesting not only in the pattern of results that emerge but also in terms of issues of research design. Hecht and Proffitt (1995) assessed water-level task performance in six different groups of participants: wait-resses, housewives, female undergraduates, male undergraduates, male bar-tenders and male bus-drivers. Their results suggested that participants with experience in the most pertinent occupations, waitresses and bartenders, performed relatively poorly. In order to account for this these authors suggested that it is possible in this task to pay attention to different frames of reference: environmental horizontality which guides judgement of the water-level and an object relative frame where participants make the water-level judgement in relation to the oblique sides of the object.

Hecht and Proffitt (1995) argued that an 'adoption of an object-relative perspective introduces a perceptual bias' (p. 91). They further suggested that waitresses and bartenders would be required to attend to the object (rim)–water-level information in order to avoid spillage. Thus participants in these occupations would have occupational biases leading to greater error in the standard water-level task context. However, Vasta *et al.* (1997) drew attention to design anomalies in the Hecht and Proffitt study: namely the lack of control for sex, age, education and job experience in each of the groups. The Vasta *et al.* study found an inverse pattern of results, with bartenders and servers (waiters and waitresses) showing better task performance in comparison with clerical and sales participants. It should be noted that in both of these studies performance accuracy was significantly greater in men than women. The Vasta *et al.* study also noted that the level of knowledge of the effects of gravity upon water-level was significantly associated with task performance.

Pulos (1997) explicitly manipulated this factor, providing cues which were aimed at facilitating retrieval of this knowledge during water-level task performance. Pulos observed that only students with greater science experience benefited from the cue. Given that boys may have more ready access to this knowledge (Robert and Berthiaume 2002) a part of the reason why men perform more accurately could lie in their ability to retrieve this knowledge. This observation has two immediate implications. In order to make distinct groups more equivalent, Vasta *et al.* could have controlled this knowledge in their analysis, covarying knowledge of the effect of gravity with an ANCOVA rather than an ANOVA. Better still would be to assess this knowledge initially and then allocate matched participants to groups. However, it may be that the explicit activation of the gravity knowledge could be seen as a biasing factor in the research design, if it precedes actual task performance.

This latter suggestion raises the concern of the impact of explicit knowledge upon perceptual task performance. Pulos raises this issue within the broader 'imagery debate' where tacit (semantic or prepositional) knowledge could support performance in what appears to be a fully non-verbal task. This issue will be discussed in more detail in the next chapter. Research by Miyake *et al.* (2001) has attempted to identify the relationship between hidden figures tasks such as this and working memory, and this feature of the task demands will be discussed in Chapter 3.

The water-level task raises the issue of participant utilization of available perceptual cues in the testing context. Both the rod-and-frame task and the water-level task demand that participants make use of cues other than the immediate visual framing of the stimulus. Such a perceptual cue could be proprioceptive feedback. Whichever non-visual cues are employed, it is possible to consider that similar processes underlie field independence. The research into embedded figures and water-level suggests that women may be more susceptible to the influence of the immediate visual frame than men. However, a recent study prompts further consideration of the use of visual frames by women and men.

Line Orientation

Collaer and Nelson (2002) made use of a line orientation judgement procedure to identify perceptual differences in men and women. In the line orientation example shown in Figure 2.9, the participant has to match the two lines, A and B, with two identical orientations within the 13-line fan stimulus. The actual orientations are 12 and 5, respectively, for both fan orientations. Collaer and Nelson found that men were more accurate in this task, the effect size being large, $d = 0.85$. The task demands ventral system activation, as a conscious explicit orientation judgement is required (Milner and Goodale 1995).

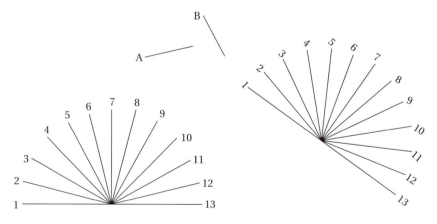

Figure 2.9 Line orientation stimuli, frame-dependent and frame-independent formats

The findings suggest that when the matched lines are oblique in nature (lines 3, 4, 5, 9, 10 and 11) men are relatively more accurate in the task.

One should note that overall, the findings indicate that the data from both sexes show a conventional oblique effect, that is poorer performance when making judgements about oblique orientations. The authors identified similarities in the line orientation task and the water-level task, where the greatest errors in water-level task accuracy also occurred when the bottle holding the water was tilted at an oblique angle. Collaer and Nelson (2002) carried out an additional experimental procedure whereby the orientation of the fan stimulus was rotated on the page (right-hand stimulus in Figure 2.9). This meant that the previously horizontal lines 1 and 13 and the vertical line, 7, possessed orientations which were no longer commensurate with the frame context provided by the edges of the page on which the stimuli were presented.

When the fan stimulus was rotated (angled) in relation to the page frame, the performance of men and women did not differ significantly. The data indicated that the male participants' performance suffered under this manipulation. Collaer and Nelson argued that:

> [T]he normally oriented task provides potentially useful cues to task geometry via the horizontal and vertical aspects of page frame (and this appears to be the only available geometric references cue). Males appear more likely than females to spontaneously attend to or use this environmental geometry, thus improving their task performance. (p. 7)

Their interpretation, an emphasis upon men utilizing local visual frames in order to facilitate task performance, is in contrast to the common interpretation in the embedded-figure task procedures and the water-level task, where men are presumed not to give salience to the local, but now misleading, visual information. Should subsequent research suggest that men indeed are able to select between useful and less useful local visual cues it would suggest that these sex differences may arise from higher-level visual selective attention strategies rather than lower-level perceptual processes *per se.*

A recent study has attempted to elucidate the neural processes underlying line orientation judgement (Gur *et al.* 2000). This study looked at brain activation in two regions, the planum temporale in both hemispheres and the inferior parietal region in both hemispheres, with two tasks, a verbal analogy task and the line orientation task. The authors found that during the line orientation task, a sex difference in performance occurred, favouring men. The emphasis in this study was upon the pattern of neuroimaging activity. They found that in 'the spatial task men showed more extensive and bilateral activation' (p. 164). However, they also found more right-hemisphere activation in the men. As discussed in Chapter 1 regarding the advantages of a process-oriented approach, a difficulty in interpreting such a pattern of activity is that two distinct factors could contribute to the difference in right-hemispheric activity: a genuine sex difference, or a difference due to performance level. In this study these two factors are confounded as both sex and performance level could contribute to increased activity level.

Face Perception

Face perception is one of the most important perceptual acts humans undertake; it is the process which forms the platform for one of the most important social cognition acts we perform: the interaction with others. Face perception is an integral component of 'mind-reading', which allows individuals to interact successfully with others within a social context. These social cognition processes were fundamental to the social modules discussed by Geary (1998) and are described in Chapter 9. Consequently, the neural system underpinning face perception is understandably complex (Haxby *et al.* 2002). Two major sources of information are available in a face:

1. The invariant characteristics of a face which allow the recognition of a face, and the featural, configurational and holistic qualities (Rakover 2002) which permit individual recognition.

2. The dynamic aspects of the face, such as eye gaze, emotional expression and lip movements which facilitate social interaction.

Neural processes in the fusiform area of the posterior cortex contribute to the identification processes; however complex prefrontal cortex and subcortical systems (for example the limbic system) contribute to extracting the pertinent information relating to social communication. An important structure in this latter system is the amygdala, which has been implicated in the process of recognizing emotion in faces (Campbell *et al.* 2002). These authors also cite research that indicates that there may be sexually dimorphic differences in the amygdala.

When dealing with such a complex system, research methodology has to be correspondingly sophisticated, thus when studying face recognition not only do facial features such as hair have to be controlled for between stimuli, but facial emotion, gaze and so on have also to be controlled. Campbell *et al.* (2002) investigated both facial recognition and facial emotion recognition and found different patterns of association between the two processes in men and women. Thus in women there was a significant correlation between recognition of emotions and recognition of faces (both familiar and unfamiliar). This relationship did not hold for men. In addition, women were generally better at recognizing facial expressions. The authors attempted to explain this by reference to sex differences in the amygdala–hippocampal systems underlying task performance.

This competency in recognizing emotions provides support for sex difference in the social modules discussed by Geary. While the Campbell *et al.*

study did not provide evidence for any sex difference in facial recognition *per se*, other research has suggested differences in this process. Lewin and Herlitz (2002) found that women were more efficient at recognizing female faces, but both sexes were equally competent at recognizing male faces. To add to the complexity of findings, the findings in Wright and Sladden (2003) suggested an *own gender* bias, where women were more accurate at recognizing female faces and the men more accurate in the recognition of male faces. Further replication research is required in order to reveal which of these patterns is the most accurate.

Auditory Perception

Neural and Cognitive Processes

Sound performs an important signalling function for humans and other species. It has an ancient evolutionary function, which warns us of potential danger, for example an approaching predator, or more recently, the sound of a smoke alarm. Fundamental for humans is the communication function, speech and interpretation, and its production is important for most human interaction scenarios. However, in many cultures individuals also appreciate the importance of non-speech sounds in the form of music.

Although at first glance the auditory system in humans appears to be fundamentally different from the visual system, and while this may be the case at the structural level, at a functional level there are many similarities. These similarities begin when considering how an auditory event may be described. A sound event will cause air pressure changes, which are labelled sound waves. These waves can be described in terms of frequencies (cycles per second, Hz) and amplitude (loudness). This description is similar to the spatial frequency and contrast characteristics described above for grating stimuli employed in vision research. Goldstein (2002) provides an example of different frequencies or pitch on a piano: the keys on the left produce low frequencies of about 30 Hz while those on the extreme right produce pitches of about 4000 Hz. Humans can typically detect frequencies up to 15 kHz. However, there is increasing loss of higher frequencies throughout development and adulthood (see also Chapter 8).

The anatomy of the ears reveals a distinction between three sets of structures:

- The outer ear, which contains the pinna and the auditory canal.

- The middle ear, which contains the ossicles, three small bones which serve to amplify the pressure waves by acting on the oval window, the barrier between the middle and inner ear.

- The inner ear which contains the liquid-filled cochlea; an important structure is the organ of Corti, which possesses inner and outer hair cells.

The cilia, which project from the hair cells, bend when the fluid in the cochlea is disturbed by distortions of the oval window. This bending leads to transduction, whereby electrical energy is produced by the hair cells in the form of action potentials. Transduction also occurs in the retina. At the oval window end of the cochlea, hair cells respond best to low frequencies. Moving along the cochlea, it is possible to identify a systematic shift in preferred frequency, with a preference for increasing higher tones. This organization is known as *tonotopic* and is repeated within the auditory cortex itself. The axons of the hair cells form the auditory nerve and carry information to the auditory cortex.

Recent research has suggested that, as in the visual system, there is segregated processing within the two major cortical pathways (Ducommun *et al.* 2002; Maeder *et al.* 2001). A ventral *what* pathway, for the identification of sound objects, this system includes the auditory cortex, rostral superior temporal cortex, and prefrontal regions. In addition there is a dorsal *where* pathway, for the spatial location of a sound stimulus, which incorporates the caudal superior temporal cortex, parietal cortex and prefrontal regions. Ducommun *et al.* have further argued for subdivisions of the dorsal pathway, reflecting spatial location and auditory motion information respectively. The extraction of these 'low-level' characteristics of sound events is complemented by the ability of humans to extract meaning from speech utterances.

As with most acts of perception, most individuals experience speech perception in such a successful manner that it appears a straightforward process. However, production of, and perception of, speech is one of the most sophisticated and complex of human actions. A native speaker of English (or any language) can readily separate or parse the sounds and the words which make up a spoken sentence in their native language. This can occur despite the fact that were the speech analysed over time, the speech signal would appear to be continuous. Our language efficacy allows us to break down this continuous flow into discrete sounds that we know as words. This competency is in sharp contrast to our experience of a spoken language to which we are not familiar. In this context, the speech inevitably sounds as if it is continuous with no apparent breaks for word segmentation. This segmentation process acts implicitly and effectively when listening to one's native speech.

Speech sounds are broken down into more manageable chunks, labelled phonemes – basic units of speech. Sequences of phonemes are grouped to form morphemes or words. A change in the morpheme will affect how we give meaning to the word. Thus the phonemes /b/a/t/ make up the word *bat*; if the leading phoneme is changed from 'b' to /p/ then the word changes to /p/a/t/. In English there are 48 different phoneme sounds. In some languages the number is much less. In some South African languages, the number is a many as 60 (Goldstein 2002). Not only does the production of phonemes appear continuous; there is variability in the phoneme's sound depending upon its context, that is phonemes are produced amongst other phonemes and the same phoneme, surrounded by differing phonemes, will possess different frequencies. Thus the listener's perception must take into account the context of the speech sounds when processing each phoneme. There is also variability in the production of phonemes arising from dialect, how quickly an individual speaks, their sex and so forth. This variation in phoneme production emphasizes just how competent our speech perception has to be in order to perceive what is being said.

In order to understand the process of speech perception against this background of production variability, one could look at the characteristics of the speech itself or adopt a more cognitive approach. Thus invariant acoustic features of the stimulus, and categorical perceptual processes associated with *voice onset time*, aid our recognition of individual phonemes. At a higher cognitive level, the meaning of the sentence can offer aid to the perceptual processing. This meaning also aids our segmentation of morphemes.

Sex Differences in Auditory Perception

Baker (1987) reviewed an extensive literature on individual differences in sensory processes in hearing. The vast majority of studies found that when differences occurred there was typically an advantage for women. These tasks ranged from pure tone (frequency) thresholds to tasks of just noticeable differences (JND) in loudness decisions. Baker noted that these differences were emphasized when the stimulation was high in frequency. In early adulthood (32 years of age), men begin to lose sensitivity to frequencies above 2000 Hz. The loss of threshold and suprathreshold (above-threshold) sensitivity may account for the difference between the sexes in determining a change in the spatial location of a sound source. Some subsequent research has identified sex differences in sensorimotor gating in the auditory system, with women displaying smaller pre-pulse inhibition (Kumari *et al.* 2003).

Despite the early research indicating sex differences in auditory sensory processing favouring women, little research has found sex-individual differences in phonological processing. One such exception is the work of Majeres (1999), who in a series of tasks aimed at identifying phonological competencies, matching five-letter strings, words with phonologically inconsistent spellings and so on, found a consistent advantage for women. Citing neuroimaging research which observed right-hemispheric phonological biases for women (Pugh *et al.* 1997), Majeres concluded that their superior access to these representations may underlie several competencies exhibited by women. He also suggests that difficulties with phonological processing may have implications for learning to read and articulation. It should be noted though that recent research has suggested more complex neural systems in phonological processing (Gandour *et al.* 2003; Siok *et al.* 2003; Weber-Fox *et al.* 2003).

Other Senses

Olfaction

There are many factors which influence odour perception, one of which is the sex of the individual (Brand and Millot 2001). Various methodologies have been employed to assess odour sensitivity:

- Threshold sensitivity, which for many smells reveals an advantage for women (Baker 1987).

- Intensity rating, where the findings suggest that female participants indicate higher intensities than the male participants (Brand and Millot 2001). However, one must ensure that any differences do not arise from cognitive biases in the rating process.

- The rating of how pleasant or unpleasant the odour appears, where again rating biases could be present.

- Discrimination, recognition and identification procedures, which were also employed (Brand and Millot 2001). Again the suggestion is that women are more efficient.

Oberg *et al.* (2002) carried out a study with young adults and employed a range of methods. The only sex differences which occurred were in odour memory and recognition. These authors were concerned with the role of verbal mediation, and once they had controlled for odour-naming ability the differences were removed. This emphasis on cognitive processing other than odour perception was highlighted by Bengtsson *et al.* (2001), whose neuroimaging study found no differences between the neural systems employed by women and men. Given the similarity in neural processing of odour information they concluded that sex differences could arise from other cognitive processes, for example reporting bias or verbal scaffolding. The concern with verbal support in tasks, which are putatively non-verbal, is an issue which consistently runs through the sex differences literature and will re-emerge in the following two chapters.

Touch

Baker (1987) reviewed research that assessed individual differences to somatosensory or touch information. Women were found to be more sensitive to touch, 2 g versus 3 g. However, in spatial-localization performance women were less accurate, in both absolute and two-point discrimination. Thus the direction of the sex difference depended upon the precise somatosensory task. Two-point discrimination is a measurement of spatial acuity on the surface of the body. Individuals with good acuity can discriminate two points of pressure which are spatially close to one another.

More recent research has confirmed sex differences in spatial location favouring men (Aglioti and Tomaiuolo 2000). In addition there also appear to be differences in the underlying functional neuroanatomy in response to touch (Sadato *et al.* 2000). These authors found that activation in the dorsal pre-motor cortex was asymmetric in men, whereas it was symmetric in women. Research has also suggested that women are also less sensitive to temporal acuity as well as spatial acuity (Geffen *et al.* 2000). This research found that women were likely to judge two tactile stimuli as being simultaneous at longer ISI intervals than men. Thus the research in somatosensory processing suggests some advantages for women and some for men dependent upon the task demands.

Conclusions

This chapter has considered the presence of individual differences across a range of sensory and perceptual modalities. In visual perception, there appear to be low-level dynamic visual acuity differences favouring men, but research with static grating acuity is more equivocal. One drawback of such threshold studies is that they assess quite extreme information contexts: suprathreshold measurements may be more meaningful. There is extensive research to suggest that in dynamic visuomotor tasks there is a clear advantage for men. However, the complex nature of these tasks makes it difficult to identify which particular cognitive processes contribute to the differences. Research has attempted to deconstruct the influence of these processes.

The recent meta-analysis by (Voyer *et al.* 1995) suggests that sex differences in spatial ability depend critically upon the nature of the tasks. Mental rotation tasks (discussed in Chapter 4) show evidence of large effect sizes favouring males, while spatial visualization tasks such as embedded figures tasks display small effect sizes. Research that has focused upon visuospatial procedures such as water-level tasks and line orientation has produced equivocal results. The greater accuracy in water-level judgements in male participants is related to the notion of field independence: men do not appear to be biased by oriented frame of the water container. However, in line orientation judgement the accurate performance of men has been explained by their use of the perceptual frame of the page on which the stimuli are presented. Thus in different contexts men appear capable of ignoring or deploying frame cues in order to perform the task effectively.

Not all studies in visual perception indicate an advantage for men. In facial perception studies, particularly the recognition of facial emotions, women may be more effective in identifying the expressions. These findings provide support for Geary's (1998) suggestion of sex differences in social and physical modules. In addition, the research suggests that in auditory perception many sex differences occur, typically favouring women. These differences exist at the sensory level, in frequency detection and in JND protocols, and may occur in more complex contexts, for example phonological processing. Research into odour perception also suggests that sex differences may be present; however there is an ongoing debate as to the extent that this is due to verbal scaffolding as opposed to actual sensory differences. Sex differences occur in somatosensory processing, but the direction of effect depends upon the task demands.

Research to Do

Declerck and De Brabander (2002) suggest that performance in the Poggendorff illusion is related to performance in a broader range of spatial tasks. Consider how you could attempt to identify which perceptual processes contribute to task performance in these different contexts. Would these processes be equally important for women and for men?

3 Attention and Memory

Aim and Overview

This chapter will consider the evidence for sex differences associated with the processes of attention and memory. The attention component will initially provide the cognitive framework associated with attentional processes. This section will consider basic attention research and the principles and processes of attention which have emerged from the research. The previous chapter highlighted the extensive parallel processing which occurs in the human nervous system. Essentially, the human sensory systems are exposed to a wealth of environmental information and thus attention may be seen as a means of filtering, selecting or constraining what is fully processed. Thus a critical element in the discussion will be the notion of a limited capacity or resource constraining the attention process. Constructs such as the *single channel* will be considered.

The next section will highlight an early model of attention, which demonstrates the complexity of attention and the diversity of factors (physiological, cognitive and social) that have an impact upon performance in attention tasks. This model and its more recent derivatives have relevance for the interpretation of the research which purports to show spatial memory differences between men and women. This component will also consider briefly the extent to which attentional resources could be considered as executive resources in working memory. Indeed it could be argued that these issues have as much relevance for research into working memory findings as the research into attention processes. This consideration demonstrates the close relationship between working memory and attention. For many psychologists, the two processes are inseparable.

The discussion of individual-differences research will emphasize the use of dual-task methodology. Interestingly, this literature has not employed dual-task methods in order to identify different resource constraints in the two sexes; rather the methodology has been employed to illustrate the differences between how men and women appear to attend to and process information. Much of this research discusses the underlying functional neuroanatomy contributing to performance levels. This discussion will conclude with a consideration of different strategy deployment by women and men during attention tasks within a more applied context. This latter research indicates the cognitive complexities associated with attention.

The next component of this chapter identifies the presence of sex differences in tasks that may make major demands upon memorial or mnemonic processes. The first of these sections looks at the functional architecture of working memory, considering different theoretical accounts of the nature of working memory. The subsequent section will consider empirical observations of the individual differences associated with working memory, and given the visual spatial content of the previous chapter, an emphasis will be on sex differences in visuospatial working memory. The next section will briefly outline constructs associated with long-term memory, with the emphasis on processes that in the main are likely to be verbally mediated, so that the concepts of semantic memory, episodic memory, autobiographical memory and procedural memory will be discussed.

What will become obvious again in this chapter is the difficulty in separating the contribution of discrete cognitive processes to particular task performance, an issue discussed previously in the text. Thus for example the imagery research by Loring-Meier and Halpern (1999) discussed in the next chapter was envisaged by the authors themselves as research into visuospatial working memory. One major approach to working memory (Engle *et al.* 1999) considers the role of attention, to be discussed in the earlier sections of the chapter, as a key to the understanding of the role of executive or control processes in working memory. Indeed, one researcher who has focused upon sex differences in spatial location memory emphasizes the contribution of attentional differences (McGivern *et al.* 1997). The reader should remember that processes such as attention are likely to interface with many other cognitive processes and that the placing of attention research into one chapter or another does not negate this observation.

Many researchers consider working memory to be at the centre of a whole host of cognitive processes and task performances (Baddeley *et al.* 1998; Kane and Engle 2002; Miyake *et al.* 2001; Tuholski *et al.* 2001). This chapter will begin a consideration of this suggestion by discussing explicitly the relationship between WM processes and some of the perception and spatial ability tasks dealt with in the previous two chapters.

Attention

Cognitive Processes

Attention was one of the first cognitive constructs to be considered by psychologists in general and one of the earliest experimental psychologists, William

James (1890), in particular. The first consideration was how humans could actually make sense out of all the sensory information that is processed, moment-by-moment, in the nervous system. This process of focusing upon one source of information – visual, auditory or other – is known as *selective attention*, the selection of one source of information among many.

One source of experimental momentum for this research was the use in the 1950s of a dichotic listening task procedure. In this procedure, participants are exposed to two auditory information sources via stereophonic headphones and have to attend to, or shadow, one of the sources. An interesting aspect of this data was the suggestion that non-shadowed, non-attended, information tended not to be perceptually processed. For example, a change of language from English to German in the non-shadowed ear would typically not be detected!

Findings such as these were to shape the first major information-processing model in cognitive psychology, Broadbent's (1958) model of attention. This model explicitly assumed that perception was resource-constrained and inserted a filter to allow only the selected information to receive further (perceptual) processing. It also allowed for parallel sensory processing but a serial attention process protected the limited-capacity perceptual system. Subsequent research was to suggest that non-shadowed information could be perceptually processed, for example the participant's name (an observation labelled the 'cocktail party phenomenon'). This stimulated research into *divided attention*, the processing of information in parallel (this research orientation is reflected in the construction of Baddeley and Hitch's (1974) model of working memory).

The typical procedure in divided attention research is the dual-task paradigm. The participant has to carry out one task, for example perceptually processing heard words, while carrying out a second task, for example attending to visual information on a PC screen. The measure of dual-task (or divided-attention) efficacy is the extent to which the two tasks can effectively be carried out together as opposed to individually. This paradigm is employed extensively in both attention and working-memory research. Another aspect of attention, which has received much research interest, is the *visual search* paradigm where the participant has to locate a target among a set of non-targets or distractors. This type of task is shown in Figure 3.1.

The visual search task shown in Figure 3.1a illustrates a visual search task where the target is the letter O. In the left-hand array, the target is relatively easy to detect; however, in the right-hand array, where the non-targets possess curves, a conscious visual search is typically undertaken in order to find the target. In Figure 3.1b, the target is the filled-in circle, again in the left-hand array, the target typically is rapidly detected, an effect called 'pop-out'. However, a visual search typically has to be carried out with the array on the right. These stimuli demonstrate parallel processes at work in the two left-hand arrays, and a serial, visual search process in the right-hand arrays.

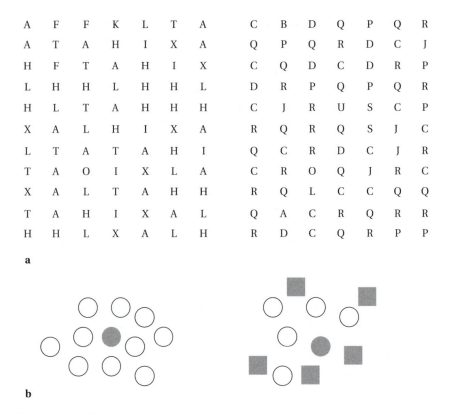

A	F	F	K	L	T	A		C	B	D	Q	P	Q	R
A	T	A	H	I	X	A		Q	P	Q	R	D	C	J
H	F	T	A	H	I	X		C	Q	D	C	D	R	P
L	H	H	L	H	H	L		D	R	P	Q	P	Q	R
H	L	T	A	H	H	H		C	J	R	U	S	C	P
X	A	L	H	I	X	A		R	Q	R	Q	S	J	C
L	T	A	T	A	H	I		Q	C	R	D	C	J	R
T	A	O	I	X	L	A		C	R	O	Q	J	R	C
X	A	L	T	A	H	H		R	Q	L	C	C	Q	Q
T	A	H	I	X	A	L		Q	A	C	R	Q	R	R
H	H	L	X	A	L	H		R	D	C	Q	R	P	P

a

b

Figure 3.1   Visual attention protocols

The targets in the left-hand arrays possess a feature which is unique; in Figure 3.1a, the letter O is the only letter with curves and thus can be detected by looking for a curved feature in the letter. In 3.1b the target is the only shaded circle, so the target can be detected by looking for the unique feature, the shading. Typically, this is a parallel search, with pop-out. In the right-hand figures, the target does not possess a unique feature, thus in 3.1b half of the distractors share the same shape, that is are circular, and the other half possess shading. However, the target has a unique combination (conjoining) of these two features, the only circle with shading. When the target is only unique in terms of its combination of features it is labelled a conjoint search and typically (but not always) involves an explicit serial visual search. Presumably this is similar in nature to the conscious visual search process employed in the right-hand panel of Figure 3.1a.

Recent research has more extensively investigated inhibitory processes in attention, for example the paradigms associated with the Stroop effect (Stroop 1935) and inhibition of return. One of the earliest procedures employed with the Stroop test was a colour-processing task where participants had to

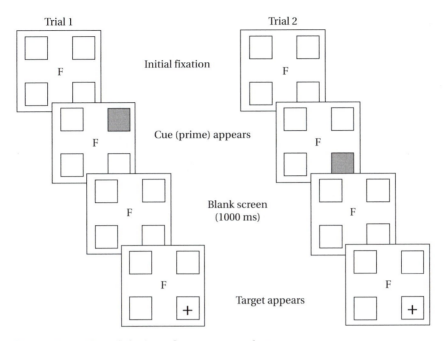

Trial 1   Trial 2

Initial fixation

Cue (prime) appears

Blank screen
(1000 ms)

Target appears

Figure 3.2   The inhibition of return procedure

attend to the ink colour of the text while ignoring the semantic content, two examples being as follows:

1. What is the colour of the text?   BLACK

2. What is the colour of the text?   BLUE

In the first example the colour of the text is the same as (congruent with) the text meaning and RT is quick. However in the second example the text meaning conflicts (is incongruent) with the text ink colour and consequently RT slows down. Both meaning and ink colour are perceptually processed, but the irrelevant information, text meaning, needs to be suppressed or inhibited before the appropriate response can be made.

Inhibition of Return (IOR) is a process which has been implicated in visual search (Klein 2000; Klein and MacInnes 1999). A typical IOR procedure is shown in Figure 3.2. The participant has to detect a target (+) within one of the four squares in the array. On some trials a cue appears in a square approximately 1 second prior to the target appearance. On some of these trials (for example trial 2), the cue appears in the same square as the target.

Two distinct types of trial are shown in Figure 3.2. In trial 1 the cue or prime appears in the top right square; one second later the target appears in the bottom right square and the participant's reaction time is measured. In trial 2, the prime appears in the same location as the target and now the RT is slowed down. The presence of the prime elicits orientation to that square; however, given that the prime is not the target, the square is labelled as a non-target location. Thus when the target appears a second later in the same square there is a conflict of response (as in the Stroop task above), a memory tag implying non-target location and a stimulus which suggests target location. This conflict slows down the response of the participant. According to Klein and co-workers (1999, 2000) this ability to place tags on non-target locations would aid the visual search process by preventing the participant from continually returning to previous (unsuccessful) locations during the search. This would be an important component in visual search of a target object in an array or a food within ambient vegetation.

A final form of attention paradigm employed has been *vigilance* or sustained attention. In this context the participant has to attend to an event which may occur repeatedly over a prolonged period of time. An applied example of this sort of task would be the radar operator on a naval ship who had to monitor, over a period of hours, the radar screen for incoming objects (planes and/or missiles) located in space around the ship.

Sex Differences in Attention

It is probably the case that the major aim of the dual-task literature on individual differences has been to gain insight into sex differences in parallel processing, rather than to look at attentional resource differences *per se*.

McGowan and Duka (2000) looked at the effects of a manual and verbal task combination. In the verbal task, participants had to recite words presented either visually or aurally. The manual task was either right or left finger tapping. Generally there were no differences in the performance of women and men apart from one context: when aural presentation was combined with right finger tapping, the disruptive effects were greater in women. Goddard *et al.* (1998) looked at the effect of dual-task interference upon complex tasks of memory retrieval and problem-solving. Again they found that women were more susceptible to resource demands being increased. The implications of this finding for sex differences in lateralization was emphasized by subsequent meta-analysis by Medland *et al.* (2002). Their review indicated that dual-task demands revealed a slighter greater degree of lateralization in men.

An important element in many of these studies is the use of selective dual-task interference in order to identify the processing or strategy style of the participants. Thus Pezaris and Casey (1991) asked participants to carry out a mental rotation task while simultaneously memorizing either verbal digits (verbal working memory load) or dot locations (visuospatial working memory load). The adolescent girls and boys displayed different patterns of interference (see Chapter 4 for an elaboration of this study). Saucier *et al.* (2003)

carried out a navigation memory task where participants either concurrently repeated the days of the week (verbal interference), or tapped a spatial pattern (visuospatial memory load). These authors found differences in susceptibility to interference between the sexes: men were equally affected by the two forms of interference, whereas women were affected more by the articulation (articulatory suppression) format. This observation will be discussed in more detail later in this chapter.

An interesting paper by Palmer and Folds-Bennett (1998) indicated individual differences in the Stroop task. In this study participants were placed into competitive and non-competitive conditions by being informed that performance would be ranked. The results suggested that men were more susceptible to interference (slower RT) than women in the competitive condition. This suggests that in this context the social cognitions associated with the task and task instructions had a greater impact upon the men (see the section 'Social Cognition, Anxiety and Working Memory Task Performance' below). Schirmer and Kotz (2003) found a different pattern of results in a speech recognition procedure. The participants had to attend to the emotional valence of the words 'happy', 'neutral' or 'angry' while ignoring the prosodic (intonation) information of the speech, or vice versa. The interaction pattern between task and sex of participant indicated that women more quickly matched the available prosodic and valence information. The dual-task studies discussed above consider the pools of resources or the cognitive processes employed across a range of tasks. A consistent feature of the findings is that women and men may draw upon different cognitive resources in order to complete the same task.

Perhaps the most interesting observation of research into inhibitory processes in attention is the relative lack of research into IOR. This attention process appears to have a substantial theoretical framework, suggesting the presence of sex differences favouring women. Klein (2000) explicitly links the IOR process with ancient foraging behaviour; he suggests that:

> Efficient foraging for food (or other desirable objects, places, playmates) involves not only voluntary control over orienting but also the use of information in memory about one's previous orienting behaviour. Once discovered, the locus of a food source that is not exhausted should be remembered as a place to return to. By contrast, places one has searched and not found what one is looking for, should be remembered to be avoided. (p. 138)

Silverman and Eals (1992) suggested that a major factor in the emergence of a sexually dimorphic difference in spatial ability was the division of labour during early hominid evolution. They suggested that men were more likely to be hunters (see the previous chapter on visuomotor processes) while women were more likely to be foragers. The authors developed a task which purported to reveal spatial location memory differences in men and women. This memory task will be discussed in detail later in this chapter.

However, the strongest implication for a sex difference emanating from the division-of-labour-theory would be in a study of IOR rather than an attention/memory task procedure, though IOR itself has been linked to working memory (Castel *et al.* 2003). Koshino *et al.* (2000) in an IOR study found a difference in reaction time between women and men, where men were quicker. However this RT advantage was also apparent in the semantic negative priming procedure and so may actually have reflected a general processing speed difference with no evidence of an IOR specific processing difference (see also the Chapter 8 section, 'Theoretical Frameworks' on speed of processing). Koshino *et al.* also found that positive spatial priming performance (where the cue and target are in the same spatial location) was correlated with MRT. However, this pattern was only evident in women in the sample.

A more recent study by Bayliss *et al.* (2005) also investigated spatial IOR in women and men. Their results were consistent with those of Koshino *et al.* (2000), with no difference in IOR performance between the men and women. An interesting social attention protocol was also employed in this study, where the participants were presented with a centrally located facial stimulus with eye fixation to the left or to the right. This stimulus was followed by presentation of a letter to the left or right of the display. Participants had to respond to the identity of the letter. On some trials the direction of eye gaze predicted the letter appearance (valid trials); on other occasions eye gaze direction was not related to letter appearance (invalid trials). Bayliss *et al.* found sex differences in this task, with women responding relatively more slowly in the invalid cue condition. The authors concluded that this was a result of the women encoding gaze so effectively that they could not inhibit the stimulus in the invalid trials. Sex differences in response to eye gaze is predicted by the Baron-Cohen (2002) suggestion that autism, which is associated with impaired social cognition processes, is a form of extreme maleness.

Several studies have investigated the presence of sex differences in sustained attention or vigilance. Many have observed sex differences (for example Giambra and Quilter 1989) while some have not (for example Chan 2001). Dittmar *et al.* (1993) utilized a vigilance task where participants had to maintain their attention to a pair of lines which were repeatedly presented. The lines could change in appearance in two ways: line length could change (labelled a spatial change) or the duration of appearance could change (a temporal change). The authors employed signal detection measures to identify the performance level of men and women. They observed that men were more sensitive to the spatial change (line length) but no sex differences were found in the temporal change.

This suggests that task-specific sex differences may occur in vigilance. Prinzel and Freeman (1997) also found evidence of these task-specific differences. In addition they assessed the perception of the participants towards the task and found task-specific levels of boredom. Consequently, individual differences in these vigilance measures may in part be cognitive, but may also in part be motivational. This research is a good example of where cognition and social cognition processes may interact and contribute to task performance.

Working Memory Models

According to Baddeley (1997) working memory can be viewed as 'a system for temporarily holding and manipulating information as part of a wide range of essential cognitive tasks such as learning, reasoning and comprehending' (p. 49). An early model constructed to capture the essence of working memory is the model by Baddeley and Hitch (1974).

According to this original working memory model by Baddeley and Hitch (1974), working memory comprises three components: the *phonological loop* (PL), the *visuospatial sketchpad* (VSSP) and the *central executive* (CE). The first and second components were characterized by Baddeley and Hitch (1974) as 'slave systems' that are specialized for the processing and manipulation of limited amounts of information within highly specific modality domains. In contrast to the highly specific informational domains in which these two slave systems operate, the CE is capable of performing a range of high-level functions. The PL system was considered to possess a passive phonological store component and an active rehearsal system based upon inner speech. The visuospatial sketchpad was viewed as 'a system involved in generating and manipulating visuo-spatial images' (Baddeley 1986, p. 72).

Baddeley (1996) identified several key central executive functions:

1. The coordination of performance with two tasks, a component of the dual-task paradigm which was discussed in the previous chapter.

2. The ability to switch retrieval strategies, exemplified in the random number generation task where participants are asked to orally (or by key press) generate a random sequence of digits from 1 to 5 or from 1 to 10.

3. The ability to selectively attend to some information source while concurrently inhibiting other information.

4. The capacity to hold and manipulate information in long-term memory (LTM); thus the executive process is the interface between working memory and LTM, observed in verbal fluency procedures (see below).

Miyake *et al.* (2000) also made explicit the processes of set-shifting, inhibition and memory-updating (monitoring) in executive functioning. An extension of the Baddeley and Hitch (1974) model of working memory was carried out by Logie (1995). Logie elaborated the rather nebulous notion of a visuospatial sketchpad and identified two processes: a passive visual store, the *visual cache,* and an active rehearsal process, the *inner scribe.* According to Logie, 'the scribe provides a means of "redrawing" the contents of the visual cache, offering a service of visual and spatial rehearsal, manipulation and transformation' (Logie 1995, p. 3).

These models generated in Europe emphasized the functional architecture of the slave systems in working memory; models originating in North America articulated the functioning of the executive processes within the system, one such model being shown in Figure 3.3.

In this model of working memory by Engle and colleagues (1999; see also Kane *et al.* 2001; Kane and Engle 2002) a major emphasis is placed upon the nature of executive processes. A key element in this model is the role of focused attention upon the contents of working memory. Short-term memory (STM) is perceived as activated long-term memory; however attention further activates some selected portion of the STM information. The research of Awh and co-workers (1998, 2000; see also Awh and Jonides 2001) has attempted to identify precisely the role of attention in location memory task procedures. These authors argued that their results implicate selective spatial attention as a rehearsal mechanism for spatial working memory. In this sense, the spatial rehearsal mechanism in VSWM could be a spatial attention process. Imagine undertaking the Corsi block task described below. One way in which to rehearse the locations of the touched blocks would be to visually scan across the blocks in a sequence which mimicked the original touching sequence.

More recently Cornoldi and Vecchi (2003) have developed an alternative '*continuity model*' in order to account for individual differences in working memory. In the Cornoldi and Vecchi model the horizontal axis represents modality-specific processes – verbal, visual, spatial haptic and so on. These

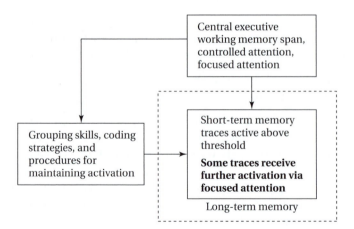

Figure 3.3   A controlled attention view of working memory (*Source*: Engle *et al.* (1999) 'Working memory, short-term memory, and general fluid intelligences' *Journal of Experimental Psychology: General*, 128, 309–31, Figure 4.1, p. 106. With permission from the American Psychological Association)

memory processes may occur independently and in parallel. Thus the authors suggest that there discrete pools of resources associated with the initial mnemonic processing of information derived from domain-specific perceptual processes. The vertical axis emphasizes the level of processing associated with any given task, from passive tasks such as digit span through to tasks demanding extensive active or control processing, such as mental rotation. In contrast to the Baddeley and Hitch type models discussed above, Cornoldi and Vecchi also suggest the presence of pools of resources for more active control (executive-like) processes. The authors have employed this model in the interpretation of individual differences associated with sex (discussed below in this chapter), age and visual impairment. They have argued that individual differences such as sex differences are more likely to occur when task demands recruit more active processes. An example of this is the manipulation and transformation of spatial information in mental rotation procedures.

Working Memory, Perception and Spatial Ability

The research of Loring-Meier and Halpern (1999), although nominally into imagery task performance, could also be considered to be demanding of visuospatial working memory resources (Bruyer and Scailquin 1998). Is it possible that many of the tasks discussed in the next chapter actually make demands upon VSWM? If so, then any observed sex differences may not originate in perceptual or imagery processes but rather may actually be due to individual differences in working memory. Thus Miyake *et al.* (2001b) have suggested that tasks measuring field dependence/independence (see Chapter 2) may make extensive VSWM demands. Miyake *et al.* (2001a) have suggested that spatial-visualization, spatial-relations and perceptual-speed processes are all associated with visuospatial storage and executive resources.

Hamilton and Wolsey (2001) made explicit the interface between visuospatial working memory (VSWM) and imagery. They modified the model of MRT suggested by Bauer and Jolicoeur (1996) to incorporate the categorical and coordinate spatial relations processes discussed in the previous chapter. This account is shown in Figure 3.4.

In this proposal it is presumed that the actual rotation and checking for integrity of the parts is carried out by the categorical and coordinate spatial-relations processes which are not integral to working memory itself (Morton and Morris 1995). However, the interim outputs from the rotation, and the integration of the spatial relations and working memory processes, are considered to be VSWM processes. The work of Salway and Logie (1995) and Bruyer and Scailquin (1998) has provided experimental, secondary-task interference evidence for the significant contribution of the *central-executive* process in the mental rotation process. Thus Bruyer and Scailquin employed a dual-task paradigm where the primary task was mental rotation of a two-dimensional

Original stimulus pair.

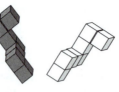

Coordinate spatial
processes rotate one of
the stimuli, but only
through a small angle.

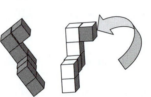

Newly rotated image is
maintained in visuospatial
working memory.
Categorical processes then
check the integrity of the
parts.

Processes are integrated by the central executive

Coordinate spatial
processes rotate the
stimulus a few more
degrees.

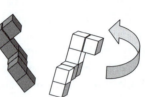

Newly rotated image is
again maintained in
working memory.
Categorical processes
again check the parts.

Processes are integrated by the central executive

Ultimately, coordinate
spatial processes rotate
the stimulus the final few
degrees.

Final matching of the two
stimuli.

Figure 3.4 The relationship between VisuoSpatial Working Memory
(VSWM) and mental rotation

shape (see Figure 4.5 depicting mental rotation formats in the next chapter)
and the secondary task made demands either on the phonological loop, VSSP
or on executive resources. The interference affect upon mental rotation was
greatest when the secondary task made demands upon executive resources.

Sex Differences in Working Memory

Methods in Working Memory Research

A variety of tasks are employed to selectively tap the discrete VSWM processes.
A summary of three typical tasks is shown in Figure 3.5. One conventional
measure of visual memory is the matrix task (Phillips and Christie 1977) or
visual patterns task (Della Sala *et al.* 1999). In this task the participant is shown
a matrix with filled-in cells; after a period of maintenance of the matrix image
the participant has to identify the filled-in cells. The more competent the

Task *Putative process*	Encode	Maintenance intervals ~2–10 seconds	Retrieval
Matrix or visual patterns task *Visual cache matrix task* (Della Sala *et al.* 1999)	 Remember the filled-in-cells		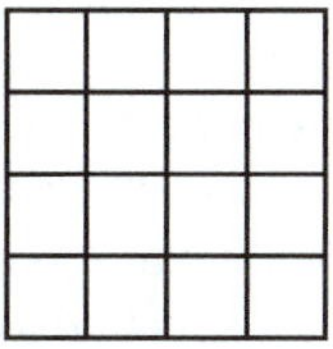 Identify the filled-in-cells.
Corsi blocks task *Inner scribe* (Della Sala *et al.* 1999)	 Researcher taps a sequence of blocks.		 Participant repeats the sequence of taps.
Visuospatial complex span task *Visuospatial executive* (Shah and Miyake 1996)	 Are the letters the same or mirror reversed? Remember the spot's location		Complete the mental rotation judgements then identify the spot's locations, or sequence of locations.

Figure 3.5   Typical VSWM task procedures

participant the more complex (more cells) the matrix becomes. The Corsi blocks task is viewed as a task demanding inner-scribe processes (Della Sala *et al.* 1999; Hanley *et al.* 1991; Morton and Morris 1995). In this task the researcher taps a sequence of blocks, typically at a rate of one second per tap, and the participant has to repeat the sequence of taps in the correct order. The procedure demands a combination of spatial location information and spatio-temporal sequence. The more competent the participant, the more blocks will be tapped.

A key element of a working memory or complex span task is that it demands concurrent maintenance and processing from the participant. The complex spatial span paradigm employed by Shah and Miyake (1996) is shown in the bottom row of Figure 3.5. In this task the participant has to maintain the location of the top of the rotated letter (shown in grey). At the same time the participant has to perform mental rotation on the pair of letters to judge whether the letter stimuli are the same as or mirror images of one another. Then subsequently the participant has to identify the location of the top of the letter (grey spot). Thus the participant has to maintain location information and carry out a concurrent process (mental rotation). More competent participants will have more mental rotations and locations to carry out and memorize. Shah and Miyake found in their undergraduate sample that typically participants could carry out three mental rotations and recall the three associated locations (although the range was large, from 1 to 5).

The typical measure of the phonological-loop measure is the digit span task, where a series of digits is presented to the participant and the series has to be recalled in the same order. Complex verbal executive tasks also demand concurrent verbal maintenance and processing. Thus a common task is the backward digit span, where the participant has to recall a series of digits, but in reverse order. Thus the participant has to maintain the original items and then reorganize (processing element) the order. The most typical verbal executive task is a derivative of the reading span task output (Daneman and Carpenter 1980) where a sentence is read (processing element) and the last word in each sentence has to be remembered (maintenance element).

Sex Differences in Visuospatial Working Memory

Work by Orsini *et al.* (1987) investigated the importance of age and sex in the performance of the Corsi block task. This task was employed initially as a visuospatial measure within a clinical context (Milner 1971). The task is shown in the middle row of Figure 3.5 above. Orsini *et al.* found that a sex difference in task performances emerged in young adulthood, with men achieving higher span scores. While this research does appear to highlight individual differences in visuospatial working memory it is difficult to pinpoint exactly where the difference in performance emerges. Is the cognitive locus in the *visual cache*, in the *inner scribe* or in the *central executive*? This task is amenable to a variety of strategies and thus across participants the task may make demands upon the various components of VSWM.

These diverse demands are highlighted by dual-task studies (Fisk and Sharp 2003; Hamilton *et al.* 2003; Vandierendonck *et al.* 2004; Vecchi and Richardson 2001), where both spatial tapping and executive secondary tasks reduced the performance in the Corsi task. Research by Fisk and Sharp (2003) further emphasizes the importance of executive processes in VSWM task performance. Consequently, identifying the locus of the Corsi block sex difference within VSWM is problematic. It should also be noted that the difference in task performance between women and men is not always found in smaller samples (Postma *et al.* 2004). In addition, it has been observed that long-term learning of the Corsi block task is not associated with sex differences (Capitani *et al.* 1991). The lack of confidence in identifying the cognitive locus (or loci) of the individual differences in the Corsi block task is a difficulty encountered before in this book, and a problem which will re-emerge in this and later chapters.

The Orsini *et al.* (1987) finding stands in contrast to a series of other studies on object location memory which have tended to find that women perform the object location recall task more effectively. Silverman and Eals (1992) and Eals and Silverman (1994) working within an evolutionary framework assessed the performance of participants in an object memory task. In this task 27 objects were placed in an array and then subsequently some objects were added and ultimately some of the original objects were moved. Typical object location procedures are shown in Figure 3.6.

The first array indicates the original locations; in the second stimulus array, objects have been added and participants have to cross out these additional objects (some are marked with arrows). Silverman and Eals described this procedure as an *object memory* task. In the final stimulus array, pairs of objects from the original array have their locations exchanged. These relocated stimuli in the figure are again indicated by the arrows. This was labelled a *location memory* task. Their results indicated that female participants performed significantly better in both the object memory procedure and in the object location memory context.

In the second phase of their original study, Silverman and Eals placed participants within 'a naturalistic setting' where real objects and their locations in a room had to be recalled; again female participants performed significantly better. The final procedures reported in this study indicated that object memory performance favoured female participants only when the memory task was incidental, that is, where memory recall was unexpected. In contrast, location memory performance consistently favoured women in both incidental and directed (where participants were explicitly instructed to memorize objects in the room) conditions.

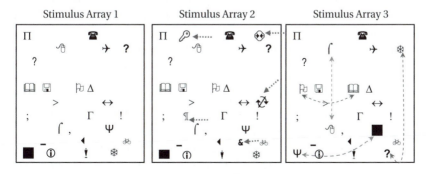

Figure 3.6   The object location task protocols

A subsequent replication by Eals and Silverman (1994) controlling for verbal labelling of the objects found essentially the same pattern of results. These studies provided evidence that female participants had high ability in spatial memory tasks. The conclusions made by these authors was that these spatial skills emerged in early hominid ancestry where women exhibited foraging behaviour and so consequently the ability to remember and locate appropriate food sources would have been a highly adaptive function (see Klein and MacInnes 1999; Klein 2000, above for a similar argument). These studies have had a major impact upon subsequent sex differences research in spatial memory; the Eals and Silverman (1994) paper had over 100 citations at the point where this book was being prepared.

Despite its citation success, there are many procedural difficulties with the task. As a consequence it is difficult to identify where in the task the advantage for women occurs: it could be in the initial phase where participants have to allocate their attention across the array; it could be in working memory where object location is maintained; or it could be that performance is supported by some long-term memory (LTM) process which is required in order to maintain the array during the one-minute inter-stimulus interval. The complexities of the task procedure have been examined extensively in subsequent research.

McGivern *et al.* (1997) considered that the advantage for women in the object location task was related to the initial attention component. These authors based their predictions upon the work of Meyers-Levy (1989), whose research in advertising led her to suggest that men are more likely to direct attention to stimuli which are pertinent to themselves. Thus McGivern *et al.* predicted that while women would perform well with objects which possessed either stereotypical 'feminine' or 'neutral' labels, men would perform well with objects which possessed 'masculine' associations. Their results supported these predictions: men were as competent as women with the recall of 'masculine' object locations, women were more efficient with random ('neutral') and 'feminine' object locations. Thus in a task that may make demands upon working memory and LTM maintenance, McGivern *et al.* concluded that the difference between men and women lay in their allocation of attention to the objects in the array, a key central executive process (Engle *et al.* 1999).

Cherney and Ryalls (1999) replicated the more naturalistic context from the Eals and Silverman studies. They had a particular interest in the incidental memory nature of the original studies. They exposed men and women to an array of 30 gender-stereotyped objects within a room. After two minutes' exposure and a 5-minute filler period they had to recall the objects and then the locations of the objects. Cherney and Ryalls found that women and men recalled more stereotypic congruent objects and object locations. They suggested that this pattern of results (similar to McGivern *et al.* 1997, above) was unlikely to be explained by a 'hunter-gatherer' theory but could be readily

accounted for by gender-schema theory (see Chapters 6 and 10). This interpretation raises another important issue in the Eals and Silverman procedures.
The objects may be subject to stereotypical labelling, labels which are allocated to cultural artefacts typically constructed and employed differentially
by men and women within the last few centuries. If so, it appears a rather
inappropriate research context in which to assess an evolutionary advantage
for women in natural-object (food) location. The issue of ecological validity
was raised by Neave *et al.* (2005). In order to overcome this problem they carried out a study where the objects were plants and were embedded within
natural foliage contexts. In these contexts when sex differences occurred
they favoured women.

McBurney *et al.* (1997) devised an alternative procedure for memory location
based upon recalling pairs of stimuli among an array of locations. The advantage for women in this object location memory task was large ($d = -0.89$)
and the authors interpreted the results in line with the evolutionary explanation of foraging. This observation had been replicated for static and
dynamic arrays (Tottenham *et al.* 2003). Duff and Hampson (2001), employing a similar procedure, further replicated the observation of an advantage
for women. More importantly they attempted to control for various other
factors that may have contributed to the more efficient performance of
women: attention, perceptual speed, verbal ability such as access to verbal
labels and incidental processing. The large difference between the sexes
existed after these factors were controlled for.

It is interesting to note that this sex difference occurred in the absence of any
such difference in the Eals and Silverman procedure with the same participants. Duff and Hampson concluded that the sex difference 'was due to its
spatial working memory components *per se* and was not secondary to a
female advantage in some other potentially task-related ability' (2001, p. 481).
More recent research by Choi and L'Hirondelle (2005) has contested this
conclusion, suggesting that in a concrete object location context, where
women performed at a higher level than men, the sex difference was removed
when verbal memory was controlled.

Another issue for these task protocols is the duration retention interval; as
in the original Eals and Silverman procedure, task performance occurs over
several minutes, and consequently it is difficult to rule out the contribution
of an LTM process, which was not considered in the Duff and Hampson study.
Zimmer *et al.* (2003), employing the dual-task paradigm, argued that object
location memory and the Corsi task made differential demands upon memory.
While the latter made extensive demands upon spatial attention (see Awh
and Jonides 2001, above), object location memory made use of episodic
processes in LTM, where the information about object property was bound
with location information. This argument has been applied to the sex differences literature by James and Kimura (1997), who suggested that the advantage
for women arose from the integration of object information with location

information. This emphasis upon object to location processing was high-lighted in the approach of Postma and his colleagues (Postma and De Haan 1996; Postma *et al.* 1998; Postma *et al.* 2004; Postma *et al.* 1999).

Postma and his co-workers have worked within a visuospatial working memory framework and have identified at least two discrete processes at work in object location memory. The first component is a positional encoding system based upon fine metric information provided by the coordinate spatial relations system, and an object-to-location process potentially based upon the verbal categorical spatial relations system. Postma *et al.* (1998) found that there was no sex difference in a task condition which demanded object-to-position assignment. In addition, articulatory suppression (a dual-task procedure employed to impair verbal working memory) impaired performance on the task equally for men and women.

Thus despite the attempt by Duff and Hampson (2001) to control for verbal processes, this finding does implicate verbal working memory processes in object location memory. However, the Postma study also incorporated a condition whereby only locations had to be remembered. In this condition object memory processes could not contribute to task performance. Errors in location were measured in millimetres; thus performance required fine-grained location memory. In this condition there was a sex difference favour-ing men; however, articulatory suppression again affected men and women equally. In a later study Postma *et al.* (2004) replicated this pattern of results but in the same participants did not observe a sex difference in either the Corsi span task or the Silverman and Eals procedure.

This dissociation between Corsi and object location memory supports the observation by Zimmer *et al.* (2003) that suggests that the two tasks do not draw entirely on the same cognitive processes. In this case, where the sex dif-ference arose from recall of precise metric location information in the Postma studies, it is unlikely to be present in the Corsi, where spatial separation of the block locations is in the order of centimetres rather than millimetres. It should be noted that Postma *et al.* (1998) observed that articulatory sup-pression had an impact upon the recall of fine metric location. This observa-tion presents another anomaly in this research literature. It is presumed by Postma and his co-workers that recall of metric, coordinate information would not be dependent upon verbal processes in the left hemisphere (Kessels *et al.* 2002). Yet articulatory suppression is viewed as making demands upon left-hemispheric phonological processes (Logie *et al.* 2003).

In summary, the initial observations by Silverman and Eals revealing an advantage for women in an object location memory protocol have failed to be systematically replicated and are difficult to interpret. The original protocol compromises the identification of the precise cognitive locus underlying the individual differences. Are the sex differences a consequence of attention biases, visuospatial working memory differences, or are they mediated by verbal long-term memory processes? Procedures which emphasize the precise spatial location (a coordinate spatial relations process) have found no advantage for women, but in fact the reverse (Postma *et al.* 1998).

An alternative approach to explaining sex differences in visuospatial working memory has been the suggestion of Vecchi and Girelli (1998). In this task procedure the participant views the block matrix pattern and has to memorize the location of the filled-in blocks (passive task). The participant then has to visualize a blank block matrix and, in response to oral instructions, mentally follow a pathway through the block to its termination (active task). Then the participant has to indicate the location of the terminal block in the pathway. The participant then indicates the locations of the filled-in cubes. Vecchi and Girelli found that there was no sex difference in the passive component, the recall of the locations. However, in the active task, the recall of the terminal position in the mental pathway, the men performed better than the women ($d = 0.5$ with 2-D stimuli, $d = 0.60$ with 3-D stimuli). This pattern of results supports the notion of Cornoldi and Vecchi (2003) that individual differences are most likely to be found in tasks demanding extensive active processing (see also Richardson 1999, in the next chapter).

Closer examination of the Vecchi and Girelli task procedure makes apparent the close similarity of these task procedures and the processes demanded by complex working memory span tasks (see above). Their procedure demands concurrent maintenance and active processing within each trial. Typically, complex span tasks assess performance in only the maintenance component: the Vecchi and Girelli procedure measured both the maintenance and the processing components. If the task is viewed as a complex span task then this offers the suggestion that men possess a greater VSWM capacity than women. Vecchi and Girelli considered this possibility and went on to investigate whether there was a sex difference with the maintenance of complex block matrix stimuli. Their results did not suggest a difference and they concluded that this 'result does not support the hypothesis that a difference in VSWM capacity is indeed responsible for the gender effect reported' (Vecchi and Girelli 1998, pp. 13–14).

However, this presumes that there is one resource available for passive and active processing within this one modality (Cornoldi and Vecchi 2003). The Baddeley and Hitch model (1974) would argue for multiple pools of resources, with discrete resources for maintenance and processing (Cocchini *et al.* 2002; Duff and Logie 2001). Within this view, there may be still a difference in VSWM capacity, but limited to executive resourcing.

Vecchi and Girelli also investigated the consequence of combining visuospatial working memory with verbal memory demands to identify the verbal contribution to task performance. This combination produced three task variants:

- Memory location component (passive) with mental pathway component (active processing) – the original task.

- Memory location (passive) with verbal task (active processing).

- Mental pathway visuospatial task with verbal task (passive).

Their results provided several interesting patterns. Combining the active verbal task with the memory location task reduced performance; this indicates a verbal contribution to the memory location component. In addition, both women and men were affected equally, suggesting no strategy differences between the sexes. A final observation was that the mental pathway process was not affected by a passive verbal task. The Baddeley and Hitch working memory model could equally accommodate these findings. In fact Shah and Miyake (1996) observed similar effects in their complex span performance when the location maintenance component was paired with an executive verbal process, namely sentence verification. In this context, the mean number of locations retrieved when completed alone was 3.89 but in combination with sentence verification was reduced to 3.04. Figure 5b in Shah and Miyake (1996, p. 20) also indicates a putative contribution of verbal processing to the location memory task.

Thus, in the Vecchi and Girelli protocol, a task which on the surface demands visuospatial working memory, may also recruit verbal executive resources (see also Fisk and Sharp 2003; Hamilton *et al.* 2003). Consequently, a common thread in this chapter so far has been the consideration of verbal 'intrusion' into participant performance in tasks conventionally labelled visuospatial in nature. The advantage in employing a process-oriented approach allows one to identify the complexity of functional architecture underlying visuospatial working memory task performance. The next section considers explicitly whether sex differences could actually occur in verbal working memory task performance.

Sex Differences in Verbal Working Memory

The research by Orsini *et al.* (1987) identified above also investigated verbal competencies in men and women. They employed the digit span task and found a non-significant trend towards women being more efficient. This would suggest that women might have more efficient phonological working memory processes, as Kimura (1999) also reported an advantage for women in this task. Majeres (1999) carried out a series of experiments varying phonological demands and found women were quicker at accessing and utilizing phonological and lexical representations. Majeres linked his findings to the observations that boys were more likely to experience reading-related problems. It should be noted that this is an instance of verbal working memory processes being scaffolded by verbal LTM, an interfacing that can occur in many contexts, for example redintegration. It should be noted that not all studies indicate a sex difference favouring women; thus Duff and

Hampson (2001) failed to detect any evidence for a sex difference in digit span performance.

Duff and Hampson also observed verbal complex span task performances in their participants. In a backward-digit-span procedure again they found no difference in task performance between women and men, however in a second complex WM task they did observe a difference. In the *digit-ordering task* the participant has to randomly order the digits between 1 and 10 without repeating or omitting any of the digits. This task would demand some of the executive resources deployed in the random number generation process identified by Baddeley (1996) above and in addition requires the maintenance of digits recently articulated. Duff and Hampson did not employ measures of randomness, merely the overall number of errors. Men made 30 per cent more errors than women in this task.

Research by Block *et al.* (1989) also employed a task with the critical characteristics of concurrent verbal maintenance and processing elements. In this task the participant is presented with a word with a particular consonant–vowel pattern and has to match the stimulus word with another word with a similar pattern in a list of alternatives:

Consonant vowel task (CV task)
HEATH: DARES SLIDE   LEARN TREAT
The solution is the word LEARN (CVVCC).

This task requires the pattern to be maintained and then compared with the consonant–vowel pattern of a different word. The combination of maintenance and manipulation (comparison process) is again present and again in this task women outperform men. The results revealed an exceptionally large effect size in favour of women ($d = 1.3$). Thus these two studies suggest that when verbally based tasks make demands upon central executive resources, women show a significant advantage in performance.

A further example of a sex difference in a verbally based central executive function is task performance in verbal fluency, another one of the executive functions identified by Baddeley (1996) above. In the verbal fluency procedure participants have to recall a set of words from long-term verbal memory, and thus make demands upon central executive resources. In the lexical fluency procedure, participants are instructed to generate a list of words beginning with a specific letter, for example the letter F. In category fluency, participants have to retrieve words from within a semantic category, for example animals. Findings indicating an advantage for women have been consistently demonstrated (Herlitz *et al.* 1997; Kimura 1999; Weiss *et al.* 2003).

The sex difference appears to be dependent upon the format of verbal fluency; there is a consistent and large difference in lexical fluency, Weiss *et al.* finding an effect size of $d = 0.45$. However categorical fluency can sometimes show an advantage for men. Kimura contrasts searching through the category 'things round' as leading to an advantage for men whereas searching for 'red things' favours women, possibly because of the advantage women have in accessing colour information in LTM (Duff and Hampson 2001; Kimura 1999; but see also Alexander 2003, in Chapter 2). Research by Kosmidis *et al.* (2004) also highlights the variability of individual differences across discrete fluency categories. The variability of individual differences in verbal fluency suggest that the locus for some of the sex differences observed may lie in the structure, organization and function of long-term memory, rather than in central executive efficacy *per se.*

Sex Differences in Long-Term Memory

Psychologists have conducted extensive research into the nature and function of long-term memory (LTM). While there may be general agreement as to varying forms of LTM representation, the precise details and organization are still debated. Consequently, this section will give a brief overview of the general characteristics of LTM before discussing research in detail.

Declarative or explicit memory processes are those we can consciously access. Recalling the details of what we did last night would be an example of explicit episodic memory relating to events of the night before. Remembering that Tesco is the major supermarket chain in Britain would be explicit retrieval of general or semantic knowledge of the world. On the other hand, many memory processes cannot be accessed consciously; these are implicit or nondeclarative memory processes. Thus we have no explicit access to the motor or cognitive skill processes we possess (procedural memory). In addition we have no explicit access to representations which arise through classical conditioning or processes such as habituation. Most of the research to be discussed below refers to episodic and semantic memory. However, the distinction between explicit and implicit memory processes has already been identified in the research by Silverman and Eals (1992) discussed earlier in this chapter.

An important issue which should be raised at this point is the consideration of long-term visual memory (LTVM). The notion of LTVM has already been referred to implicitly in the discussion of image generation in the previous chapter. It may be presumed that images generated and maintained in visuospatial working memory are retrieved from LTVM. However, the nature of this representation is contentious: is it in an analogue or a propositional format? This is the imagery debate revisited. It is possible that long-term knowledge of a map route could be held in some analogue format and a 'maplike' representation retrieved, and for some individuals the map is subsequently inspected in a survey-like manner (Pazzaglia and De Beni 2001). However, it may be equally plausible that a propositional representation is made of the map information. Thus, I could represent in long term memory the route from a local rail station to my university department by means of a set of categorical spatial statements; turn left out of the station, walk for about fifty yards, turn right, walk along the road for about two hundred yards to the traffic lights etc. In this account the role of VSWM may be to reformat this long term propositional account into an analogue format in order to aid with the navigation. It is difficult though to imagine how propositional statements could fully capture the coordinate spatial relations detail required for face recognition However, the discussion in this text will not make a presumption as to which representation is more appropriate; the research into map and route retrieval will constitute a separate section.

Many of the memory processes to be discussed underpin the general concept of 'verbal ability' (Hyde and Linn 1988), however the emphasis will remain on cognitive processes. In their meta-analysis Hyde and Linn identified five verbal processes:

- Retrieval of the definition of a word, vocabulary assessment, demanding retrieval from semantic memory, mediated by executive processes.

- Retrieval of the name of a picture.

- Analysis of the relation between words, for example analogies; this demands reasoning as well retrieval.

- Selection of relevant information from extensive information, for example comprehension assessments.

- Verbal production, spoken or written.

Their meta-analysis indicated that in all five processes effect sizes were small, with the 'largest size', $d = -0.12$, for retrieval of the name of a picture indicating a small advantage for boys and men. Their conclusions appeared quite unequivocal: 'We are prepared to assert that there are no gender differences in verbal ability, at least at this time, in American culture' (Hyde and Linn 1988, p. 62).

However, in 4 of the 5 processes (not analogies) there was a significant nonhomogeneity. Consequently, these general categories of processes may well have confounded the patterns of effect sizes. Hyde and Linn recognized this, and went on to suggest there was a need for future research to undertake a finer-grained analysis of cognitive processes. An example of such a development is the research discussed above which motivated a consideration of lexical versus categorical verbal fluency.

Sex Differences in Semantic and Episodic Memory

There has been prior discussion in this chapter of research which suggests sex differences in access and retrieval from semantic memory; thus studies on verbal fluency suggest a general advantage favouring women (Weiss *et al.* 2003). The contribution of both central executive and semantic memory functions are presumed to contribute to this difference. In order to look specifically at semantic memory one could consider gross differences or finer differences. Thus Lynn and Irwing (2002) suggested that men and women differed significantly ($d = 0.5$) in their general knowledge, with men displaying greater knowledge in a number of semantic categories: general science, games, finance, and literature. Women were more knowledgeable in medicine and fashion. The majority of studies have looked at more specific semantic processing competencies in procedures where information is presented and then retrieved from memory. Authors such as Herlitz (Herlitz *et al.* 1997, 1999; Herlitz and Yonker 2002) view this format as episodic memory, where participants have to recall information from a presentation made some time before. Therefore participants have to recall information from a particular presentation event.

Both Kimura (1999) and Halpern (2000) suggested that verbal retrieval is more efficient in women. Herlitz *et al.* (1999) suggested that women were more efficient in word recall, word recall in focused and divided attention conditions, face and name recall, spatial recall (see above) and odour recognition. In their study they found evidence for women being more efficient in the free recall of abstract words, and the recall and recognition of concrete pictures. However, Chipman and Kimura (1998) in a study of incidental (implicit) recall found that the advantage for women in recalling pictorial stimuli could be mediated by the verbal ability women possess. Consequently, Herlitz *et al.* employed verbal measures, fluency and synonyms, and spatial measures, water-level task and mental rotation as control measures. When the combined verbal measures were employed as a covariate the advantage for women in the abstract word recall was lost, although over all stimuli material a significant sex effect was maintained. These authors concluded that 'verbal skill does have an impact upon episodic memory performance, although it cannot fully explain women's higher performance' (Chipman and Kimura 1998, p. 595).

In a later study by Herlitz and Yonker (2002), psychometrically defined intelligence was also identified as a further measure related to episodic efficacy, a finding supported by other research (Kimura and Clarke 2002). Consequently, in future studies IQ may need to be matched and controlled for in the statistical analysis. Research findings suggest that there are sex differences across a range of memory retrieval contexts: emotional content (Cahill and van Stegeren 2003), everyday memory (Colley *et al.* 2002), autobiographical memory (Davis 1999; Goddard *et al.* 1998) and memory for the appearance of others (Horgan *et al.* 2004). Sex differences favouring women in olfactory or odour recollection were identified in Chapter 2; however it should be noted that once again this advantage may be mediated (in part) by the general verbal efficacy of women (Larrson *et al.* 2003). In general, therefore, there is extensive and diverse evidence for an advantage for women in LTM retrieval.

Route and Map Memory in Women and Men

Information in semantic and episodic memory generally produces a verbal representation output in working memory, in the form of writing or speech. However, certain LTM representations brought into working memory may not produce solely a verbal representation, for example a face, an image of one's home and so on. One such source of LTM is the knowledge of geographical information, both local and more global. There are distinct sources of evidence which imply that this form of information is generated in visuo-spatial working memory. Garden *et al.* (2002) carried out a dual-task study whereby participants had to learn a route from a map and did so under conditions of articulatory suppression or spatial tapping. The results suggested that spatial interference had a greater impact upon route learning, suggesting that participants employed VSWM during recognition of the route. Interestingly, a second part of the study, which employed an actual route through an Italian town, found that only high-spatial-ability participants were more sensitive to a secondary spatial task, spatial tapping. Subsequent research has also found evidence for VSWM involvement during a navigation task (Saucier *et al.* 2003).

There is substantial evidence for differences between men and women in the way that they represent such information. Kimura (1999) noted that research had indicated that men and women give different types of advice when giving directions. Women are more likely to employ landmarks, for example 'Drive towards the school then at the traffic lights turn right towards the railway station', whereas men are more likely to employ directions such as 'Drive north for half of a mile (about 0.75 km) then at the lights turn east and drive east for 2 miles (about 3 km)'. Making use of readily verbally labelled structures such as the school or station to give directions is an example of the use of a *landmark* or *route* representation. Descriptions which employ cardinal directions such as north or east are typical of a *survey* format of representation. Pazzaglia and De Beni (2001) provided evidence that individuals employing the survey strategy had relatively higher mental rotation performance. However, this association between memory for cardinal directions (Euclidian) and mental rotation has not always been found (Dabbs *et al.* 1998).

Galea and Kimura (1993) found evidence for sex differences in memory for routes. Participants had to observe a route being traced through a map with street names and buildings and objects located on it. Participants had to learn the route without making any errors. Men learnt the route in fewer trials and less time. Interestingly subsequent retrieval of information from the procedure indicated that women recalled more landmarks and street names while men recalled more details on directions and distances. In this study learning of the route was correlated with mental rotation performance. Subsequent research (Dabbs *et al.* 1998; Montello *et al.* 1999) has found similar patterns of results, with women displaying relatively good landmark retrieval and men displaying better retrieval of Euclidean features such as directions and distances.

This strategy of survey deployment and its demands upon VSWM make men more susceptible to spatial tapping interference, while the strategy of women to employ landmark information makes them more susceptible to articulatory suppression (Saucier *et al.* 2003). An advantage for men in navigation memory has also been observed in virtual reality contexts (Astur *et al.* 1998). The deployment of some form of Euclidean representation in men has also been evidenced in these virtual maze contexts (Lawton and Morrin 1999; Sandstrom *et al.* 1998). The former study also provided evidence that with appropriate learning experience, both women and men improved their performance to an equivalent extent (see Baenninger and Newcombe 1989 in Chapter 10). Research by Saucier *et al.* (2003) suggests that the differential use of strategies by men and women is quite rigid. Thus when encouraged to utilize a non-typical strategy, men were poorer when employing landmarks and women were poorer with the Euclidean strategy. It is tempting to suggest that this observation implies a structural limitation in working memory functional architecture in the two sexes. However, it may simply mean that extensive training is required before well-established strategy deployment can become more flexible.

Neuropsychological Research in Memory

Neuropsychological research has attempted to identify whether there are sex differences in the neural systems involved in memory procedures. An issue to reconsider at this point is that such studies are much more informative when performance in women and men is equated and thus performance difference does not confound the results (see Chapter 1).

Recent research has suggested that verbal working memory tasks make demand upon left-hemispheric processes (Logie *et al.* 2003; Smith and Jonides 1997). Logie *et al.* identified three particular structures: the inferior parietal gyrus and the inferior and middle frontal gyri. However, Saucier and Elias (2002) have suggested that the findings are not entirely equivocal. They employed a phonological memory task within a divided field format, where stimuli are presented briefly to the left or right of the fixation point, the left visual field (LVF) and right visual field (RVF) respectively. Stimuli presented to the LVF will initially be processed in the right hemisphere; RVF stimuli will be processed, in the first instance, in the left hemisphere. Their findings suggested that not only did the stimuli format (letter versus number) and stimulus load affect the extent of lateralization but the sex of the participant also had an impact. Typically there was an RVF advantage in the tasks, suggesting that the left hemisphere was the more efficient one in this procedure. However, the extent of lateralization varied across task and sex, with men more asymmetric in the letter format and women more asymmetric in the number task.

Research by Weiss *et al.* (2003) carried out an fMRI study of verbal fluency where the women and men were selected on the basis of equivalent high performance. Thus, with this matched design, performance difference could not act as a confounding variable. The verbal fluency task was lexical in nature, generating words with the initial letters B, A, F and S. The task performance pattern of results confirmed the matched nature of the design. Common areas of activation were observed: left prefrontal cortex, right prefrontal, cingulate gyrus, and the right cerebellum. The authors concluded that when performance is equated there are no sex differences in the recruitment of neural systems underlying verbal fluency.

Ragland *et al.* (2000) looked at regional cerebral blood flow (rCBF) in immediate and delayed verbal memory procedures. These authors noted that a sex difference in resting rCBF existed between men and women. More importantly the relationship between blood flow in the left temporal lobe and verbal memory performance was significant in women only. The authors suggested that the temporal regions were more important for providing information about objects and relations rather than memory retrieval *per se*. A study by Nyberg *et al.* (2000) looked more directly at the retrieval process and right prefrontal activation. They observed that right prefrontal and cingulate activity was increased in both men and women. No performance differences were observed. However, despite the similarity in regional activation there were again sex differences in the intensity of the activation, with three specific regions in the anterior cingulate and right prefrontal areas where the increase in activation was greater for women.

These authors speculated that 'higher activation of anterior cingulate for females underlies their tendency to perform better than males on attention demanding tasks that require response selection, such as recall and fluency tasks' (Nyberg *et al.* p. 190). Note though that the authors' own results suggest no sex difference in overall task performance and that in general activation level is sometimes difficult to interpret.

Research indicating sex differences in the lateralization of semantic memory was found by Baxter *et al.* (2003). They carried out a semantic comparison task where participants had to identify the extent to which two words were semantically related, for example category and exemplar such as 'beverage' and 'milk'. No difference in task performance was observed. Overall the pattern of results emphasized the importance of the superior temporal gyrus and inferior frontal gyrus regions. Analysis on women and men separately indicated lateral differences, with very little right-hemispheric activation in men, who displayed more diffuse left-hemispheric patterns (see also Chapter 9). Thus women showed relatively more bilateral activation.

It was noted above that there appear to be sex differences in the retrieval of autobiographical memories with an emotional content. The work of Cahill and his colleagues (Cahill 2003a, 2003b; Cahill *et al.* 2001; Cahill and van Stegeren 2003) has investigated the importance of underlying neural systems in this difference. Thus Cahill *et al.* (2001) observed in a PET study that men and women differ in their amygdala activation when presented with twelve commercial film clips with negatively arousing content. The results suggested that women were more likely to have left amygdala activation while men demonstrated right activation. This finding supports the earlier suggestion by Coney and Fitzgerald (2000) of sex differences in the lateralization of emotional processing.

Later research (Cahill and van Stegeren 2003) emphasized the interaction between the amygdala and hemispheric processing of local and global attention processes. In this study participants viewed a set of slides which contained emotional scenes and which sequentially made up a coherent story. The story possessed 'central' and 'peripheral' components: 'central' information might refer to the character in the slide, for example a mother and her son, while 'peripheral' information might refer to something a character was carrying, for example a teddy bear. By blocking amygdala influence the authors demonstrated that men and women were selectively impaired in the recall of global and local information.

The research discussed above on memory for routes and maps strongly suggests that men and women deploy different strategies, with women making use of landmark information and men making more use of survey representations. This appeared to be the case in a variety of contexts; active exploration, paper and pen and virtual reality. Gron *et al.* (2000) carried out a functional MRI study with men and women performing three variants of a virtual reality maze. While many common areas were activated in women and men, hippocampal and parietal regions, sex differences in the extent of the activation were noted. Women displayed greater levels of activation in the right medial frontal gyrus and left superior parietal regions while men showed greater activation levels in the left parahippocampal gyrus. However caution is needed in interpreting these findings, as men were quicker at completing the maze one cannot disentangle the contribution of differential task performance to these sex differences in functional architecture during task performance.

Social Cognition, Anxiety and Working Memory Task Performance

While the discussion above focused upon putative sex differences in recruitment of the underlying neural systems employed in memory task procedures, other research has emphasized the importance of social cognition in memory task procedures (Ashcraft and Kirk 2001; Dutke and Stober 2001). This research has employed the notion of 'the processing efficiency theory' (Eysenck and Calvo 1992). This theory suggests that decrements in performance in highly test-anxious individuals result from impaired working memory efficacy. According to Dutke and Stober (2001) these individuals 'experience task-irrelevant thoughts such as worries and concerns about self-evaluative aspects of failure which partially occupy working memory capacity' (Dutke and Stober 2001, p. 381).

It is possible that these individuals are unable to inhibit these distracting thoughts and thus although the slave system capacity may be impaired in anxious individuals it is likely that executive processes may also be impaired. Both Ashcraft and Kirk and Dutke and Stober manipulated task demands in order to reveal complex span limitations in anxious individuals. This suggests the importance of complex span (and potentially executive) limitations in anxious participants. One potential issue associated with these observations is that rather than anxiety leading to on-line reduction in working memory efficacy, it could be the case that poor working memory leads to performance in a given task context which in turns leads to anxiety associated with that particular context. Thus with non-experimental observations such as these the direction of causality can be problematic.

While the processing efficiency theory considers a generic impact of anxiety in particular contexts, it could be argued that specific anxiety resulting from *stereotype threat* (see also Chapter 5) could lead to impaired WM capacity (Schmader and Johns 2003). This research explicitly assumed that that stereotype threat interferes with test performance because it reduces the individual's working memory capacity. Their research manipulated the context of the working memory procedure by suggesting to participants in one condition that the memory procedure was 'a test related to mathematical ability'. This manipulation led to significantly reduced working memory performance in women only. This experimental manipulation provides more direct support that induced anxiety, in this case potentially mediated by stereotype threat, can reduce working memory performance.

These observations suggest that anxiety, when undertaking tasks demanding working memory processes, can actually result in reduced working memory capacity. Potentially, most of the task procedures discussed in this chapter could elicit anxiety. Thus Lawton and Kallai (2002) in a cross-cultural study noted that women in the USA and Hungary were more likely to indicate a higher level of anxiety, despite a lack of trait anxiety difference between women and men. Trait anxiety reflects the existence of stable individual differences in the tendency to respond to general situations with anxiety; in contrast, state anxiety is elicited by a particular or specific context, for example a cognitive task assessment. The authors identified that women in both countries indicated lower ratings of personal safety than men and concluded that this accounted for the higher levels of way-finding anxiety.

Research by O'Laughlin and Brubaker (1998) also suggested that women possessed relatively negative views of their performance, despite equivalent performance in a mapping procedure. A further example of the research, which has begun to tease apart the impact of anxiety, is that of Miller and

Bichsel (2004). These authors suggested that mathematics anxiety had a discrete impact upon working memory from state and trait anxiety. In particular they suggest the association is greater with visuospatial working memory than verbal working memory. Their results provided partial support for the processing efficiency theory discussed above.

The studies discussed above indicate that while there may be sex differences in the underlying neuropsychological mechanisms in memory tasks it is also important to consider the social cognitions participants bring to the research.

Conclusions

This chapter has considered research looking at attention and memory processes. To emphasize the link between these processes the first research findings discussed employed the dual-task paradigm, which is commonly employed in working memory and formed the basis for several attention studies discussed in Chapter 3. Thus Medland *et al.* (2002), McGowan and Duka (2000) and Goddard *et al.* (1998) all found interaction effects in their studies, suggesting that women and men were allocating attention in a distinct manner. Inhibitory processes in attention were also considered with evidence for differences in Stroop test conditions. The spatially based inhibition-of-return procedure has the most theoretically informed predictions (Klein, 2000; Silverman and Eals 1992).

The research to date has not however found specific sex differences in IOR processing, though spatial priming appeared to differ in men and women (Koshino *et al.* 2000). More research is required in this area, given its important theoretical scaffolding. The research on sustained attention or vigilance provided some evidence for sex differences but again indicated that an interpretation of performance had to consider motivational factors as well as purely cognitive processes.

This chapter has outlined a diverse range of research studies into memory, and in many research contexts sex differences have been consistently found. Perhaps the most complex pattern of results has been evidenced in studies purporting to assess visuospatial working memory. While early studies suggested men were superior in the Corsi block task performance later studies in object location memory suggested that women performed more effectively. It may be the case that these two task formats make different demands upon VSWM, with the former demanding spatial attention and the latter demanding LTM scaffolding. Thus the difference in individual differences may be a result of sex differences in different component processes of the tasks. Where men may have an advantage in object location is where the task demands require fine, metric, coordinate spatial relations processing. In contrast there appears to more consistent evidence of women being more efficient in verbal complex working memory tasks.

This verbal processing advantage in women is observed in a variety of verbal task procedures: episodic, emotional, autobiographical memory retrieval. This sophistication in verbal representation provides difficulty when interpreting the strategy women employ in tasks that are perceived as visuospatial in nature. Many of the VSWM tasks in the research literature make demands upon executive resources and therefore may be subject to verbal intrusion or scaffolding. This should be more likely in women who possess relatively sophisticated verbal representations in memory. This use of verbally based strategy is apparent in the research literature into map and route memory retrieval, where women are more susceptible to articulatory suppression and men are more susceptible to spatial interference.

Research into sex differences in the neuropsychology of memory has suggested that there are strong similarities in the neural systems employed by women and men. Some sex differences do occur, notably in the level of activation of particular regions. An important consideration is the social cognition context of the research procedure. Extensive research has indicated that task anxiety, for instance mediated by stereotype threat, has significant impact upon the functional efficacy of working memory processes. This has implications not only for tasks directly measuring working memory processes, but also for tasks such as route and map memory which may demand working memory resources.

Research To Do

The notion of stereotype threat has typically been applied in visuospatial (perceptual and mnemonic) contexts when considering the performance of women. However, stereotype threat can also occur of course in the performance of men (Aronson *et al.* 1999) and within ethnic groups and age-groups (Hess *et al.* 2003). The research above which indicated relative competencies for women in verbal retrieval from LTM did not discuss the possibility that men may be susceptible to stereotype threat in contexts where the existing stereotype knowledge may suggest performance will be better in women. Adopt the procedures from a study such as Aronson *et al.*'s research and modify the instruction set to make them appropriate for a verbal retrieval context and observe the impact upon men and women. Alternatively, attempt to alleviate the putative stereotype threat experienced by men in a verbal task by attempting to reduce the impact. The research of McIntyre *et al.* (2003) provides the rationale and methodology for this form of quasi-experimental design.

4 Imagery

Aim and Overview

This chapter will consider the evidence for sex differences in the processes associated with visual imagery. This field, including mental rotation, is possibly the most researched process in the sex differences literature.

The first section of the chapter will begin with a discussion of what is meant by visual imagery and consider the 'imagery debate' between those psychologists who consider that imagery can be likened to a visual or analogue representation of the physical world and others who consider that the imagery tasks, to be identified below, can be carried out with verbally based or propositional processes. Often these verbal processes can be implicit or tacit. This debate has major implications for how psychologists interpret the findings from tasks which purport to be visuospatial, that is non-verbal. Following this discussion there will be a description of the typical methodology employed in the cognitive research into imagery.

The imagery section will consider sex differences across a range of imagery measures. This field of research is by far the most extensive research area in the field of individual differences associated with sex, and the extent and diversity of the research will be evident. Again an important element of the section will be the consideration of the task demands made by the various imagery task procedures, and the extent to which it is possible to identify the cognitive loci of the individual differences. This 'process-oriented' approach is exemplified by the work of Halpern (1996–2000). The discussion will also consider explicitly the range of issues associated with the mental rotation research literature: performance factors, the social cognitions and the underlying functional neuroanatomy.

Imagery

Cognitive Processes

Richardson (1999) identified four strands in the psychological research into imagery. The first method was to consider imagery as a 'subjective' experience, involving self-report measures. Richardson noted the construction of an imagery questionnaire by Galton as early as 1880. A popular contemporary inventory is Marks's (1973) Vividness of Visual Imagery Questionnaire. The second approach is to consider imagery as some form of internal representation; this is the approach which will be most extensively considered in this chapter. It is presumed that many spatial ability tasks draw upon visual imagery in order to complete the tasks. The methodology of Kosslyn (Kosslyn 1994; Dror and Kosslyn 1994) will be discussed in detail below. The third approach is to consider imagery as a characteristic of a stimulus. Thus participants may be asked to rate how easy it is to form an image of the words 'crayon' or 'idea'. Most participants would find the former much easier to image: crayon is an example of a *concrete* word, while idea is a more *abstract* word, difficult to image. The final strand identified by Richardson was the use of imagery as a mnemonic strategy, most commonly deployed in learning paradigms.

Kosslyn decomposed the imagery process into several steps and this *componential* approach allowed the construction of tasks which could be designed to identify a more precise cognitive process. These subprocesses included image *generation*, image *maintenance*, image *scanning*, and *transformations* such as mental rotation. Image generation involves the construction of an image from long-term visual memory and placing it within short term memory or a *visual buffer*. A procedure for investigating individual differences in the generation process is shown in Figure 4.1.

In the initial phase of the study, the training phase, the participant has to associate a blocked upper case E image with a lower-case e stimulus. Once this association has been learnt, mere presentation of the e stimulus should enable the participant to generate an image of the blocked upper case E. Notice that that the blocked E is framed in all phases of the procedure by four brackets. This ensures that the image is accurately anchored upon the screen. The image is generated for 500 ms then an X-stimulus appears within the brackets. The participants' decision is to judge whether the X-stimulus falls upon their

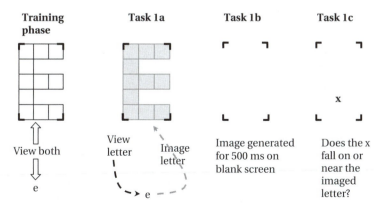

Figure 4.1 Image generation task procedure

imaged letter. If the letter is still in the process of being generated, performance will be poor. In the example shown, the X actually falls near to the imaged
letter. The temporal appearance of the X can be varied in order to identify how
long it takes to generate letters of varying complexity. The dependent variable
is typically the reaction time in making the judgement. A procedure for assessing variability in the maintenance process is shown in Figure 4.2.

In the image maintenance procedure, the image is not generated from long-
term memory; the image is presented on the screen (within the brackets
again) and the participant then has to maintain the image for 2.5 seconds.
The X stimulus then appears and the participant has to indicate whether the
X falls on or near the maintained image. In the example below the X would fall
on the image. Poor maintenance of the image will lead to poor performance.

Image scanning can be carried out in a variety of formats; the format below
presents the stimulus and the participant maintains the image for 50 ms, giving
particular emphasis to the location of the filled cells. After 50 ms an arrow
appears and the participant has to judge whether the arrow points towards
one of the filled squares or not. This procedure is shown in Figure 4.3.

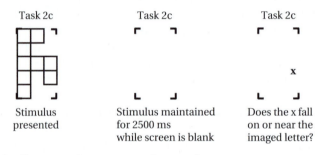

Figure 4.2   Image maintenance task procedure

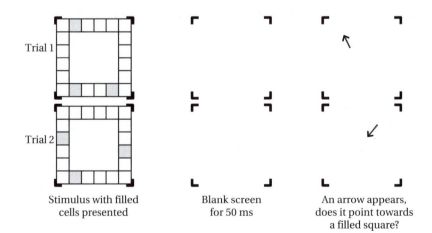

Figure 4.3   Image scanning task procedure

In the image-scanning procedure RT would typically be the dependent variable measure, however fine manipulation of the arrowhead direction would allow a measure of the accuracy of the scanning process. This task involves the participant mentally scanning from the arrowhead towards the cells. In the two trials above the arrow actually does point towards a filled cell, one would expect trial 2 to produce a longer RT as the scanning required is over a longer distance.

The final image scanning procedure is mental rotation, and this paradigm is probably the most researched tasks in the individual-differences literature. The procedure is shown in Figure 4.4.

In this procedure illustrated in Figure 4.4 the participant has to identify whether two stimuli are the same, merely rotated in different orientations, or mirror images of one another at different orientations. Using the blocked cell stimuli, the figure shows a reference pattern and four other identical patterns but in four different rotations, with a final mirror image pattern varying in orientation by 90°. Mental rotation forms vary immensely and Figure 4.5 indicates some of the formats.

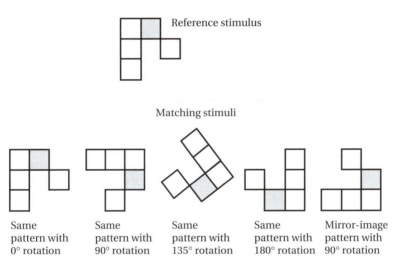

Figure 4.4   Mental rotation formats

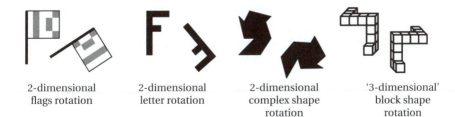

Figure 4.5   Variety of mental rotation formats

The meta-analysis by Voyer *et al.* (1995) suggests that mental rotation tasks with 2-D stimuli show smaller effect sizes than tasks employing the 3-D cube stimuli (shown in the right-hand panel) originally employed by Shepard and Metzler (1971).

Sex Differences in Imagery

Richardson (1999) identified several imagery studies where apparent differences between men and women were evident. Women tended to rate their images (in response to questionnaire questions) as more vivid. Richardson discussed the importance of item presentation, random versus blocked, for the emergence of this difference. Gender differences also appeared when participants had to rate the concreteness of words. However, the difference in rating of vividness may be specific to static images rather than dynamic images. Richardson suggested that 'women tend to be more efficient than men in the generation and maintenance of information ... men tend to be more efficient than women in the manipulation and transformation of that information' (Richardson 1999, p. 108). These suggestions by Richardson were directly assessed in subsequent research by Loring-Meier and Halpern (1999).

A Process-Orientated Approach in Imagery

Halpern (Halpern 1992; Halpern 2000; Loring-Meier and Halpern 1999; Halpern and Wright 1996) has argued that rather than consider tasks in the psychometric manner of the conventional individual-differences approach, a more appropriate manner would be to consider the cognitive processes demanded by these tasks. She labelled this approach a process-oriented one, and essentially attempted to place cognition at the heart of the sex differences research. This is the explicit rationale of this book. Her research (Loring-Meier and Halpern (1999)) adopted the componential approach of Kosslyn (Kosslyn 1980; Kosslyn 1994; Dror and Kosslyn 1994). This allowed Halpern to assess sex differences in image generation, maintenance and scanning, as well as manipulation (mental rotation).

In the image generation task, reaction time and error rate were both measured. In addition, letter generation complexity (simple, H generation versus complex, S generation) was assessed. This latter manipulation is a check to identify that the image generation process was carried out in the anticipated manner.

Loring-Meier and Halpern (1999) found that while there was no sex difference in mental rotation error rate, men had quicker responses than women. This pattern of no error rate differences but faster reaction times in men was evidenced in both the image maintenance and scanning data. The mental rotation data displayed a similar pattern but with one interesting difference. There was an interaction between sex of subject and degree of rotation. Typically, as the degree of angular rotation between the two stimuli increases so does the reaction time. Their data indicates that as the two task stimuli increasingly differ in orientation, the reaction time appears to increase for both men and women. The significant interaction found by the authors suggests that the increase in RT as a function of orientation (angular) disparity was greater for women than for men.

This is an important observation. The differences in reaction time observed in image generation, maintenance and scanning might not result from greater efficacy in the male participants' imagery processing. These observed differences may be due to some general speed of processing factor (Kail and Salthouse 1994; Reed *et al.* 2004) and not related to spatial processing differences between the sexes. However, the reaction time interaction pattern in Loring-Meier and Halpern's study allows us to separate generic speed of processing from processing times related to the mental rotation itself.

When the two stimuli are the same and have the same orientation, the reaction time does not reflect actual mental rotation but encoding and matching processing time. The interaction effect found by Loring-Meier and Halpern indicates that the slowing down is proportionately greater for women than for men. Thus the largest difference in mean RT between men and women is present in the 180-degree condition. This finding supports the earlier observation of Thomas and Kail (1991). These findings suggest that in all aspects of imagery processing, including image generation and maintenance, men are more efficient. This would appear to contradict the suggestion by Richardson (1999) above. However, it could be argued that reaction time may not be the most appropriate measure of the *quality* of image generation and maintenance. Thus it is possible that self-rating scales and reaction time measures may measure distinct components of imagery processes.

Issues in the Mental Rotation Literature

The research literature on mental rotation is extensive and it is not surprising that issues have arisen over the contribution of the methodology to the observed sex differences. This section will consider the nature of these issues and the research highlighting putative problems in the interpretation of sex differences.

Stimulus Format

As identified above, mental rotation tasks can possess a variety of stimuli and presentation may also vary substantially: conventional pen-and-paper procedures, slide projection or computer presentation. The Voyer *et al.* (1995)

meta-analysis explicitly indicates that different presentational formats are associated with different effect sizes, $d = 0.31$ for 2-D stimuli, 0.67 for '3-D' stimuli (note: this refers to the representation of a 3-D image on a 2-D plane; see Figure 4.5, right-hand panel), and 0.37 for stimuli presented on a computer or slide projection. Thus while the difference in performance between men and women varies as a function of the type of spatial task, it is evident that the difference also varies within mental rotation research.

The difference between 2-D and 3-D stimuli has recently been considered (Collins and Kimura 1997). These authors identified two alternative explanations:

- It is explicitly the change from 2-D to 3-D representation which leads to the change in effect size because the advantage in men may stem from men's ancient experience in navigation in 3-D space (Geary 1995, 1996, 1998).
- It may be the case that typical 3-D stimuli are actually more complex than 2-D stimuli and thus rotation becomes more difficult (McWilliams *et al.* 1997).

Collins and Kimura (1997) employed three tasks: the Vandenberg MRT (the most frequently employed pen-and-paper procedure based upon the original Shepard and Metzler (1971) 3-D procedure) and an easy and a hard version of a 2-D 'clocks' task. In the clocks task the participant has to judge whether two complex line patterns were either the same at different orientations or mirror reversed pairs. In one condition the line pattern was framed by a clock face (easy condition) and in the second version there was no clock frame (difficult). The effect size for the Vandenberg was $d = 0.86$, for the easy 2-D task, $d = 0.43$, whereas for the more difficult 2-D task the effect size was $d = 1.1$. In all cases the difference favoured men. This suggest that it is not merely a change in 2-D to 3-D stimulus which contributes to the difference between men and women.

This conclusion is supported by research directly manipulating the actual 3-D properties of the stimulus (Robert and Chevrier 2003). In this study actual 3-D stimuli were employed within both a visual and a haptic stimulus context in conjunction with a 2-D representation of 3-D stimuli. There were consistent sex differences in response times (though not accuracy) across all three formats. This appears to make it less likely that the 2-D to 3-D distinction is as important as first believed, but research (Roberts and Bell 2003) has suggested that women and men differentially engage lateralized parietal processes during 2-D and 3-D task performance.

Research subsequent to the Voyer *et al.* (1995) meta-analysis has supported the notion that with PC-presented stimuli, the effect size is much reduced (Parsons *et al.* 2004; Roberts and Bell 2000). Parsons *et al.* suggest the contribution of motor processes to the change in effect size between formats. Bearing in mind the dorsal visuomotor research discussed in the previous chapter and the importance of motor processes for mental rotation (Kimura 1999; Kosslyn 1994) this may be a fruitful way forward for future research.

Performance Factors

An extensive literature has accumulated in the past 15 years indicating that many factors within the mental rotation task procedure may influence task performance. A major assumption in many of these studies is that men and women encounter differential cultural experiences and, as a consequence, men and women bring different expectations to a study (see Chapter 10). Factors such as confidence and knowledge of the time constraints in the task could exert a differential impact upon women and men (Goldstein *et al.* 1990).

Goldstein *et al.* investigated the role of 'performance factors' in completion of mental rotation tasks. The authors employed the Vandenberg task procedure but scored performance in two ways: either the raw score or a ratio score (number correct/number attempted). The typical pattern was found with the raw scores, however with the ratio score no sex difference was observed. Voyer *et al.* (1995) observed that the effect size associated with the Vandenberg procedure varied according to whether the scoring was out of 40 ($d = 0.70$) or out of 20 ($d = 0.94$). They attributed this to the possibility that women guessed more (Delgado and Prieto 1996; Prieto and Delgado 1999). In a second study, Goldstein *et al.* demonstrated that in an untimed procedure there was no sex difference in performance even with the raw scores taken as the measure. This pattern of results suggests that MRT differences between men and women may occur only in certain situations, for example under time constraints.

Subsequent research investigating the importance of these factors has been equivocal. Voyer (1997) replicated the procedures and found that the effect size favouring men was lost when the procedure changed from timed to untimed. In addition, a ratio score reduced the effect size favouring men, though it did not eliminate it. Voyer concluded that a generic speed of processing factor could account for the observed sex differences in MRT. However, subsequent research by Masters (1998) found no effect of timed versus untimed manipulation.

The importance of the instruction given to men and women has been observed in studies by Prieto and Delgado (1999), Scali *et al.* (2000) and Sharps *et al.* (1993, 1994). Sharps *et al.* (1993) manipulated the explicit labelling of the tasks given to women and men. In a map task demanding spatial memory and in the Vandenberg task procedure, map or spatial labels tended to result in a male advantage. However, with a non-spatial instruction set, performance became equivalent. The authors refer to the notion of *situated cognition*, whereby cognitive performance has to be interpreted in the light of the context (task instructions in this case) of the assessment.

These findings were replicated and extended by Sharps *et al.* (1994) observing that instruction set only had an impact with difficult stimuli (that is with 3-D Shepard–Metzler stimuli). Scali *et al.* (2000) manipulated the instruction set given to participants emphasizing either speed or accuracy. They found that men outperformed women in a MRT procedure only when accuracy was emphasized. The pattern of results suggested that men improved their performance under accuracy instructions whereas women appeared less dependent upon the nature of the instructions. The results were discussed in terms of women's efficacy beliefs about performing tasks explicitly designated as spatial in nature.

These studies emphasizing the social cognition processes at work in the task context are akin to the research on *stereotype threat*. This concept arises in the context where an individual in a particular situation is aware of the social stereotypes about that individual's group. For example, a young girl may know that the cultural expectations for women undertaking advanced mathematics courses are quite negative. The girl therefore becomes aware that should she sign up for such a course her performance will be evaluated against this stereotype. The findings by Spencer *et al.* (1999) suggest that in this particular context the individual will experience self-threat, and this social cognition will interfere with performance. The implication of stereotype threat for working memory and mathematics performance will be discussed in the next chapter.

Although the emphasis on these studies suggests that the social cognitions women may possess would lead them to possess particular expectations about completing visuospatial tasks, expectations by themselves cannot account for all patterns of results. For instance, consider the case where participants in a study carry out more than one spatial task; for example in the Hamilton (1995) study participants were asked to complete a mental rotation task and an embedded figures task. There was no explicit reference in the instructions to the fact that both of these tasks were spatial in nature. Women participating in this study would be likely to be aware of UK cultural expectations of women carrying out visuospatial tasks; consequently, negative tasks expectations were likely to have occurred.

However, it is difficult to imagine that these participants would be aware that sex differences are typically found only in mental rotation procedures (unless they have read Voyer *et al.* 1995!). Thus task expectations would be likely to be similar for both tasks; the instruction examples for both tasks implicitly highlight the spatial nature of the tasks, so consequently the ongoing social cognitions about the two tasks would be expected to be equally negative. However, task performance indicated that while sex differences occurred in the mental rotation task, the embedded figures task showed no such difference. Consequently, these social cognitions may come into play only with particular task items, for example particular mental rotation items (Kerkman *et al.* 2000; Qubeck 1997).

Kerkman *et al.* (2000) observed the performance of men and women undertaking a mental rotation of a visual scene involving a train yard or depot. Thus for example a station building may have a train in front of it and a shunting engine behind it. Perhaps the most interesting aspect of the data was the observation that although overall the men appeared to be more efficient in the task, this was only where the stimuli pair could not be possibly rotated, that is when the two stimuli were mirror images. In the men, there was a strong correlation between performance with the possible and with the 'impossible' rotations; this suggests common processes at work in the two types of trials. However, in women there was no correlation between performance on the 'possible' and 'impossible' trials.

This interpretation suggests that for women in the 'impossible' item context, a different process or processes may be at work. It may well be the case that in a context where the stimuli pair appear not to match (mirror images), the anxiety associated with stereotype threat is at its greatest. In addition, the participants carried out interference tasks, memorizing seven digits (verbal interference), or memory for seven dot locations (spatial interference). The only effect of interference was upon RT in the 'impossible' trials which evidenced a complex pattern (see below for further details on this study).

Strategy Deployment

The research by Kerkman *et al.* (2000) investigated in part the contribution of differential strategy deployment by women and men when undertaking a mental rotation procedure. Pezaris and Casey (1991) also considered the suggestion that when women undertake mental rotation procedures they are liable to utilize verbal strategies to resolve the task. In contrast it is suggested that men are more likely to deploy visuospatial strategies. It is difficult to consider that the mental rotation stimuli displayed in Figure 4.5 could be represented in a verbal manner. However, this very issue is the essence of the imagery debate identified in the introduction to this chapter. Consider the stimuli in Figure 4.6.

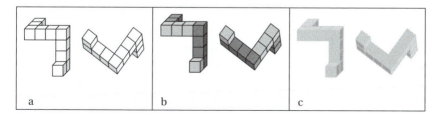

Figure 4.6 Implicit verbal cueing in MRT stimuli

The standard Shepard and Metzler (1971) stimuli are shown in Figure 4.6a and although the stimuli look unlikely candidates for verbal representation, this may not be too difficult to achieve. For the stimulus on the left of this figure, one could describe the object as follows:

1. One cube extending in front, at the base of a column.

2. Four cubes arranged in the vertical column.

3. Three cubes extending to the left from the top of the column.

4. Two cubes extending backwards from last of the three cubes.

A representation of the stimuli in this categorical manner would most likely mediate a verbal strategy.

The cubes are easy to segment and could be represented thus. In Figure 4.6b, this putative representation is primed by the deliberate shading of the four components. This form of stimulus should allow an even easier categorical description of the stimulus. The stimuli in Figure 4.6c are designed to minimize the cube boundaries and therefore act against this categorical representation. These latter stimuli may require a more coordinate representation and may be less amenable to a verbal strategy.

Kerkman *et al.* (2000) investigated strategy use in men and women by asking participants to carry out the mental rotation procedure while maintaining in memory seven digits or dot locations. This is the dual-task principle discussed in the previous chapter. It was presumed that digit maintenance would interfere with verbal working memory (see the previous chapter's section, 'Sex Differences in Verbal Working Memory'), and thus with a verbal strategy employed in MRT. It is presumed, in the light of the Pezaris and Casey (1991) study above, that this would therefore affect women more. Maintaining dot location should impair men's performance as they were presumed to be using a visuospatial strategy (and visuospatial working memory). However, the observations by Kerkman *et al.* suggest a pattern which is almost the opposite in nature.

Kerkman *et al.* indicated that mental rotation RT with mirror images actually decreased in women when the secondary interference task was digit maintenance. In men RT decreased when dot location was required. In order to account for this pattern Kerkman *et al.* suggested that participants were acting in a strategic manner to reduce reaction time. Thus for women, digit maintenance and mental rotation using a verbal strategy would demand shared resources in verbal working memory. Consequently, women would attempt to complete the MRT processing as quickly as possible in order to ensure digit maintenance was maintained. With dot location maintenance, discrete resources would be required and thus verbal mediation of MRT and dot location could be carried out in parallel, with no need to speed up the

MRT process. Kerkman *et al.* labelled this strategy 'rapid off-loading of the intervening task'.

There are several points of interest in these findings on interference:

1. MRT reaction time is subject to strategic influence and thus one cannot be entirely sure of the precise processes underlying a particular RT.

2. The impact of interference was only in mirror-image trials, emphasizing their importance for sex differences.

3. The observation that women and men were differentially affected by different interference procedures does suggest that men and women may deploy different strategies during mental rotation.

The latter implication along with the Pezaris and Casey (1991) findings can be related to the suggestion that men and women make different demands upon right- and left-hemisphere processes.

Hemispheric Contribution to Mental Rotation Task Performance

The conventional consideration of hemispheric contribution to visuospatial ability was that it was highly dependent upon right-hemisphere neural processes. This belief was so strong that Crucian and Berenbaum (1998) entitled their paper 'Sex Differences in Right Hemisphere Tasks'. One of the tasks in their study was MRT. Corballis (1997) considered earlier research which had labelled MRT as the 'prototypical' right-hemisphere task; he then proceeded to discuss other research which suggested that this notion was misplaced and that left-hemispheric processes also contributed significantly to mental rotation processing. This evidence was derived from a range of studies which also included neuropsychological evidence (Mehta and Newcombe 1991, Morton and Morris 1995).

These observations suggest that the left hemisphere contributes to tasks such as mental rotation (see Chapter 9). Extensive neuroimaging research has been carried out on mental rotation and although stimulus formats have differed and the underlying active neural systems have also shown variance, there are consistent findings suggesting that the left hemisphere is active during mental rotation (Alivisatos and Petrides 1997; Carpenter *et al.* 1999; Cohen *et al.* 1996; Deutsch *et al.* 1988; Just and Carpenter 1985; Just *et al.* 2001; Podzebenko *et al.* 2002; Tagaris *et al.* 1997, 1998; Vingerhoets *et al.* 2001; Wendt and Risberg 1994; Zacks *et al.* 2003).

Despite the consistent evidence for bilateral contribution to mental rotation processes, there remains a consistent belief that considers the mental rotation task to be solely right-parietal in nature. Thus Deutsch *et al.* (1988) are often cited as evidence for right-hemispheric parietal contribution; however a closer look at their data offers a different insight. Mental rotation does increase right-parietal processes more than left-parietal processes. However, their findings (Figure 3) suggested that mental rotation also activates the left parietal. In addition they noted that 'The most robust regional asymmetry observed was a right frontal activation' (p. 449). This study also found evidence for sex differences in neural activation. Women displayed higher levels of activity in rest and task contexts. However, more importantly, there was no pattern of differential dependency upon the right hemisphere during MRT (or indeed line orientation) processing, that is men and women showed similar patterns of hemispheric activation. Women displayed a relatively higher level of activity in the right hemisphere, as did the men. This lack of sex differences in dependence upon the right hemisphere is also evident in studies with brain-damaged individuals (Kimura 1999). Kimura demonstrated that women, like men, had more impaired performance after right-hemispheric than left-hemispheric damage. However, it should be noted that both men and women also had impaired MRT performance after left-hemispheric damage.

Deutsch *et al.* (1988) suggested that the factor contributing to elevated activity in women could be due to the greater effort women put into the task. However, this highlights a problem present in many neuroimaging studies: how to interpret differences in activation. When comparing men's and women's MRT activation this difficulty is exacerbated; if differences in neural activation are observed, is this due to the possibility that men and women may be undertaking different cognitive strategies or is it due to a difference in task performance level? This is an example of where individual differences can actually be better understood when there is no behavioural difference in performance (Jordan *et al.* 2002). Jordan *et al.* carried out a neuroimaging study in a sample of men and women who did not differ behaviourally in MRT performance. Under these circumstances, neural activation patterns between the sexes did differ:

1. Women had more bilateral activation in the inferior temporal gyrus and precentral gyrus regions.

2. Men had more bilateral activity in the primary motor cortex, the left intraparietal sulcus and the right parieto-occipital sulcus regions.

The authors concluded that three different (not necessarily independent) explanations could account for the pattern of results: strategy differences, allocation of attention within the task and 'sex-specific' neural systems employed during mental rotations. They suggested that women might be paying particular attention to the object components of the stimuli, performing a piecemeal or analytic process to the task, while men may adopt a gestalt like strategy, which allocates attention to the 'surface visual-spatial characteristics'. The difference between the women and the men could be due to any combination of these hypotheses, however, the improved design ensured that the putative confound of performance level was removed from the interpretation.

A subsequent neuroimaging study by Weiss *et al.* (2003) also found evidence for differentially active regions in men and women with very good, and equivalent, MRT performance. They found that women had more activity in the right temporal gyrus and right frontal regions. Men had more activity in the inferior parietal lobe. Again these authors concluded that these differences were the result of different strategy use between the sexes. They argued that men's use of 'gestalt-like' strategies was based upon parietal systems, whereas women were presumed to make use of a more analytic strategy based upon right-frontal systems. The Jordan *et al.* (2002) and Weiss *et al.* (2003) studies come to the same conclusion over differential deployment of strategies but used different regional activations to account for the strategies. Jordan *et al.* highlighted the inferior temporal gyrus in women as the basis for their analytic processing, Weiss *et al.* focused upon the right frontal regions.

Conclusions

This chapter has considered the presence of individual differences in imagery processes. Although these processes are in a chapter distinct from working memory it should be emphasized that most cognitive psychologists would presume that attention, imagery and visuospatial working memory are intimately related to one another. Thus explicit links between the processes in the two chapters were made in this and the prior chapter. Imagery research has formed one of the most popular research areas in the sex differences literature. As a consequence, many research issues/limitations have been identified which are discussed in the chapter.

Non-experimental research findings related to self-report questionnaires have suggested that women experience a richer level of imagery experience, as measured by vividness rating. Richardson (1999) suggested that this could imply that women were more effective in their image generation and maintenance processing. However, Loring-Meier and Halpern (1999) using reaction time as the DV found no evidence for greater imagery efficacy in women, but rather the reverse pattern. In their study men displayed faster RTs across image generation, maintenance, scanning and rotation procedures. It was suggested that RT measures might not accurately tap the quality of the image generation and maintenance processes. In addition, there is a need to consider whether general speed of processing might underlie the advantage for men in these tasks.

The chapter has also considered issues related to mental rotation research. The Voyer *et al.* (1995) meta-analysis suggested that the effect size associated with sex differences varied as a function of the MRT format, being largest with the Shepard and Metzler (1971) '3-D' stimuli on a paper format and smaller with 2-D paper stimuli and also with computerized presentations. The Collins and Kimura (1997) study suggested that complex 2-D stimuli could also produce a large effect size, so it may not be the 2-D/3-D dichotomy alone which contributes to the variability in effect size. Research is required which aims to understand why changing the format from paper and pen to PC monitor results in a reduction of the effect size.

The early research of Goldstein *et al.* (1990) focused attention upon the procedural factors, which might exacerbate sex difference in MRT performance. They argued that scoring and timing factors might induce a sex difference in performance, which might not otherwise be present. Voyer (1997) among others also found such effects. However, this finding is not unequivocal; studies such as Masters (1998) have not found any major change in the effect size when scoring or timing is altered. An important element of the procedure is the instruction set provided to participants: the research of Sharps and her co-workers (1993–1994) suggest that explicit labelling of the tasks as being spatial in nature activates social cognitions in female participants which lead to impaired performance. This activation of negatively based task schemata has been observed in studies of stereotype threat, and will be discussed further in the next chapter.

A further issue related whether the difference between women and men arose only where the pair of MRT stimuli were mirror images, so that rotation to match was impossible (Kerkman *et al.* 2000). This research also considered the deployment of different strategies by men and women. This difference in strategy arises through the possibility that women may represent the stimuli in a verbal format, while men retain a 'gestalt-like' representation. The Kerkman *et al.* study indicates that if differential strategy use is employed then MRT reaction times may be under strategic control, which further undermines their use as the sole indicators of mental rotation processing.

The issue of strategic differences between women and men was also observed in the neuroimaging research aimed at identifying hemispheric contribution to MRT processing. This research found consistent evidence for bilateral activation during MRT performance. Jordan *et al.* (2002) and Weiss *et al.* (2003) found some evidence for sex differences in activation and explained these differences by the selective use of serial/analytic versus gestalt-like strategies in women and men respectively. It should be noted that these strategy differences did not relate to differential use of the left and right hemispheres by women and men; rather, they were related to the differential use of parietal and other regions (though these regions were not consistent in the two studies). An important element of the research design in these neuroimaging studies is that by controlling for performance level in women and men, sex differences in neural activation would not be confounded by differences in performance level.

Research to Do

The mental rotation research discussed in this and in previous chapters suggests that despite having the appearance of a prototypical visuospatial task, mental rotation tasks may be subject to 'verbal intrusions'. In order to investigate this in a quasi-experimental design you could construct mental rotation stimuli with the modifications shown in Figure 4.6. Thus you could manipulate the nature of the representations employed by the participants. The stimuli in Figure 4.6b have their components shaded differently which could encourage categorical representations of the stimulus, e.g. in the left-hand figure of the pair, the stimulus could be represented as 2 dark shaded blocks on top, joining 3 light shaded blocks, which sits on top of 4 dark shaded blocks, which has a single light shaded block attached to the bottom. However, in Figure 4.6c, the shading is changed to make this categorical compartmentalization more difficult to achieve, and thus force a more global or gestalt representation which would require coordinate representations of the arms of the stimulus.

5 Intelligence and Educational Achievement

Aim and Overview

This chapter, the last to focus directly upon individual differences between women and men, considers sex differences in arguably the most complex of cognitive assessment contexts: intelligence and educational achievement. Consistent with the previous chapters in this part of the book, the initial components of these two topics will consider the contribution of cognitive processes to task performance. In particular the contribution of working memory processes to intelligence (Conway *et al.* 2003; Engle *et al.* 1999; Kane and Engle 2002) and the contribution of these processes to scholastic achievement will be emphasized (for example De Beni and Palladino 2000; Furst and Hitch 2000; Gathercole *et al.* 2003; Swanson and Berninger 1996a, 1996b).

The complexity of the educational context necessitates an understanding of a broad range of theoretical explanations of academic achievement: cognitive, social cognition accounts, which embrace self-efficacy, affective and motivational processes and socio-cultural issues (for example Eccles 1987; Hyde and Kling 2001; Rouxel 2000; Van Houtte 2004). Important in this discussion will be the interaction of cognitive and affective processes, for example the impact of stereotype anxiety upon working memory capacity and mathematics (Ashcraft 2002; Ashcraft and Kirk 2001; Hopko *et al.* 1998; Schmader and Johns 2003), considered in a preliminary manner in the previous chapter.

This introductory section on the factors underlying educational achievement will conclude with a consideration of socio-cultural influences within education that have an impact upon the performance of boys and girls and women and men (Hargens and Long 2002; Rustemeyer 1999). The interaction of social cognition and socio-cultural factors will be made explicit in the discussion of distinct cultures and varying masculinities within the classroom setting (Skelton 2001; Van Houtte 2004). The section will finish with a review of scholastic achievement across a range of countries, looking at achievement in children and adolescents within a compulsory schooling context and young adults in higher education.

It should be noted that although this chapter will consider individual differences in intelligence and educational achievement in children, the discussion will focus only on these two aspects. Chapter 11 will consider a broader range of cognitive processes within a developmental framework.

The Nature of Intelligence and Its Measurement

Before any discussion of the factors contributing to individual differences in intelligence it is worth while briefly considering the nature of intelligence. The definition of intelligence is itself a contentious issue, particularly when nature–nurture issues are considered. This discussion will concentrate on intelligence assessed through the psychometric methodologies of intelligence tests such as the Stanford–Binet (Stanford–Binet Intelligence Scale) and the Wechsler (for example the Wechsler Adult Intelligence Scale) measures.

Measures of Intelligence

The Stanford–Binet measures a range of abilities: verbal, quantitative, nonverbal or performance and memory. Typical verbal measures are:

- Vocabulary (define the word 'envelope').

- Comprehension ('Where do people buy food?').

- Verbal relations, reasoning ('Identify how the first three items are similar and how they differ from the fourth: lecturer, teacher, professor, banker').

Quantitative measures may ask the participant to generate the next number in a given sequence (for example 2, 5, 9, 14, …) or construct an equation from a set of digits and operations (for example 4, 6, 8, 3 and $\div$, $\times$, $=$; one correct answer is $4 \times 6 \div 8 = 3$).

Non-verbal tasks include the block design task, which assesses how well the participant can construct a 3-D copy from a picture of block designs.

Further examples are the digit symbol substitution procedure where the participant has to match a digit with a non-verbal pattern. The participant's task is to write down the matching digits as quickly as possible. This measure is commonly taken as a speed-of-processing measure (discussed earlier in Chapter 4).

In the matrices task the participant has to fill in the missing matrix pattern using the cues from the array. Although the task would appear to be a visuo-spatial/perceptual task, it is considered to be, in the main, a reasoning task. The participant has to logically deduct the change in pattern across and down the array and from these logical deductions should be able to identify the missing matrix pattern. While this may be considered to be a spatial reasoning task, Abad *et al.* 2004 provided evidence to qualify this conclusion (see below).

In addition many intelligence task measures directly tap or require some aspect of working memory, typically the verbal short-term memory component using a task such as digit span or short-term memory for letters or words (see below).

An important distinction that has been made in the intelligence literature concerns *fluid* and *crystallized* intelligences. Crystallized intelligence involves the demonstration of previously acquired knowledge, skills and ways of thinking. These competencies are presumed to be culturally driven and are evidenced in tasks discussed above which assess vocabulary and comprehension. Such tasks are culture-specific and to deploy them outside the culture (or subculture) for which they were devised is inappropriate and unwarranted. Fluid intelligence tasks require new approaches and ways of thinking and employ procedures that will be novel to the participant. They are presumed to be independent of cultural experience and are labelled *culture-fair* or *culture-free*. These two forms of intelligence exhibit distinct developmental trajectories: crystallized intelligence performance improves markedly in childhood and thereafter only gradually in adulthood, whereas fluid intelligence performance also improves markedly in childhood, but peaks in young adulthood and then declines in middle and late adulthood (see Chapter 8).

Factor theories have attempted to deconstruct the functional organization of intelligence. A simple consideration would be a model with general intelligence and group factors such as verbal and spatial intelligence. A recent example of a factorial structure highlighted by Eysenck (1994) was based on the work of Carroll (1993). In this structure, the notion of general intelligence (g) is at the peak of the hierarchy straddling a series of group or primary factors. At the base of the figure are highly specific factors of intelligence, for example lexical verbal fluency or mental rotation. The model indicates a range of abilities, including visual and auditory processes, memory capacity and a measure for speed of processing which reflects extensive recent research on speed of information processing. The digit symbol task identified above is one such task which is a putative measure of speed of processing.

The Contribution of Working Memory to Intelligence Test Performance

The factor model discussed by Eysenck (1994) identified the importance of a memory capacity component; consequently it should not be surprising that a significant relationship exists between working memory measures and intelligence scores. The work of Engle and his colleagues (Conway *et al.* 2003; Engle *et al.* 1999; Kane and Engle 2002; Kane *et al.* 2004) was mentioned in the previous chapter and has been a major contribution to the understanding of the relationship between WM and intelligence. Conway *et al.* (2003) reviewed early research which identified strong relationships between WM performance and intelligence scores, with correlations as high as 0.8 to 0.9. Extensive research has suggested that there are important relationships between WM and intelligence measures (Embretson 1995; Hutton and Towse 2001; Mackintosh and Bennett 2003 and this relationship may not be fully explained by speed of processing (Fry and Hale 1996; Necka 1992).

The memory tests typically employed by intelligence batteries appear to demand phonological memory resources (and redintegration). This would suggest that it is the domain-specific WM resources that are important in the relationship with intelligence and there is some evidence for domain specificity (Mackintosh and Bennett 2003; Shah and Miyake 1996). The carefully designed and constructed research by Engle and colleagues has enabled a more precise understanding of which working memory processes are important. Kane *et al.* (2004) assessed in detail the relationship between WM and intelligence. They employed 9 WM tasks and 13 reasoning tasks and extracted a number of latent variables: a verbal (phonological) STM variable, a visuospatial STM variable, a WM executive (working memory capacity) variable, a verbal reasoning variable, a spatial reasoning variable, and a general fluid reasoning (*g*) measure. In separate analyses they established that the executive variable was the most important predictor of general fluid (Gf) intelligence, however there was some element of domain specificity in that verbal STM variable accounted for variance in the verbal reasoning variable, while the visuospatial STM variable was a significant predictor of spatial reasoning. In addition, the authors noted that the visuospatial variable also predicted general fluid intelligence.

The presence of substantial common variance between the working memory latent variables and the fluid intelligence variables has implications for how one interprets individual differences in intelligence test performance. The presence of sex differences on these measures could be a consequence of individual differences in working memory processes. The previous chapter indicated sex differences in tasks demanding verbal executive resources, with women performing better. Men appeared to perform better in visuospatial STM procedures. On the basis of these differences one might expect to observe differences in different types of intelligence tests. In addition, research such as that of Dutke and Stober (2001), which observed that test anxiety impaired intelligence test performance, could be accounted for by the impact of anxiety upon executive processes in WM (Ashcraft and Kirk 2001). This impact of anxiety upon WM processes will be returned to below in the context of mathematics anxiety.

Sex Differences in Intelligence Test Performance

Halpern and LaMay (2000) have suggested that intelligence tests are explicitly constructed so that there is no overall advantage in performance for one sex over the other. However, Halpern did note that:

> Full scale IQ scores represent an average of heterogeneous subtests, and although on average there are no differences between males and females

on the IQ scores obtained, there are group differences on the subtests, suggesting that females and males differ on at least some of the abilities assessed with intelligence tests. (p. 232)

Recent work by Colom and colleagues has identified subtest performance differences between the sexes (Colom and Garcia-Lopez 2002; Colom and Lynn 2004; Colom et al. 1999). Colom et al. (1999) compared the performance of over 4000 young men and women, with an average age of 18 years, who undertook two intelligence tasks in either 1979 or 1995. Each sample was presumed to be representative of its age-group. The tasks employed were the differential aptitude test (DAT) and the primary mental abilities (PMA) task. Colom et al. observed advantages for women in inductive reasoning and advantages for men in verbal reasoning, numerical ability, spatial relations, mechanical reasoning and mental rotation. Interestingly, some of these differences had remained unchanged in the two time samples observed. However, the advantage for men in abstract reasoning and the advantage for women in vocabulary did appear to display a reduced level in performance over the two time periods. This latter finding, of a decreasing vocabulary advantage for women, reflects a change in a crystallized intelligence measure rather than fluid intelligence.

Lynn (Lynn and Tse-Chan 2003; Lynn et al. 2004a, 2004b, 2005) has suggested that there are sex differences in intellectual development. He has argued that girls mature faster and evince relatively higher scores on intelligences tests, but after the age of 15 years the development of boys leads them to improve their performance so that they outperform girls. In order to provide evidence for his claim Lynn collated progressive matrices data from across several countries: Estonia, Hong Kong, Mexico, Spain and New Zealand. He has suggested that 'the male advantage of 3.8 IQ points is consistent with, and caused by, the larger males brain, which from the age of 15 years onward is about 10% greater than the average female brain' (Lynn et al. 2005, p.1250).

This biological argument, a form of biological determinism, will be briefly considered in Chapter 9. However, alternative explanations for the advantage for young men in the matrices task have been forwarded.

The work of Abad et al. (2004) attempted to identify whether particular items on Raven's advanced progressive matrices were so visuospatial in nature that they acted against the performance by women in the task. Differential item functioning provided evidence of several such items; however, even after these items were not included in the overall measure a (reduced) sex difference favouring men was still evident. The authors considered the possibility that the remaining 19 items could also possibly demand visuospatial processing and commented that when performance on the rotation task of the PMA battery is employed as a statistical control, the matrices performance difference between women and men becomes non-significant. This conclusion has been supported by other recent research (Colom *et al.* 2004). Given the close relationship between mental rotation and working memory, this observation emphasizes the close relationship between working memory efficacy and intelligence task performance (Colom *et al.* 2003).

Sex Differences in Scholastic Achievement

The research discussed immediately above suggests that it is worth while considering not only individual differences in a complex behaviour itself, that is intelligence measurement, but also the factors contributing to the behaviour. Thus it is possible that sex differences in intelligence test performance could be due in part to individual differences in cognitive processes such as working memory. The rationale of the introductory component of this section is similar: a consideration of the factors that may impact upon educational achievement, and an identification of the individual differences associated with these factors. This will be followed by a review of the research and statistics which suggest the presence (or absence) of sex differences in educational achievement.

Cognitive Influences upon Scholastic Achievement

There is extensive evidence to suggest that working memory (WM) processes contribute significantly to achievement within schools and colleges (though see Chanquoy and Alamargot 2002, for a rather different view). The work of Engle and others above has stressed the importance of executive resources in the relationship between WM and intelligence. There is also accumulating evidence indicating the importance of executive contributions to scholastic achievement, in a generic executive context (Adams and Snowling 2001; DeStefano and LeFevre 2004; Swanson 1999; Swanson and Berninger 1996). Further research has been carried out in a more specific executive process context (Bull and Scerif 2001; Palladino *et al.* 2001; van der Sluis *et al.* 2004). In addition research has also considered the importance of working memory slave system contributions to language and mathematics (Baddeley *et al.* 1998; Demont and Botzung 2003; Hecht and Shackelford 2001; Venneri *et al.* 2003). Research has also been directed at both normative and atypical educational development contexts (Gathercole and Pickering 2000; Gathercole *et al.* 2003).

There is ongoing research aimed at delineating the precise contributions of these components of WM architecture to language and mathematics (Furst and Hitch 2000; Lee and Kang 2002; Passolunghi and Siegel 2001; Pastells and Roca 2003; Trbovich and LeFevre 2003). This research is necessary before one can establish the precise nature of WM contribution to language and mathematics competence within the classroom. In addition, given the relationship between general intelligence and scholastic achievement (deJonge and deJong, 1996; Floyd *et al.* 2003; Hale *et al.* 2003) and between working memory and intelligence (above), more research is required to separate out the impact of Gf from working memory influences upon educational achievement.

General spatial ability has also been consistently associated with mathematical achievement (Casey *et al.* 2001; Geary 1996, 1998). However the research findings on the matter are equivocal. Early research by Pattison and Grieve (1984) asked participants to undertake a battery of spatial tasks (including the Vandenberg and Kuse mental rotation task procedure discussed in the previous chapter) and a series of mathematics problems. A sex difference was found in both the spatial battery and mathematics problems. However, the sex difference in mathematics did not disappear when spatial ability was statistically controlled for. Research by Manger and Eikeland (1998) with a sample of 13-year-olds also found no support for the importance of spatial visualization in mathematical achievement. Further research has found evidence for the impact of spatial ability upon mathematics performance (Casey *et al.* 1995, 1997, 2001; Geary *et al.* 2000). In these studies spatial ability acted as a unique predictor of mathematics performance.

However, the precise nature of this relationship is dependent upon the spatial task(s) employed (that is mental rotation) and the sex of the student, with the relationship between spatial ability and mathematics being stronger in women (Casey *et al.* 1992b; Friedman 1995). Manger and Eikeland (1998) employed a 3-D spatial visualization procedure similar to the block design procedure and employed a sample with the modal age of 13 years. For both girls and boys there was a significant relationship between spatial visualization and mathematics performance ($r = +0.47$). However, much of the research described above employed mental rotation task procedures, where large sex differences do occur, and it appears that it is the cognitive processes underlying this type of task which appear more important in the maintenance of individual differences in these mathematical contexts. The discrepancy between the early and more recent results may also lie in the nature of the mathematics topic assessed as well as in the type of spatial task.

Delgado and Prieto (2003) observed that verbal fluency or lexical access performance was related to a range of mathematical domains, whereas MRT (Vandenberg and Kuse version) predicted only geometry and word problem-solving. This observation supports those by McGuinness (1985) who noted that the DAT spatial relations task is a strong predictor of geometry in women and men, but not so strong a predictor of arithmetic and particular forms of algebra. The Casey *et al.* (1992b) study provided support for the theory, to be discussed further below and in Chapter 11, which suggests that women with an appropriate combination of handedness (a family member with sinistral tendencies) and educational experience will show patterns of spatial ability/mathematics relationships similar to men. In addition, Stumpf and Haldimann (1997) observed that spatial ability (including block mental rotation and visual memory) was a significant predictor of generic academic achievement in sixth-formers. The importance of spatial ability in academic importance has led to attempts to improve or 'train' visuospatial ability in order to successfully facilitate calculus problem-solving (Ferrini-Mundy 1987). Interestingly, the results of this particular study suggested that women's calculus performance benefited more from training than the men's performance.

Biological Influences upon Scholastic Achievement

The work of Casey *et al.* (1992b) highlighted the putative contribution of the underlying neural systems to mathematics performance. Geary (1996, 2004) strongly argues for the importance of neural processes in mathematics. Geary (1996) suggested that:

> In some respects, all forms of cognition are supported by neurocognitive systems that have evolved to serve some function or functions related to reproduction or survival ... in terms of children's cognitive development, the interface between culture and biology involves the cooptation of highly specialized neurocognitive systems to meet culturally relevant goals. (p. 230)

Geary (1996, 1998) identified two sets of components pertinent to cognition: *biologically primary processes*, processes which have evolved in humans and are independent of the current culture, and culturally driven, *biologically secondary processes*. Thus infants and non-human primates show evidence of such a primary process through subitizing, an ability to discriminate and identify small quantities of objects. Geary argued that such biologically primary abilities were dependent upon a system of *skeletal* processes; in counting, the principle of a 'one-to-one correspondence' underpins early counting competencies. A further aspect of these skeletal processes is that knowledge, which is implicit in these systems, can be made explicit in order to scaffold other cognitive competencies. He thus argued that the development of geometry as a formal discipline (culturally driven and thus a biologically secondary process) involved the recruitment of neurocognitive systems evolved in the first instance to facilitate navigation of 3-D physical environments (these are Geary's (1998) *physical* modules, to be discussed in Chapter 9).

Geary (1996) suggested that boys and girls do not differ in their ability to discriminate small numerosities (biologically primary abilities). However, he argued that sex differences in mathematics performance might be expected where the topic draws on the neurocognitive systems involved in navigation (see Piazza and Dehaene 2004, for some of the putative parietal systems important for arithmetical competence). Geary (1996) constructed a model accounting for cognitive and mathematics abilities which draws upon evolutionary and socio-cultural factors.

Geary's model identified the evolution of neural systems, interacting with cognitive and social cognition processes as the key processes underlying sex differences in mathematics. One point emphasized by Geary is that the level of mathematical achievement influences the extent of observable sex differences. He argued that sex differences in mathematics are more likely to be evidenced in cultures with prolonged formal mathematical teaching (this accommodates the influence of experience in mathematics courses upon mathematics competencies.). However, the model would also suggest that were the courses taken by the student statistically controlled there would still be sex differences in specific mathematics topics such as problem-solving and geometry. This remaining difference would be attributed to the underlying cognitive systems that evolved to mediate environmental navigation (more effectively) in men, that is in spatial abilities. The complexity of interactions shown in the model, for example the interaction between cognitive systems in navigation and experience in mathematics courses, preclude a narrow explanation of individual differences in mathematics. Thus the major strength of this model is the integration of a variety of psychological perspectives. The emphasis in this model is of the primary impact that sexual selection has upon the neural and cognitive systems underlying mathematics performance; the section below contrasts with this and highlights the importance of social cognition processes.

Social Cognition Influences on Scholastic Choice and Achievement

Many psychologists have emphasized the importance of motivation, beliefs, values and goals within an educational context (Eccles 1987; Eccles and Wigfield 2002; Hyde and Kling 2001). The fundamental framework of this perspective is the socio-cultural context in which the child is embedded. This approach articulates, more extensively, the social cognitions of the developing child – for example the child's perception of culturally determined gender roles; the child's interpretations of their experience of the culture; their locus of control – and the goals which emerge from these cognitions. Moderating these influences are the child's expectations of success and the values and costs associated with the particular tasks or courses. Expectation of success is dependent upon the individual's goals, their self-perception of ability and their perception of task demands. The task or course value is influenced by previous achievement-related experiences, attributional processes and the child's affective memories.

Hyde and Kling (2001) cited research which suggested that boys were more likely to possess higher expectations of success in mathematics, sports and English. While a girl may feel self-confident about her mathematics and English ability, a belief that she is more able in English will lead her to choose

English courses rather than courses in mathematics. However, if there is no perceived value in the course then there will be no motivation to choose the course (the notion of utility is also part of the Geary model above). Thus girls are more likely to perceive mathematics as less important, less useful and less enjoyable. These cognitions are influenced by socialization processes, which include family, educators and the media. It should be noted that the model also identifies a cost factor associated with task or course selection; Eccles and Wigfield (2002) defined the cost as 'the negative aspects of engaging in the task, such as performance anxiety and fear of both failure and success' (p. 120). This element is similar to the concept of stereotype threat discussed in the previous chapter.

This model articulates extensively the importance of the social cognitions the child may experience. However, a disappointing aspect of the model, and of the subsequent research incorporating the model, is the lack of explicit emphasis upon the individual differences the child may bring to these social cognitions (the differential-aptitude-of-*child* factor in the model). The Geary model above identifies these contributions more extensively.

Consider how the observation by Casey *et al.* (1992b) discussed above could be incorporated into the Eccles model. According to Casey these girls would possess appropriate neural systems that would mediate competent visuo-spatial ability (*differential aptitude*) which would lead to positive (success-ful) spatial activities. This in turn could bias the girls' attributions regarding their contribution to its success (internal attribution as opposed to the more typical external attribution). One would expect that the development of the girls' self-schemata would adopt more 'masculine' characteristics (see Chapter 6) and, consequently, both expectations and perceived course val-ues would motivate these girls to undertake more mathematics courses which would lead to greater mathematical achievement. One must assume that even within this model, factors such as the cultural milieu and socializ-ers' beliefs would tend to act in an inhibitory manner for the development towards mathematical competence in this group of girls.

The model can be related to other approaches to individual differences in mathematics achievement. Fennema and Peterson (1985) constructed an autonomous learning behaviour (ALB) model which attempted to account for how social cognitions could account for sex differences in mathematics. The authors suggested that ALB is evidenced when the child is 'observed to work independently on high level tasks, persisting at such tasks, choosing to do and achieving success in such tasks' (p. 20).

The Eccles model described above identifies the importance of the internal motivational beliefs and socializing factors, one of which is the importance of pupil–teacher interaction. The Fennema and Peterson model acts a medi-ator between the internal processes and the mathematics achievement. Eccles's model emphasizes the relationship between self-perceived compe-tency and expectation of success. The notion of an individual's beliefs about their own competency is reflected in self-efficacy theories. Eccles and Wigfield (2002) in discussing the Bandura *et al.* (1996) model defined self-efficacy as the 'individuals' confidence in their ability to organize and execute a given course of action to solve a problem or accomplish a task' (p. 110).

An example of research employing these constructs was Rouxel (2000). Rouxel studied the relative importance of self-efficacy and (state) anxiety in academic performance. (State anxiety is arousal associated with a specific situation or context the individual is in.) Her results suggested that boys' performance in a French (first language) examination was associated with state measured anxiety. They felt more anxious before the French exam than a mathematics exam. On the other hand the performance of girls in the mathematics exam was related more to their self-efficacy.

Stereotype Threat and Mathematics Performance

In the previous chapter reference was made to the concept of stereotype threat and working memory capacity. According to Keller (2002), stereotype threat 'focuses upon social-cognitive processes related to the applicability of negative stereotypic expectations in a testing situation' (p. 194). The context in which stereotype threat occurs tends to be one where the task is particularly difficult, when performance is subject to evaluation and where the negative stereotype is directly applicable to the task being undertaken. This process is potentially associated with several of the processes in Eccles's model: the concurrent activation of gender role and activity stereotypes and the relationship with self-schema and cost (anxiety).

A study by Spencer *et al.* (1999) exemplifies the research which has investigated the importance of stereotype threat within a mathematics context. The authors investigated the performance of men and women in contexts where the mathematics problems were difficult or not so difficult, and where there was explicit activation of the stereotype threat. In this latter manipulation the participants were told either that the test had displayed sex differences in the past or else that the test had never shown any sex differences in the past. This latter description should interrupt the matching of a negative stereotype to the particular assessment context and is similar to the manipulation carried out by Sharps (Sharps *et al.* 1993; Sharps *et al.* 1994) discussed in Chapter 4. The explicit activation of the stereotype threat resulted in significantly poorer performance by women in the mathematics task. In the third component of their study, Spencer *et al.* (1999) attempted to identify whether the impact of stereotype threat was mediated by evaluation apprehension, self-efficacy or anxiety. The evidence suggested that the former two factors were not implicated but that anxiety may be important. The work of Keller (2002) suggested that under conditions of stereotype threat, adoption by women of a self-handicapping strategy was a significant mediator of the effect upon mathematics performance. Thus these women would be more likely to endorse inventory items such as 'How much stress have you been under lately?' in order to attribute their poor performance to an external factor.

It is possible that stereotype threat acts directly upon cognitive mediators in mathematics performance. The work of Schmader (discussed in the previous chapter) and others (Ashcraft 2002; Ashcraft and Kirk 2001; O'Brien and Crandall 2003; Schmader 2002; Schmader and Johns 2003) suggests that anxiety associated with stereotype threat reduces available executive resource capacity. This would have it greatest impact during the most difficult of mathematics tasks, when presumably working memory demands are at their greatest. This 'social-cognitive' account with its emphasis upon the working memory process tends to be underemphasized in the majority of social cognition models of achievement. The identification of the direct modification of a working memory process does not dilute the importance of dynamic social cognition processes.

On the contrary, this research offers an explanation of how social cognitions can directly influence mathematics performance, through their influence upon executive resourcing in working memory. A recognition of the contribution of these dynamic processes may lead to interventions designed to reduce the impact (O'Brien and Crandall 2003) and the observation that the impact is not restricted to women (Smith and White 2002) or issues of sex differences (Osborne 2001). An interesting academic domain for application of the concept of stereotype threat is in areas where attitudes and anxieties appear to act in opposite directions (Baloğlu 2003), so that the different factors underlying academic achievement may be more readily teased apart.

The Education Process as a Socio-Cultural Agent

Explicit in the Eccles model and most accounts of educational achievement is the importance of socializers: family, friends and educators. However social scientists such as Skelton (2001) would argue that the educational process itself is a major socialization factor; thus Young and Fraser (1994), in an Australian study, provided evidence to suggest that the effect of school is a more significant factor in science achievement than the sex of the student.

The Importance of Pupil–Teacher Interaction

Fennema *et al.* (1990) asked first-grade teachers to identify students with the lowest and highest mathematics ability and to subsequently make judgements about the characteristics of these identified pupils. The best boy student was judged as more competitive, logical and adventurous, was more likely to volunteer mathematics answers, enjoyed mathematics more and was more independent in mathematics. Fennema *et al.* noted that the teachers perceived boys as demonstrating more autonomous learning behaviours (see above). An important difference in the perception of pupils lay in the attributions given to success in the highest-achieving boy and girl. The teachers were more likely to attribute the boy's success to ability, whereas the girl's success was more likely to be attributed to effort (see Hyde and Kling 2001, for a further discussion of these issues). These results suggest a systematic bias in these teachers' perceptions, and lead to a concern over teacher expectancy effects within the classroom (see also Kuklinski and Weinstein 2001).

Research by Burnett (2002) in Australia observed that boys in years 3 to 6 were more likely to receive negative teacher feedback than girls; boys also received significantly greater *ability feedback* ('Gee, you're a good student.') than girls. Girls were more likely to report a better relationship with their teachers. A study by Kim *et al.* (2000) in Korea also assessed the experience of children within the classroom. In contrast to Burnett (2002) this study observed that boys (in grade 8) tended to have a more positive classroom perception, for example in teacher support, involvement and general attitude. These inconsistent findings regarding boys' experience in schools have not prevented Van Houtte (2004) from suggesting that a major factor in educational differences in men and women arises from boys and girls experiencing different cultures within school. The author suggests that boys do not have a study culture: 'Educational achievement or displaying other school attitudes is antithetical to typical masculine – that is, macho – behaviour, which is a condition of popularity for boys' (p. 160).

The Australian and Korean evidence above suggests that boys do not universally have a similar school experience. Skelton (2001) would argue that within the same classroom, boys with different masculinities have distinct experiences. This approach suggests that rather than consider boys as a homogeneous group, one must also consider the variability that exists within each of the sexes. This emphasis forms the rationale for the next chapter and part of this book, a within-sex consideration.

Assessment within Education

The use of examinations may elicit stereotype threat (discussed above) in individuals, for example Hyde and Kling (2001) have suggested that when women undertake the Math SAT they may be similarly subject to the stereotype threat. The SAT is a United States college entrance examination and is assumed to be a significant predictor of freshman grade point average (FGPA). The correlations between SAT and freshman grade are around + 0.5 for both sexes. Historically there has been evidence of sex differences in the SAT tasks (see Halpern 2000) and more recent data suggest that although the Math SAT difference is relatively slightly smaller than in previous years, there is still a significant sex difference.

While the SAT performances are of interest themselves, it is the function and deployment of the SAT which have led to the greatest criticism. Hyde and

Kling (2001) highlighted research evidence that suggested that although the SAT is a predictor of FGPA, it tends to overestimate men's college grades and underestimate women's college grades. Thus Lynn (Lau & Lynn 2001; Lynn & Mau 2001) followed a sample of over 10,000 students and found the typical advantage for men (50.1 points) in the Math SAT and an advantage for men in the American College Test (ACT). However, in the subsequent GPA taken across the college years, women significantly outperformed the men in the sample. Lau and Lynn concluded that the discrepancy in the pattern of results occurred as a consequence of nature of assessment. Hyde and Kling would argue that if colleges selected purely on the basis of SAT marks, independently of the sex of the applicant, then female applicants would be discriminated against. In addition if scholarship special programmes are determined by the SAT performance then women may be additionally discriminated against.

The Organizational Structure of Education

Many social scientists argue that the educational process is by its very nature resistant to the implementation of equal opportunities. Skelton (2001) discussed the concept of a *gender regime*, which according to Skelton is 'the pattern of practices that construct various kinds of masculinity among staff and students, orders them in terms of prestige and power, and constructs a sexual division of labor within the institution' (p. 23).

One source of evidence which has been employed in this debate is the data concerning the academic staff profile across higher-educational institutions in a range of countries. Throughout the course of the last 120 years there have been more men on the faculty staff. Interestingly, the 1999 data identify the highest proportion of women (about 41 per cent) in the twentieth century and it is the only year in the USA sample where the proportion of women is greater than in the 1879 data (National Center for Education Statistics, 2002). However, in the light of Skelton's comments above perhaps a more appropriate consideration should be of the sex profile within the faculty, particularly in relation to positions of 'power' and 'prestige', that is the senior positions.

Within Australian academic faculties, women make up a disproportionate number of high- and low-status positions – underrepresented at the more senior positions, overrepresented at the lower faculty levels. However, it should be noted that in the 6-year period between 1997 and 2003, the proportion of senior female staff did increase by over 30 per cent (DEST 2005). The faculty profile changes in Sweden over the period 1996–2000 also indicate a small change in the proportion of senior female staff (George 2002). While the figures for the proportion of female professors appear relatively low, the figure actually masks a large variability in the proportions which is dependent upon the academic discipline. In 1999, the overall figure for female professors was 13 per cent, however in humanities the proportion was 23.5 per cent while for mathematics it was 2.7 per cent.

The corresponding academic staff profile for the United Kingdom indicates a profile not dissimilar from the other countries identified above (Higher Education Statistics Agency 1995, 2001).

The highest proportion of women professors, about 24 per cent, is in psychology. However, in some of the other science and medicine disciplines the proportion is below 5 per cent. Apart from mathematics there is evidence, as in Sweden and Australia, of a recent increase in the proportion of women faculty members at a senior level. However, despite these relative increases, the absolute proportion of female professors still remains disproportionately low. Consequently, there is a large discrepancy in the academic career achievement of men and women within faculties. This may be a result of the inherent characteristics of employment processes within higher education; it could also be the result of a lack of appropriately qualified women applicants. A consideration of graduate numbers may help answer such a question and this will be addressed below.

The Educational Achievement of Girls and Boys

Feingold (1988) considered the trends over time in competencies such as spelling, language and numerical ability, items taken from the DAT (see above). In spelling, large sex differences ($d > 0.45$) were evident in favour of girls from grade-8 through to grade-12 students. In language a similar advantage was found favouring girls. Feingold noted that between 1947 and 1980 these differences actually decreased. In numerical ability the sex difference favouring boys occurred in the older students in the earlier samples but by 1980 no sex difference was evidenced. The lack of quantitative differences in girls and boys was reinforced by evidence from a meta-analysis study (Hyde *et al.* 1990). A general consideration of the research noted small or non-significant effect sizes for problem-solving, arithmetic, algebra and geometry. Calculus had an effect size of $d = 0.20$ favouring boys, computation a similar effect size but favouring girls. However, it should be noted that the arithmetical and geometry data were non-homogeneous, suggesting other variables were having an impact. The effect size was dependent upon the age of the students in the sample; older students displayed a larger effect size. In addition, when the sample was highly selective (see below) then effect size was $d = 0.54$ in favour of boys (and men).

However, later research by Nowell and Hedges (1998) does not entirely support the evidence found in these earlier studies. This later meta-analytic study considered a range of educational measures: vocabulary, reading, mathematics, writing, arithmetic, numerical operations and science. Assessment performances of grade-12 students in the USA were analysed. Large effect sizes favouring female students were found in reading and writing, and these effect sizes were not dependent upon the survey year. Mathematics and science showed effect sizes favouring boys, the former a small effect size and the latter a medium one. There was a tendency for both mathematics and science effect sizes to become smaller in more recent surveys.

One of the most important observations in this research was that boys displayed a greater overall variance than girls in their achievements. The proportion of boys to girls varied as a function of the percentile. Thus, in the top 1 per cent of mathematics scores, boys were overrepresented by a ratio typically greater than 2:1. In science, in the 1992 cohort, there was a ratio of greater than 5 boys to 1 girl in the top 1 per cent. While boys were overrepresented in the bottom 5 per cent of the reading scores, girls were not overrepresented in the top 1 per cent. This greater variance in the boys' scores will be discussed later in this chapter and the within-sex variability will form the basis of the next part of the book.

The Third International Mathematics and Science Study (TIMSS)

The major international research study (Mullis *et al.* 1999) collated pupil performance in mathematics and in science in the mid 1990s across grades 4 to the final year of compulsory secondary schooling, and thus provides an invaluable snapshot of individual differences in these curricula areas.

In a sample of 17 countries the study found only one overall sex difference in mathematics performance in grade-4 pupils, in Korea. However, when the curriculum content was broken down, significant sex differences were found across the curriculum, predominantly (but not exclusively) indicating an advantage for boys. The mathematics area with the most frequent sex difference was measurement, estimation and number sense. At grade 8, again only Korea showed an overall sex difference. Sex differences within the curriculum were not as frequent. However, in the final year of secondary school 7 of the 8 countries sampled indicated an overall sex difference favouring male students. In advanced mathematics courses 8 of the 10 countries displayed significant sex differences favouring young men.

In science, 6 of the 17 countries sampled reported a sex difference in grade 4 science. The differences all favoured boys, with the major sex difference being in Earth sciences and in physical sciences. In grade 8, all 25 countries reported boys as achieving higher science scores; in 16 of the countries this difference was significant. The most frequent sex differences favouring male pupils were found in Earth sciences, physics and chemistry. The one sex difference favouring girls was in life sciences, in Cyprus. In the final year of secondary education all 8 countries reported sex differences favouring the male students. In physics, all 11 countries reported higher achievement in male students, with 10 showing significant differences.

Distribution of Scores in the TIMSS Study
The study also provides a breakdown of the proportion of students throughout the distribution of scores. The study indicates that as the children become

older and presumably as the cognitive demands of the mathematics curriculum increases, boys tend to be overrepresented. This pattern is mimicked in science achievement, which indicates that in the older students there is a large overrepresentation of boys performing well.

Mathematics and Science Examples

Mathematics Fourth Grade
Solves a comparison problem by associating elements of a bar graph with a verbal description – showed an advantage for girls in 15 countries.
Reads information from a simple bar graph – showed an advantage for girls in 9 countries.
Locates a point on a rectangular grid by following specified moves – showed an advantage for boys in 7 countries.
Estimates the distance on a map given the scale – showed an advantage for boys in 16 countries.

Mathematics Eighth Grade
Sets up the correct proportion in a word problem, and solves for the missing term – an advantage for boys in 31 countries.
Compares volume by visualizing and counting cubes – an advantage for boys in 21 countries.
Subtracts to three decimal points using multiple regrouping – an advantage for girls in 13 countries.
Decides whether estimate or exact value is appropriate in a situation involving money – an advantage for girls in 10 countries.

Mathematics Final Year
Translates graphical information into a mathematical expression – an advantage for boys in 13 countries.
Solves an addition problem involving negative numbers – an advantage for boys in 15 countries.
Demonstrates the ability to estimate area in order to solve a word problem – an advantage for boys in 16 countries.
No specific items showed an advantage for female mathematics students in this age cohort .

Science Fourth Grade
Demonstrates some understanding of fluid properties by drawing the liquid surface on a frame-of-reference diagram depicting a rotated container – an advantage for boys in 17 countries.
Interprets pictorial diagram depicting angle/length of shadows at different times of day and selects the shadow cast at midday – an advantage for boys in 16 countries.
From a list of edible and inedible plants, identifies a plant not grown or food – an advantage for girls in 14 countries.
Describes one effect of environmental change (temperature) on aquatic life – an advantage for girls in 10 countries.

Science Eighth Grade
Recognizes that a human inherits traits from both parents – an advantage for girls in 21 countries.

From a list of organs, identifies the heart as an organ not situated in the abdomen – an advantage for girls in 18 countries.
Identifies a ray diagram depicting light passing through a magnifying lens – an advantage for boys in 32 countries.
Interprets a diagram of the earth's layers and identifies the centre as the hottest – an advantage for boys in 27 countries.

Science Final Year
Understands the relationship between distance and perceived size of an object – an advantage for boys in 19 countries.
Explains the relationship between mass, acceleration and force – an advantage for boys in 19 countries.
Can explain how blood types interact with one another – an advantage for girls in 5 countries.
Recognizes the nutritional value of fruits and vegetables as a source of vitamins and minerals – an advantage for girls in 3 countries.

Mullis *et al.* concluded that:

> [I]n mathematics, males tended to perform higher than females on items employing spatial reasoning, reading maps and diagrams, as well as problems involving percentages or area. Females tended to perform higher on items requiring common algorithms. In Science … males seem to have a particular advantage on science items presented via diagrams. (p. 98)

The report also considered the presence of individual differences in different assessment formats. In the final year of secondary school, whether the assessment was multiple-choice, short-answer or extended did not appear to matter, with the male mathematics students performing better across all the formats. However, in the final-year science achievement the vast majority of performances favouring male students came exclusively in the multiple-choice and short-answer formats. Interestingly, in final-year physics there was tendency for the short answers to show less-frequent sex differences.

Further Evidence of Sex Differences in School Achievement

More recent evidence from the USA contrasts literacy, mathematics and science achievement in 15-year-olds (National Center for Education Statistics, 2002). What is consistent across all the countries sampled is that girls are significantly outperforming boys in reading and literacy competencies. Where sex differences occur in mathematics, they tend to favour boys (15 countries). The results for science show less clear-cut individual differences associated with the sex of the student. According to the US National Center for Education Statistics (2004) since the mid 1990s when the TIMMS data reported above were collected, both boys and girls have improved in mathematics achievement at both grade 4 and grade 8 in the USA. In 2003 at grade 4 average performance of girls and boys was significantly different; the difference appears greater than in 1996. In 2003 at grade 8 the difference between boys and girls appeared smaller than in 1996, but was still significant. Thus, in the USA, a sex difference favouring boys has been evident in the past few years, but in the older children the size of the difference has been decreasing. In science, the advantage for boys was still apparent, but the mean difference was smallest in the oldest, grade-12, students (National Center for Education Statistics 2004).

However, a different story emerges from the statistics in the UK (Department for Education and Skills 2002). In the youngest children, key stage 1 (7 years old), a larger proportion of girls achieve the target or criterion level for that age-group in reading and writing. While both sexes improve over the 7-year sampling period in terms of achieving the criterion, the sex difference still favours girls and the reading advantage appears to have increased. In this time period the proportion of girls achieving the mathematics criterion improved to be greater than boys. The KS2 findings, over a shorter span, indicated an advantage for girls in English, little difference in mathematics and a greater improvement over time in the proportion of girls who achieved the science criterion. In the older group of students, the proportion of girls achieving the target level in English was much larger than the proportion of boys. Even although both sexes improve over the 7-year period, the proportion of girls still retains this large advantage.

In mathematics, girls show a slightly higher proportion achieving the criterion. Again in science, over the 7-year period the change in the proportion of girls achieving the target is larger than boys. In summary, there appears to be a larger proportion of girls achieving well in English (and reading and writing), in recent years the proportion of girls achieving the criteria in mathematics and sciences appears to have grown more than the proportion of boys. This pattern of improving performance over time in girls is mimicked in the GCSE examinations, which students typically take at 16 years of age in England, Wales and Northern Ireland (Department for Education and Skills, 1999, 2001).

A larger proportion of girls achieved the highest levels (A* and A) in English in both 1999 and 2003. Note however that in 1999 the girls also had a higher proportion in the G-U tail. This suggests that for this particular year and this subject, the girls' performance may have been more variable. In mathematics, a higher proportion of boys achieved the highest grades; however by 2003 the two sexes were almost equivalent. Again note that for both years, boys had a greater proportion of G-U grades and showed more variability in their achievement. In science generally, girls demonstrated an overall higher proportion of A* and A grades; however this was not the case for physics where the proportion of high grades was larger in boys. The increasing achievement in female students in England and Wales in recent years is also reflected in the Advanced Level assessments taken by 18-year-olds in the UK (Department for Education and Skills 2002).

It is only in English Advanced Level that young men achieve a higher proportion of top marks (A); in mathematics and in the science areas women achieved a higher proportion of A grades. Note that in the English profile, men had a greater proportion not only of A grades but also of U (unclassified) grades, an indication again of greater variability in male achievement. The overall advantage for women is reflected in the Scottish Higher Grade examinations, with women showing an overall advantage in 2000 Higher Grade examinations, 77 per cent versus 72 per cent achieving grades A to C (Scottish Qualifications Authority Annual Statistical Report 2001). It should be noted that while overall women showed a larger proportion of A to C grades in the sciences, there were also larger proportions of women specifically in mathematics, English and geography subjects. In accounting and finance, secretarial studies, and computing studies, men showed a larger proportion of A to C grades. Thus in the UK there is evidence that women have improved their relative proportion of high grades in the domains that the TIMMS study covered in 1995.

It is worth while noting that although women have improved their proportional achievement in the mathematics and science areas in the UK, for many of these subject areas the number of female students actually taking the course is disproportionately low. Thus in the Scottish 2000 data, over twice as many young men undertook the physics Higher Grade course; in the England and Wales 2003 data set this disproportion was even greater, with a ratio of close to 4 young men for 1 woman in A Level physics.

The TIMMS research suggested that sex differences in mathematics were greatest in advanced mathematical assessments. Recent research has investigated the cognitive processes which may mediate this difference (Gallagher *et al.* 2000). Gallagher *et al.* attempted to identify the deployment of strategies that girls and boys could use to solve problems of the type present in the mathematics SAT. Strategies included algorithms using routines taught in the classroom; logic, estimation or insight; guessing; trial and error; and no strategy. High-ability (Math SAT) students were able to switch strategies when the task changed from conventional to unconventional problems; these students were able to change from algorithmic to intuitive strategies. The research found that girls were more likely to persevere with algorithmic strategies in the unconventional problem context.

Tinklin (2003) considered a broader range of factors associated with high attainment in 16-to-17-year-old Scottish students choosing to undertake Higher Grade examinations: attitude to schooling, occupation of parents, education of parents, home ownership status, type of school (state versus independent) and so on (see also Yang and Woodhouse 2001). Tinklin concluded that the advantage for women in the Scottish Higher examinations was likely to be attributed to the observation that 'females took school more seriously than males' (p. 321).

These studies indicate the complex nature of mathematics achievement emphasized by the research which has considered a range of factors. McGuinness (1985) reviewed research assessing the importance of vocabulary, spatial ability, confidence in mathematics, stereotyping of mathematics as a 'male domain' for mathematics achievement in grade-9 and grade-11 children in the USA. Vocabulary and spatial ability were most important predictors, followed by mathematics confidence. A later meta-analysis (Hyde *et al.* 1990) considered in detail a range of affective and social cognition factors. Hyde *et al.* observed relatively small effect sizes associated with most of these variables.

However, certain variables did show larger differences between young women and young men; men were much more likely to stereotype mathematics as a male domain, and men were more likely to attribute success to ability, whereas there was a smaller trend for girls to attribute success to effort. Young women were less likely to expect success in mathematics assessment. Later research (Rouxel 2000) suggests that these factors are dependent on the course being assessed. Thus, as suggested above, young men felt more anxious when being assessed in French than in mathematics, while for young women self-efficacy was the more important factor in these two assessments.

Casey and her colleagues (Casey *et al.* 1995, 1997, 2001) looked at the relative importance of spatial competence and social cognition factors (McGuinness's statistical review was of bivariate analysis rather than a multivariate analysis). Casey *et al.* (2001) looked at mathematical problems drawn from the tasks employed in the TIMMS study discussed above. A path analysis was conducted on two subtests. One of the subtests employed items labelled as female, for example subtraction: 2.201 – 0.753. The other used 'male' items, for example a straight line on a graph passes through the points (3,2) and (4,4); which of these points also lies on the line? The sex of the student was only related to the male sub-set of items, and the path analysis indicated that the boys' better performance on these items was mediated by greater spatial ability and self-confidence. Spatial ability accounted for more variance in the 'male' sub-test items.

Women and Men in Higher Education

Despite the relative success of UK women in recent A Level and Higher Grade assessments, disparities appear to occur in the number of men and women undertaking particular courses. Thus although women may achieve some of the highest grades in mathematics and sciences, they may not pursue these courses in higher education (Ayalon 2003). Consequently, is the differential course choice in the later years of secondary school education pattern mirrored at the higher-education level in the UK?

The UK university admission figures for 2003 (Universities and Colleges Admissions Services 2003) with standard entry students (under 21 years of age) indicated significant variability in the women-to-men ratios across a variety of disciplines. In teacher training the ratio of women to men was about 8:1 while in English the ratio was about 2.53:1. In biology there was a ratio of about 1.54:1 women to men; in physics the ratio was about 0.23:1 and in mathematics about 0.58:1. A similar pattern of variability appears to be present in the USA National Center for Education Statistics 2006b). In 2000–1, 712,331 women graduated with a first degree as opposed to 531,840 men, a ratio of about 1.4:1. In some discipline areas such as biology the ratio of women to men among first-degree graduates was close to this, in others the ratio differed markedly. In education the ratio was about 3.3 women to 1 man, in English language the ratio was about 2.2:1. However, in mathematics about 0.9:1, in physics about 0.72:1.

This relatively small number of women in mathematics and physical sciences is even more emphasized when one considers the ratio of women to men undertaking doctorates in these disciplines in the USA. In mathematics the ratio of women to men was down to about 0.4:1, in physical sciences even lower, about 0.37:1. However, even in other disciplines the ratio of women to men doctoral graduations was reduced from the first-degree ratio. In biology the ratio had dropped to about 0.79:1, in education to about 1.84:1; in English language the ratio was about 1.52:1. Overall, the number of women obtaining doctoral degrees was 20,176 as opposed to 24,728 men.

In Sweden a similar first degree/doctoral change was also noted. In 2000–1, 300,800 women or 60 per cent of the student numbers were registered on first degrees. However in the same year the 2400 women achieving doctoral degrees made up only 41 per cent of the total number of doctoral degrees. It should be noted, though, that the proportion of women doctorates in Sweden had increased from 32 per cent in 1995–6.

The lower application rate of application to mathematics degree programmes by women in the UK and the USA mirrors the observation by Ayalon (2003) in Israel. This study observed that women who had a successful mathematics and sciences background in later secondary schooling were more likely to enter courses such as medicine and law, as well as courses in the humanities.

Sex Differences in Higher Education Achievement

The United States National Center for Education Statistics (National Center for Education Statistics 2002) has tabulated the number of women and men entering first degrees in the past 130 years. The pattern indicates the steady increase in the proportion of women graduates in the United States. In the earliest sample in 1879–80, women made up less than 33 per cent of the graduates; by 1999–2000 the percentage of women was about 56 per cent. Almost 2 million more women than men began first degrees in 1999. In Sweden in 1999–2000, women made up 60 per cent of the graduates (George 2002). In the UK the proportion of women in the following academic year 2000–1 was about 55 per cent (Higher Education Statistics Agency 2004). These statistics indicate that in these three countries at least, women now make up the majority of graduates. In terms of achievement, though, a finer question would be to consider the level of achievement within the degree, that is the grade point average or the degree classification.

Richardson and Woodley (2003) investigated the proportion of men and women in the UK who had achieved first-class or upper second-class degrees, categories they labelled as 'good degrees'. In 1958, 29 per cent of women and 36 per cent of men achieved good degrees; by 1984 men and women were equivalent in their achievement (33 per cent). However, Richardson and Woodley noted limitations in the earlier research, for example not all graduates from institutions of higher education were included; full-time and part-time students were not differentiated. In addition non-honours students were included, but were difficult to place on the scale of achievement associated with an honours degree. The Richardson and Woodley (2003) observation was based upon the 1995–6 cohort of UK graduates. In this cohort, 51.2 per cent of men and 57.7 per cent of women achieved good degrees. However, this advantage was not significant in the youngest (<21 years) and the oldest (>60 years) age-groups. In the Richardson and Woodley 1995–6 cohort, a higher proportion of men achieved a first-class degree (8.5 per cent versus 6.8 per cent). This has historically been the case but the trend is disappearing and by 2003 had been reversed.

The factors underlying first-degree success are likely to embrace a variety of processes ranging from cognitive through to socio-cultural processes of the sort discussed above for school achievement. A consideration of this range of factors is evident in recent research directed at understanding a difference in the degree success of women and men at Oxford University in the UK (Mellanby *et al.* 2003). These authors considered the importance of intelligence, general achievement motivation, academic achievement motivation, examination strategy, a range of mood measures, self esteem/self-efficacy measures, measures on interpersonal relationships, and working patterns.

Sex differences were found in academic self-efficacy: men had higher expectations of degree achievement, and were more likely to deploy 'high-risk' strategies in revision and examinations. There were also differences in the emotional and self-esteem measures, women displaying higher levels of depression and anxiety. However, it should be noted that degree discipline did impact upon these general findings; thus in biochemistry men were more likely to be depressed and evidenced levels of anxiety similar to those of women on this particular degree programme. In addition, in this student sample women were 'slightly higher' in their academic motivation and expectation of degree success. The authors observed that overall 24.3 per cent of men obtained first-class degrees while overall women achieved 16.2 per cent. Again this was greatly dependent upon the discipline; women achieved a greater proportion of first-class degrees in biochemistry, chemistry and physics.

The authors employed correlation and partial correlation techniques to identify which factors were important in degree achievement (marks in the final examinations). Verbal intelligence measures predicted academic achievement, but as there were no sex differences in this measure it could not account for the difference in achievement. Academic motivation predicted examination performance but again there was no sex difference in this measure. However, degree class expectation, which indicated a sex difference, did predict examination performance. It should be noted that all of these measures, in total, accounted for only 35 per cent of the variance associated with marks achieved. Research has explicitly considered the contribution of personality beyond that of intelligence and motivation (Farsides and Woodfield 2003). These studies found that while intelligence and 'application' were associated with academic success, personality factors also accounted for academic measures of success.

Conclusions

This chapter has reviewed individual differences in cognitive achievement in perhaps the most complex of contexts: in intelligence measurement and in scholastic achievement. What becomes quite apparent is that in these contexts a variety of factors may mediate the presence of individual differences, biological, social cognition and socio-cultural processes in addition to cognitive factors. The chapter initially emphasized the importance of cognitive abilities discussed in previous chapters – working memory and spatial ability – for achievement in intelligence tasks such as matrices and in scholastic areas such as mathematics. However, the models of Geary (1996) and Eccles (1987) highlight the importance of biological processes and social cognition processes respectively.

These factors should not be seen merely as competitive processes; they are most likely to be interactive, complementary or perhaps different explanations of the same process. Thus the biologically primary structures or modules discussed by Geary are presumed to underpin the processes underlying mental rotation, which presumably recruit working memory resources (see Chapters 3 and 4). However, the research on stereotype threat, which is mediated by the social cognitions of the participant, also suggests that there is an impact upon working memory (executive) resource capacity. The socio-economic background of the child, a factor associated with poorer academic achievement, is likely to impact upon working memory efficacy, perhaps mediated by experience-dependent neural systems. Consequently, the various perspectives should not be viewed as mutually exclusive, but perhaps as exclusively interactive.

As Halpern (2000) suggested, one should not expect overall sex differences in intelligence testing if the tests are deliberately constructed in order to produce no overall difference. However, individual differences in digit symbol or matrices subtests may be expected. Thus evidence has accumulated suggesting that in the Ravens matrices task there is a small advantage for young men. Some research has suggested that this performance difference is not entirely a difference in reasoning but may be mediated in part by spatial ability scaffolding performance in some of the items.

Individual differences in educational achievement are in part dependent upon the subject, level of education and country.

In mathematics achievement, the TIMMS mid nineties research suggested that sex differences occurred most clearly in the advanced mathematics courses. The advantage was evident in some topics more than others. In the USA the subsequent research suggests that there still remains a small advantage for boys in overall mathematics performance in grade-8 children. In the UK the change in female student mathematics performance has been more dramatic – with young women achieving higher mathematics grades at GCSE and Advanced Level. The advantage for women is evidenced in a range of countries and has led to the development of education programmes targeted at boys.

In the UK, this advantage for women is also reflected in recent degree results where women increased their proportion of first-class honours degrees to a greater proportion than did men. In order to begin a systematic programme of research linking cognitive processes with academic achievement one has to move away from these global measures of academic achievement, and attempt to decompose the nature of demands made in topics across the curriculum. The TIMMS survey attempted to do this in the field of mathematics and physics; however a more fruitful approach might be more akin to the research protocols discussed in the first section above.

A final characteristic identified in the chapter was the within-subject variability in exam performance in educational data, predominantly, but not exclusively, in men. This emphasis upon a within-sex characteristic suggests that it may not be entirely accurate to suggest that all boys are failing at schools. It is more accurate to say that some boys are evidencing high educational achievement levels, while others are not. Equally, some girls are displaying high educational achievement while some girls are not. Mellanby (Mellanby *et al.* 2003) suggests that factors as diverse as degree discipline and personality may impact upon the likelihood of achieving high performance in first degrees. It should be noted that research such as that of Petrides *et al.* (2005) also suggests that personality is associated with school achievement. This suggests that in educational achievement, within-sex variability accounts for an extensive amount of variance in the overall individual differences.

Part III
Within-Sex Differences
Research Findings

6 Individual Differences Associated with Gender

Aim and Overview

The final discussion of the previous chapter identified the issue of within-sex variability in academic achievement. While this was discussed primarily within a context of socio-cultural factors, the aim of the current chapter is to consider the within-sex variability associated with the psychological construct of gender. The first component of the chapter will consider the conceptual framework underpinning the approach psychologists have adopted in the conceptualization and the measurement of gender. This discussion will initially consider self-perception (self-schema) approaches, for example the Bem Sex Role Inventory (Bem 1974, 1981) and the Personal Attributes Questionnaire (Spence and Helmreich 1978; Spence *et al.* 1974). In addition, the notion of a gender schema (Bem 1981) and gender behaviour measurement (Orlofsky and O'Heron 1987) will be discussed.

The final component of this section will briefly consider the multi-faceted nature of the gender construct (Archer and Lloyd 2002). The next section of the chapter will evaluate the empirical evidence for a relationship between gender role characteristics and cognition. The initial component of the section will identify early theoretical accounts of the relationship between gender role and cognition (for example Nash 1979; Durkin 1987). The major component will consider the research evidence which has attempted to identify the presence of within-sex individual differences in cognition associated with measures of gender. The final section will look at research issues such as the diversity of conceptualization of gender and its implication for research findings.

The Conceptualization and Operationalization of Gender

Halpern (2000) described the conventional view of sex role stereotypes in Western cultures. The utilization of stereotypic perceptions of women and men formed integral components of the models of Eccles (1987) discussed in Chapter 8. An important element of these social cognitions is the repertoire of characteristics that are presumed to be associated with men and women; these characteristics form the basis of the sex roles. These characteristics will be discussed in detail below. Archer and Lloyd (2002) discussed the social roles perspective, and its suggestion that a division of labour emerged within an industrial revolution context in the UK and the USA. This led to different gender roles for women and men, women in unpaid work at home and men in paid work away from the home.

Archer and Lloyd highlighted the constraint arising from the perception of gender roles being so closely tied to the characteristics of men and women, in their discussion of particular cultures in the Middle East and North America. In the Xanith culture in Oman and the Berdache culture in North America, gender roles were not tied to the conventional Western dimorphic conventions. In both of these cultures, individual men and women displayed behaviours not typical of men and women in contemporary Western societies. As Archer and Lloyd suggest, 'moving beyond a view of physical sex differences as necessarily binary creates a space within which a society can construct other genders' (Archer and Lloyd 2002, p. 104). This conceptual freedom is reflected in Skelton's (2001) discussion of multiple masculinities and suggests that gender need not be constrained to differences between the two sexes but may refer to differences within the sexes. Such a view of gender decouples the term from that of sex and allows social scientists to consider within-sex individual differences associated with gender. It is for this reason that the terms sex and gender are discussed as discrete concepts in this textbook.

The Measurement of Self-Perceived Gender Characteristics

Conventional measures of gender stereotype characteristics make use of an adjective checklist method whereby judges are presented with a large set of adjectives and have to assign the adjectives to particular groups. The groups may be distinguished by ethnicity or by sex (Archer and Lloyd 2002). Spence (1985) discussed the history of the methodology identifying the lack of conceptual framing for the research. Indeed on occasion the characteristics employed were employed in tasks designed for other purposes. The conclusion of these early approaches was that masculinity and femininity were at opposite ends of one dimension. This unidimensional view implies that one would expect a negative correlation between the scoring in the masculine and feminine items.

However, Spence (1985), reviewing prior studies, did suggest that researchers had viewed the concept of masculinity and femininity among the 'muddiest in all of psychology' (Spence 1985, p. 63). Archer and Lloyd (2002) identified some of the characteristics associated with sexes in the findings of this early research. Characteristics such as 'ambitious', 'handsome' and 'tough' were stereotypically associated with men, whereas 'attractive', 'fickle' and 'fussy' were associated with women. Not only were these characteristics given stereotypic labels; they were also judged along an evaluative dimension. One observation of the characteristics cited by Archer and Lloyd was that while about 15 per cent of characteristics associated with men were perceived negatively, of the characteristics associated with women about 33 per cent were viewed negatively (see Pedhazur and Tetenbaum 1979).

The identification of such stereotypic characteristics allows one to then go on to measure the extent to which individuals may possess these characteristics. Bem (1974) constructed a list of 400 characteristics which she considered would be significantly associated with women (feminine-labelled items), with men (masculine items) or with neither (a neutral set of items). Both women and men acted as judges and in order for an item to be characterized as feminine or masculine both men and women had to judge the characteristic as more desirable for one sex than the other, at the $p < 0.05$ level. Table 6.1 identifies the 40 characteristics which were stereotypically associated with women and with men. In addition 20 neutral items were identified. Bem subsequently employed these to construct the Bem Sex Role Inventory (BSRI). The BSRI was subsequently given to 356 women and 561 men (university and junior college participants) who were asked to rate the extent to which they possessed the 60 characteristics.

The key feature of this approach is that participants, regardless of their sex, could possess characteristics stereotypically associated with both women and with men. Thus gender could be considered not to be a unidimensional but a multidimensional construct. Participants subsequently were rated as either *feminine* (endorsing feminine items more than masculine items) *masculine* (endorsing masculine items more than feminine), or *androgynous* (endorsing both feminine and masculine items). Note that the identification of an androgynous personality, the possession of both feminine and masculine items, could be evident only in a measure where masculine and feminine characteristics were measured independently.

Bem observed that only about 21 per cent of the women endorsed a relatively high number of feminine characteristics and only about 13 per cent of the men endorsed significantly more masculine characteristics. This pattern of results suggests that the vast majority of women and men endorsed characteristics not stereotypically associated with their own sex. The pattern in Bem's study strongly suggests that the possession of gender characteristics may vary considerably within women and within men.

Bem developed her conceptualization of the BSRI by suggesting that performance on the inventory could give an indication of the individual's gender schema (Bem 1981, 1985). This was a significant development in that it took a self-report measure which identified particular gender-labelled characteristics and considered this measure as a marker of how the individual could organize their social word through the 'lens' of a gender schema. Bem's gender schema theory has its ontological roots in both the cognitive-developmental

Table 6.1 The feminine and masculine items of the Bem Sex Role Inventory

Feminine items	Masculine items
Affectionate	Acts as a leader
Cheerful	Aggressive
Childlike	Ambitious
Compassionate	Analytical
Does not use hard language	Assertive
Eager to soothe hurt feelings	Athletic
Feminine	Competitive
Flatterable	Defends own beliefs
Gentle	Dominant
Gullible	Forceful
Loves children	Has leadership abilities
Loyal	Independent
Sensitive to the needs of others	Individualistic
Shy	Makes decisions easily
Soft spoken	Masculine
Sympathetic	Self-reliant
Tender	Self-sufficient
Understanding	Strong personality
Warm	Willing to take a stand
Yielding	Willing to take risks

and social learning accounts of sex typing. Bem suggested that, in part, sex typing arises from the assimilation of the self-concept into the gender schema. This conceptualization is accommodated by the models of Halpern (1992) and of Eccles (1987). In both models, gender stereotypes and self-concepts are intimately linked and lead on to particular social cognitions. Bem (1981) argued that women who were identified by the BSRI as possessing more feminine characteristics and men who possessed more masculine characteristics were labelled gender-schematic. Androgynous individuals or individuals who endorsed more characteristics stereotypically associated with the opposite sex were labelled gender-aschematic.

Bem (1981) asked participants to recall a large set of words in which categorization of the words at recall, called *clustering*, could indicate the extent to which participants were employing schematic organization. Thus in a wordlist including clothes, animals and occupations, should the participant recall the words, butterfly, bra, waitress, miner, tie and stallion in that order there is evidence of clustering by gender label, initially 'feminine-like' items followed by 'masculine' items. Bem found that gender-schematic participants were more likely to employ gender related clusters such as the one above than aschematic participants. However, later research has not fully replicated this pattern of results (Archer and Lloyd 2002; Spence 1991). Spence and her colleagues (Spence 1985, 1991; Spence and Helmreich 1978; Spence *et al.* 1974) have been particularly critical of the deployment of inventories such as the BSRI as a marker of more global concepts of masculinity and femininity, such as gender-schemata, attitudes and behaviour.

Spence and Helmreich (1981) instead argued that, fundamentally, measures such as the BSRI and the Personal Attributes Questionnaire (PAQ) primarily assessed the perceived possession of instrumental (agentic) and expressive personality characteristics. Spence also identified the difficulty in establishing a two-dimensional instrument (BSRI) which is then collapsed onto one dimension (gender-aschematic/schematic) in order to account for schematic processing in individuals. This particular point was emphasized in a gender-schematic task employed by Markus *et al.* (1982), who observed that feminine and masculine individuals (regardless of sex) were differentially sensitive (had a quicker RT) in their processing of feminine and masculine items respectively.

Observation of the Halpern and Eccles models discussed above and described in more detail in previous chapters clearly indicates the importance of gender stereotypes in the social cognitions associated with task performance. Typically this is taken to account for the different task expectations that women and men may possess. However, closer consideration would suggest that rather than accounting for a sex difference in task expectation, these models may actually predict gender-schematic differences in task expectation. One would presume that both men and women who are gender-aschematic would not utilize the gender-labels of the task to form differential task expectations. Essentially these social constructivist processes may well be more pertinent for within-sex differences in gender rather than differences in social cognitions associated with the sex of the participant.

This was the rationale for the Basow and Medcalf (1988) study which assessed the relationship between social cognition processes within an educational context and gender typing. In this study gender categorization was achieved by employing the BSRI. Basow and Medcalf observed that masculine and androgynous participants exhibited a differential bias; these individuals attributed successful exam performance to internal factors such as ability but significantly reduced these internal attributions when experiencing exam failure. More recent research has emphasized the contribution of gender characteristics to social cognition (Hirschy and Morris 2002; Rammstedt and Rammsayer 2002). Hirschy and Morris noted again that masculinity in men and in women was important for the attributional style adopted in success and failure contexts.

Empirical Observation of Gender and Cognition

It is possible to explore the importance of gender for quite complex social cognitions, for example in decision-making (Radecki and Jaccard 1996), in person perception (Tunnell 1981) and in interpersonal communication (Edwards and Hamilton 2004). However, this present discussion will focus upon the contribution of gender in a range of cognitive tasks already discussed earlier in the textbook. Nash (1979) considered the importance of gender (as opposed to sex) in models of social cognition processes in an article explicitly linking sex role to cognitive task performance. Nash discussed the relevance of the participants' gender characteristics in processes such as task-labelling, task expectancy, achievement motivation and fear of success. This led her to make several predictions regarding gender characteristics; however, she suggested, ' it was crucial to use a measure that assesses masculinity and femininity independently, preferably on traits relevant to cognitive functioning' (1979, p. 292).

Nash predicted that individuals who perceive themselves as high in masculinity and high in femininity characteristics (androgynous) will do well on most tasks regardless of the gender labelling of the task. In part this may be due to self-efficacy factors rather than gender-schematic processes. High-masculine – low-feminine participants would seek out and undertake most effectively 'masculine' tasks. High feminine – low masculine individuals conversely would be more likely to achieve in 'feminine' task contexts.

Low-masculine and low-feminine individuals are gender-aschematic and thus would not be greatly influenced by the task labelling. Perceived low self-efficacy in these participants would lead to reduced overall performance.

An early meta-analysis (Signorella and Jamison 1986) assessed the evidence for some of the performance predictions made by Nash (1979). The suggestion that participants with feminine characteristics would perform effectively on verbal tasks was not supported. However, there was evidence for a (positive) relationship between masculinity and verbal competence in adolescent girls. In spatial perception, there was a strong (positive) relation with masculinity, particularly with female participants. In the adolescent boys sample there was no relationship between gender and spatial perception. With mathematics the relationship was also dependent on the sex and age-group of the participants and date of the sample. In adolescent boys, in studies immediately prior to 1986, there was a trend for femininity to be related to mathematics competence.

However, in men, in women and in adolescent girls there was (positive) relationship with masculinity. In tasks of mental rotation and spatial visualization there was a more consistent pattern, with higher masculinity scores predicting greater competence. There was no support for androgynous participants evidencing higher performance across the range of cognitive tasks. Consequently, Signorella and Jamison (1986) concluded that 'the results from our meta-analysis showed consistent and significant associations between gender self-concept and cognitive performance. For the most part these associations supported Nash's (1979) hypothesis' (p. 218). The research to be discussed below considers findings which, in the main, was carried out after Signorella and Jamison's initial meta-analysis.

Balistreri and Busch-Rossnagel (1989) directly considered the importance of task labelling and subsequent task perception in participants with different gender characteristics. The BSRI was employed as the gender categorization tool. These authors manipulated the label associated with Embedded Figures Task (EFT) procedures, for example changing the task label from a 'drafting design aptitude test' to 'fashion design aptitude test'. The pilot study sample sizes of the sex and gender categories really precluded much meaningful consideration but the authors suggested that feminine (female) participant performance was susceptible to the nature of the label. In the second study there was a tendency for masculine participants to perform better in the task context with the 'masculine' task descriptions. However, the feminine participants also performed significantly better in this condition.

Thus there is no consistent pattern in the Balistreri and Busch-Rossnagel data to suggest that BSRI categorization is associated with differential task performance in Embedded Figures Task procedures. Subsequent research on the Group Embedded Figures Task (GEFT) (Bernard *et al.* 1990) also examined the relationship between gender and spatial task performance. Bernard *et al.* employed a shortened version of the BSRI. They found that in women, high masculinity – low femininity was associated with significantly better GEFT performance. In men, gender characteristics were not associated with performance. These two studies looking at Embedded Figures Tasks found consistent patterns, feminine (categorized)women were sensitive to the nature of the task. Men showed no such within-sex variability associated with gender characteristics in task performance.

The work of Hamilton (1995) also considered GEFT performance. Once again, the BSRI was employed to identify gender characteristics in the participants. In this study, the effect size associated with sex was only $d = 0.08$. However, medium-sized effect sizes were found between the performances of the different gender groups. In women the effect size between androgynous- and feminine-categorized participants was $d = 0.42$. In men, an effect size of $d = 1.15$ was found between masculine and undifferentiated (low self-rating

of both feminine and masculine characteristics) participants. Thus in an observation where sex differences did not occur, within-sex variability associated
with gender was present and with a large effect size. As in the two studies
immediately above, despite a different direction of pattern, there was a sex
difference in the extent of within-sex variability associated with gender.
Later research (Brosnan 1998) also established a relationship between masculine characteristics and GEFT performance, though the results were not
segregated into the performance of women and men.

A major social constructivist approach by Deaux and Major (1987) attempts
to place the activation of gender-related behaviour within the social interaction
context from which it emerges. This is an approach put forward to account
for sex differences in cognitive task performance and is considered in detail
in Chapter 10 (see particularly Figure 10.2). Recent research by Massa *et al.*
2005) related this model not to sex differences but to individual differences
associated with gender role. Using the BSRI to classify women and men as
masculine or feminine, these authors looked at the impact of task instruction
manipulation upon GEFT performance in men and women with either masculine or feminine characteristics. The instructions were either 'empathetic',
suggesting the task was a measure of the participant's ability to understand
other people's problems, or 'spatial', where the task was a measure of understanding objects in space. Importantly, these authors also attempted to
measure motivation providing items such as 'It is important for me to do well
on activities like the figures activities' (Massa *et al.* 2005, p. 111).

Their findings suggested that the manipulations of explicit task instructions
had a differential effect upon women who possessed either feminine or masculine characteristics. Feminine women performed more effectively in the
empathy condition, masculine women more effectively in the spatial condition. This is strong evidence that these women were susceptible to the instruction manipulation. The findings also suggested that task instruction had no
impact upon men with either feminine or masculine characteristics.
Unfortunately, the results of the motivational assessment were unclear; only
one item, the one identified above, suggested that the motivation of the feminine and masculine women was affected. However the models suggested by
Eccles (1987) and Geary (1996) might suggest that the social cognitions associated with task performance may be so well embedded cognitively that implicit
activation by the task instructions may occur and that therefore motivational
inventories given after the task may not accurately measure the initial social
cognition dynamics. Another issue associated with the motivation questionnaire being given after the task was completed is that responses may have
been driven as much by actual performance as by the initial instruction set.

The overall pattern of findings from these studies suggest that high masculinity and low femininity, as measured by the BSRI, tends to be associated
with Embedded Figures Task competency, with a potential role for social
cognitions in the process. However, what is also clear is that the importance

of gender-characteristic possession is different in women and men in this cognitive task. Only in women is the possession of feminine or masculine characteristics strongly associated with task performance.

Hamilton (1995) also considered the relationship between gender trait possession and 3-D mental rotation task performance. With this task there was a large sex difference, but variability in gender trait possession did add unique variance in the regression analyses. A measure of androgyny was significant in the overall analysis for men (though not for women). Once again, gender trait possession was important, but once again there was a sex difference in the importance of these characteristics. Ginn and Stiehl (1999) assessed the relationship between gender schema and MRT performance. Women were classified as gender-schematics if they reported relatively high feminine characteristics on the shortened BSRI; men were classified as schematic if they possessed a relatively greater extent of masculine characteristics.

In addition Ginn and Stiehl assessed the spatial experience of the participants. The authors reported the presence of sex differences in MRT performance. However, while spatial experience was associated with task performance, there was no evidence of the schematic/aschematic categorization being related to performance. Given that higher masculinity appeared related to task performance in both women and men, it would have been interesting to have seen the raw BSRI scores for masculinity and femininity placed in a hierarchical regression, regressed upon MRT performance.

Subsequent research by Saucier *et al.* (2004) further pursued the importance of gender in MRT performance. The use of the PAQ allowed the authors to identify individuals with agentic (masculine), communion (feminine) or sex-specific traits (characteristics more desirable for men). There was also a gender behaviour measurement with the Sex Role Behaviour Scale (SRBS; Orlofsky and O'Heron 1987). The path analysis of the data provided only partial support for the suggestion that gender role mediates spatial task performance. In one analysis gender role could account for only about 6 per cent of the spatial task performance. The SRBS did not account for any variance in task performance. Recent research by Ritter (2004) investigated the relationship between gender trait possession (BSRI), MRT and a verbal task, the controlled word association task. The major finding was the association of androgyny with verbal task competence. Gender trait possession was not associated with MRT task performance.

Issues in the Gender and Cognition Research

The research discussed above suggests that gender characteristics as measured by inventories such as the BSRI and PAQ may be associated with cognitive task social cognitions and performance. However, the patterns of findings were not necessarily unequivocal and it is worth considering methodological limitations that may contribute to these inconsistencies.

Measures such as the BSRI and the PAQ were constructed in the mid 1970s in the USA and it is possible that the research identified above took place within cultures which had changed over the subsequent 30 years. While recent research has attempted to determine the pertinence of such measures in cultures other than the USA (Katsurada and Sugihara 1999; Sugihara and Katsurada 2000; Zhang *et al.* 2001), perhaps the most interesting validation studies have emerged in the USA and similar cultures such as the UK. Holt and Ellis (1998) observed that 38 of the original BSRI characteristics had retained their stereotypic label; the exceptions were 'loyal' and 'childlike'. This gives an impression of sustained validity; however the authors noted that the difference in desirability of the characteristics for men and women had appeared to decrease since 1974. This suggested that participants' perceptions had become more 'liberal' or less gender stereotyped.

Research by Konrad and Harris (2002) assessed the perceptions of different ethnic groups as well as the different perceptions of men and women. The perception of gender-stereotyped characteristics in the BSRI varied with the sex of the participant; both African- and European-American women did not view the vast majority of the 'masculine' characteristics as more desirable for men in American culture. In men a small majority of items were viewed in the conventional stereotypic manner. With the feminine characteristics the women in this study again rated the vast majority of the items as no more desirable for women than for men. Again, the men in this study were more likely to view the feminine items as more desirable for women, but this only referred to about 50 per cent of the items. These observations in this USA sample are comparable to observations in the UK (Hamilton *et al.* 2002; Wilson and Francis 1997) and suggest that women may perceive that contemporary culture holds less rigid expectations for gender trait possession.

Further research by Auster and Ohm (2000) reinforced the notion of complexity of gender stereotype perceptions. These authors found 18 of the 20 BSRI feminine items and 8 of the masculine BSRI items still retained their validity. These authors also found that there were changes in the mean desirability of the items. However, perhaps the most interesting element of their data related to the third research question which asked participants to rate the importance of the traits for themselves. The men and women in this sample wished to have similar characteristics, a mix of the feminine and masculine items from the BSRI. Typically the desired items were self-sufficient or decisive masculine characteristics and sensitive and compassionate feminine items. Thus in the conventional approach to validity, the judgement of the culture's view, there was partial support for the BSRI validity, but in relation to self an androgynous viewpoint was reported.

In total, these studies suggest that the very premise of Bem's approach may be compromised in that the gender-stereotypic nature of the original items may no longer be valid with contemporary samples, particularly for women. However, this may be dependent on the research question asked of the participants. The results suggest that the BSRI items (at least) may require modification if not rejection. Should this be the case then it would be of no surprise that research employing such inventories produced inconsistent findings. However, there are also theoretical reasons why such inventories may not be appropriate tools to investigate the importance of gender schema for cognitive task performance.

Consider the gender labels in the titles of the research discussed above: sex role (Balistreri and Busch-Rossnagel 1989); sex role identity (Bernard *et al.* 1990); gender schema (Ginn and Stiehl 1999); and gender trait possession (Hamilton 1995); sex role behaviour (Orlofsky and O'Heron 1987); gender role orientation (Rammstedt and Rammsayer 2002); sex role stereotypes (Spence *et al.* 1974); gender role personality traits (Sugihara and Katsurada 2000). Spence (1985) suggested that if anything the clarity associated with psychological conceptualization of gender had decreased since the mid 1960s. The diversity in the labels identified above suggests that conceptual understanding in the area has not greatly improved.

Spence (1991) argued that both the BSRI and PAQ had many aspects in common and were intercorrelated. However, her major argument was that these inventories were essentially measures of desirable agentic and expressive gender stereotypes and these measures could not and should not be pre-sumed to be associated with a broader constellation of gender characteristics such as gender role or behaviour and gender-schematic processing. An example of the complexity in conceptualization is evidenced by the work of Signorella *et al.* (1989) who looked at the predictions made from Bem's and Spence's approach with respect to spatial task performance.

Signorella *et al.* suggested that Bem's gender schema theory approach would imply that possession of the schema (and self-concept) would lead to the individual conforming to gender stereotypic activity such as undertaking spatial activities. Consequently, the authors argued that self-concept as measured by the BSRI would have only an indirect effect upon spatial task performance, mediated by spatial experience. Spence's identity theory on the other hand would predict that self-concept and spatial ability could potentially account for independent influence upon spatial performance. The evidence provided some support for Spence's position; however some aspects of the data could have been congruent with Bem's position! Thus research which found little evidence for a strong relationship between dis-crete gender measures (for example Archer 1991; Archer *et al.* 1995) would lead one to accede to Spence's position, and as Ginn and Stiehl (1999) and earlier Hamilton (1995) would argue, in order to measure gender schemata one needs to employ tasks which directly measure schematic processing. These inconsistencies between measures substantiate Nash's (1979) sugges-tion, that the schematic task orientation should be logically related to cogni-tive performance as opposed to related to self-schematic processing.

A final issue relates to the fundamental nature of gender construction by the child. The Eccles (1987) model discussed in Chapter 5 emphasized the social constructivist account of gender and social cognition, where the child's social cognition develops as a consequence of their interactions within the cultural milieu. Little emphasis is placed upon the characteristics the child brings to these interactions, yet in many ways the child's characteristics are the foundation for the social cognition development. Research has suggested the presence of more distal influences upon the child's potential to acquire gender characteristics (Baucom *et al.* 1985; Csatho *et al.* 2003; Hines *et al.* 2002). This research, which will be discussed in detail in the next chapter, indicates that hormonal influences may affect the child's differential-aptitude component of Eccles' model. This in turn may have a statistically significant (if minor) impact upon the possession of gender characteristics.

Conclusions

This chapter has discussed the constructs and empirical evidence relating to personality and cognitive processes, which vary within the sexes, the gender characteristics of individuals. Gender has been considered at various levels of explanation: self-concept, attitudes towards others, gender behaviour and gender schema. While many such as Bem (1974, 1981, 1985) consider that the construct necessitates a relationship between all of these levels, others such as Spence and her co-workers (Spence *et al.* 1974; Spence and Helmreich 1978; Spence 1985; Spence 1991) and Archer and co-workers (Archer 1991; Archer *et al.* 1995; Archer and Lloyd 2002) suggest that essentially inventories such as the BSRI and PAQ identify the possession of agentic and expressive gender-stereotypic characteristics which may indicate little about the general characteristics of gender immediately identified above.

The vast proportion of the empirical research discussed in the chapter has assumed implicitly that self-report measures may be implicitly linked to other characteristics such as gender schema. The importance of such schema for cognitive task performance lies in the social cognition models which link gender stereotypes to concept and self-efficacy to task expectation and thus task performance. The achievement-related model of Eccles (1987) highlights the importance of the *cultural milieu* and gender role socialization in this social cognition process. However, one could argue that it is only individuals with potent gender schemata who would employ task stereotype labels in order to activate the appropriate (or inappropriate) social cognitions associated with the task. The research of Basow and Medcalf (1988), Hirschy and Morris (2002) and Massa *et al.* (2005) highlights the relationship between gender-characteristic possession and the social cognitions identified in the models of Eccles (1987) and Geary (1996).

The early meta-analytic study by Signorella and Jamison (1986) indicated that the possession of masculine traits tended to be related to performance in tasks stereotypically labelled masculine. There was no evidence of a relation between possession of self-reported feminine characteristics and feminine-labelled tasks. However, in this study the pattern of relationship was dependent upon both the sex and the age of each of the participants. It is interesting to note that the research identifying within-sex variance also reveals between-sex differences. Subsequent research while tending to show a similar trend has also shown variance in the importance of masculinity in visuospatial tasks. This variability is not surprising given the different conceptualization apparent in the research. The titles of the research articles indicate this complexity: sex role (Balistreri and Busch-Rossnagel 1989); sex role identity (Bernard *et al.* 1990); gender schema (Ginn and Stiehl 1999); gender trait possession (Hamilton 1995); sex-role behaviour (Orlofsky and O'Heron 1987); gender role orientation (Rammstedt and Rammsayer 2002); sex role stereotypes (Spence *et al.* 1974); and gender role personality traits (Sugihara and Katsurada 2000).

Such a pot pourri of terms may reflect an implicit assumption that self-report measures of gender trait characteristics do indeed indicate these other general gender characteristics, as Bem would imply. It is tempting though to consider that in fact, as Spence (1985) above related, the concept of masculinity and femininity are among the 'muddiest in all of psychology'. Should Spence be correct then despite the partial success of the literature in establishing a relationship between the possession of gender characteristics and visuospatial task performance, there is a possibility that with appropriate measures of gender schema, more consistent and substantive relationships could be identified. This will probably depend upon the use of direct measures of schematic processing, though the design of the study would need to consider the confounding impact of priming or activation which may occur between schema assessment and task performance (Archer 1991).

The chapter finished with a brief consideration of the construction of the gender schema. Conventionally this has been presumed to occur as a consequence of the child's interaction with the cultural milieu – the social constructivist view. However, there is evidence that a small but significant factor in the acquisition of gender characteristics is hormonally driven (Baucom *et al.* 1985; Csatho *et al.* 2003; Hines *et al.* 2002). This impact would be mediated by the non-gender characteristics the child brings to this developmental process. This suggests that another source of within-sex variability in cognitive task performance could reside in hormonal variation within the sexes and forms the basis of the next chapter.

7 Hormonal Influences

Aim and Overview

The previous chapter concluded with a brief section on identifying within-sex variability associated with hormonal influences on the possession of gender-stereotype characteristics. This chapter will consider in more detail the nature of hormonal influences upon human behaviour and in particular upon human cognition. While the emphasis in this chapter will be upon within-sex variability associated with hormones, between-sex comparison will be noted where appropriate, as it was in the previous chapter.

The chapter will begin with a discussion of the theoretical frameworks associated with hormones and cognition, the theoretical model or hypotheses of Geschwind and Galaburda (1985a, 1985b, 1987) and the principles of *organizational* and *activational* aspects of hormonal actions. Geschwind's suggestions relate to the influence of prenatal hormonal influences and therefore would be regarded, in the main, as organizational influences upon the CNS, hormonal influences upon the early construction and organization of the CNS which tend to be long-lasting. However, hormonal influences in humans are also subject to daily, lunar and annual fluctuations and these temporary influences in adults form the basis of the activational influences upon the CNS.

The first element of this section will consider the methodological tools employed by psychologists which have aimed to identify behavioural markers of early organizational hormonal influences: the use of handedness, footedness and more recently finger characteristics, for example digit ratios (Manning and Taylor 2001; Manning *et al.* 1998, 2001). In addition the discussion will consider clinical groups where early prenatal hormonal disruption has occurred.

The empirical research component of the chapter will consider initially the studies which have looked at proposed prenatal influences employing the behavioural markers identified above. In addition the content will also consider research assessing activational aspects of hormonal influences, in particular the menstrual cyclical associations with cognitive task perform-ance in women. The cognitive processes discussed will range from motor task/perceptual speed processes, imagery and working memory, for example mental rotation and object location, through to retrieval, both verbal and non-verbal, from long-term memory. Other research from a clinical context, where circulating hormonal levels have systematically changed, will be dis-cussed where appropriate.

Theoretical Frames

The work of Geschwind and Galaburda (1985a, 1985b, 1987) provided a major theoretical framework for the consideration of how prenatal hor-monal factors could determine the early development and organization of the CNS. They discussed the inhibitory influence of testosterone upon hemi-spheric development. Geschwind and Galaburda stated that:

> According to our hypothesis, slowed growth within certain areas of the left hemisphere is likely to result in enlargement of other cortical regions, in particular, the homologous contralateral area, but also adjacent unaffected regions. (1985b, p. 521)

They went on to suggest that this alteration in the typical cerebral asymmetry pattern would lead to the advanced development of particular 'talents' associ-ated with neural systems within these other cortical regions. Substantive research has focused upon the neural systems resident in the right hemisphere; however the statement above clearly indicates the potential for favourable development in the adjacent left-hemisphere locality. The implications of the Geschwind and Galaburda hypotheses were immense, ranging from issues of cerebral lateralization and handedness, through cognition and learning diffi-culties, to the prediction of particular diseases such as deficits in immunology. Thus Geschwind and Behan (1984) observed that 7 per cent of left-handed individuals reported some form of dyslexia as opposed to 0.3 per cent of right-handed individuals. Bishop (1990) however has suggested that the most fre-quent observation was that handedness was not associated with dyslexia.

The journal *Brain and Cognition* published a special issue, with the lead article by Bryden *et al.* (1994a, 1994b), which addressed the success of Geschwind and Galaburda hypotheses. In the main, the articles in the issue were unfavourable; however many of the issues raised involved the question of whether the hypotheses had been effectively assessed. Some authors raised the question of whether the model's emphasis on prenatal influences diverted attention from neonatal influences (Forget and Cohen 1994; Hampson and Moffat 1994). Many articles raised issues of handedness and sample size in left-handedness and clinical research (Coren 1994; Hampson and Moffat 1994; Halpern 1994; Porac 1994).

Alternative accounts such as Annett (1994) placed emphasis upon genetic models (natural variation) of cerebral lateralization rather than a model based upon pathological factors, that is an anomalous hormonal environment in the womb. Thus while handedness has been taken as a measure of prenatal hormonal activity, for example the Baucom *et al.* (1985) study discussed in Chapter 6, other research has taken handedness as a measure of genetic models, for example Casey's (1996) bent-twig model discussed in Chapter 11. Issues associated with handedness measurement will be discussed below. Bishop (1990) described numerous genetic accounts of handedness including Annett (1970) and McManus (1984). These models have been employed in order to account for within-sex cognitive differences (Annett 1999; Johnson *et al.* 2002; McKeever 1986; McKeever *et al.* 1988). These accounts will not be discussed in detail at this point, though handedness measures will be considered in the next section.

One should not presume that issues of evolutionary processes and prenatal hormonal activity are necessarily independent of one another. Authors such as Hampson (Hampson 1995) whose research will be considered in detail below have explicitly linked evolutionary accounts of sex differences in spatial ability to hormonal influences. Collaer and Hines (1995) carried out a major review of several of the hypotheses associated with hormonal influences. They identified the complexity of hormonal influences of testosterone across and within species. The pathways identified by Collaer and Hines are shown in Figure 7.1. These hormones are predominantly produced by the gonads. Testosterone (T) and dihydrotestosterone (DHT) are produced in the testes, and oestradiol and progestins in the ovaries and placenta. All are present in different degrees in both women and men.

These pathways and their impact will vary according to species, factors of timing and the presence of inhibitory processes such as oestrogen-binding agents (for example alpha-fetoprotein) and placental mechanisms.

Collaer and Hines identified several hypotheses associated with these processes:

- A *passive feminization model*, where testicular hormone activity leads to 'masculinization' and 'defeminization'; and in its absence feminization and demasculinization occur.

- A *gradient model*, where some of the oestrogens may act to slightly masculinize and defeminize.

- An *active feminization model* , where the ovarian hormones are viewed as playing a more dynamic role.

An important element of the review by Collaer and Hines was the interaction between internal and external environments and hormonal actions. The most relevant hypothesis pertinent to the Geschwind model is the first hypothesis, which emphasized the impact of prenatal androgens.

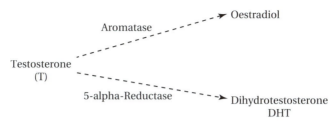

Figure 7.1   Pathways for testosterone (T) psychopharmacological action

The evidence for their first hypothesis was predominantly based upon women with Congenital Adrenal Hyperplasia (CAH). In this clinical condition the female foetus produces high levels of androgens from her own adrenal gland. In most cases this arises from a deficiency in the enzyme 21,21-hydoxylase. The impact is upon a feedback loop involving the production of cortisol. The consequence is the overproduction of the androgen 17-hydroprogesterone and progesterone. The overproduction begins prenatally and produces 'phenotypic masculinization in females at birth' (Collaer and Hines 1995, p. 64). While some CAH girls are mistaken for boys and reared appropriately, the vast majority are raised as girls. The androgen overproduction is stopped by cortisol therapy after birth. The authors considered a range of behaviours: sexual orientation, sexual identity, personality, handedness and cognitive ability. Few studies had addressed handedness, which would have allowed a consideration of the Geschwind and Galaburda hypothesis relating handedness and prenatal hormonal activation. The two studies reported by Collaer and Hines showed equivocal findings.

More importantly, Collaer and Hines reviewed the findings for cognitive abilities in women with CAH. Generally, the studies they reviewed found little evidence for major effects in verbal and performance IQ, though one study did observe impairment in performance IQ. Several studies were reported as finding enhanced performance in visuospatial tasks, 3-D and 2-D mental rotation, paper folding tests and so on. However, other studies have found little impact on performance in tasks involving block design or in the embedded-figures task. While no impact was observed on verbal processes associated with verbal fluency and perceptual speed, impaired performance was noted in certain quantitative tasks.

Collaer and Hines suggested that studies where the pattern showed no enhancement in performance, for example spatial tasks such as embedded figures or quantitative skills such as arithmetic, tapped cognitive processes where sex differences were small or even absent. This suggests that the within-sex influence of excessive prenatal androgens is associated with processes that evidence the greatest sex differences. As Hampson (1995) suggested, 'To date, neuroendocrine research in other species suggests that it is sexually dimorphic behaviors which are most subject to hormonal influence' (p. 398).

The Collaer and Hines review of their first hypothesis focused upon women and it is interesting to note that Kimura (1999) concluded

> that the levels of testosterone are non-linearly related to cognitive function, in particular to spatial abilities of the kind favouring men. Normal young men with lower levels of T perform better than young men with higher levels; but young women with higher levels perform better than those with lower levels. (p. 73)

The non-linear relationship between hormonal level and cognitive task performance identified by Kimura is evidenced in the theoretical and research work of Nyborg (1988). However, Nyborg emphasized the importance of oestradiol in spatial ability and mathematical ability. The model suggests that 'moderate oestrogenization' will move a man towards the optimum level of oestrogen for spatial ability. According to Nyborg this would account for 'androgynous' men performing well in spatial ability tasks (see Hamilton 1995 for a finding supporting this view). Nyborg (1990) also suggested that a severe deficit in oestradiol could account for the spatial impairment evidenced in women with Turner's syndrome.

Methodologies

Rather than attempt to measure testosterone and other hormones *in utero*, psychologists have attempted to identify somatic markers of these prenatal hormones: handedness measures and finger characteristics. This section will consider briefly the protocols involved in these methodologies.

Handedness Measures

The measurement of handedness has taken many forms (Bishop 1990), from hand preference inventories to hand skill tasks. Table 7.1 identifies some of the questions employed in the self-report inventories.

The sample of items shown in Table 7.1 provide an indication of how psychologists have employed self-report measures of handedness. The discussion above considered briefly the complexity of the theoretical factors underlying handedness. The examples reveal the practical issues associated with hand preference measurement. For instance, do individuals unscrew a bottle cap and open a jar with different hands? The two items relating to bottle- and jar-opening appear to make differing assumptions about the use of hands in these circumstances. In the Crovitz and Zener (1962) inventory, the presumption is that the holding hand is more important; in the Annett measure, the assumption is that the hand doing the unscrewing is more important. In addition, one could question whether respondents would necessarily be accurate in their recall of hand use (Annett 1994). Alternatively

Table 7.1 Sample of question items from handedness self-report inventories

Item	Source
(Which hand is used) to write with	C&V, A, E
(Which hand is used) to hold scissors	C&V, A, E
(Which hand is used) to throw a ball	C&V, A
(Which hand is used) to hold bottle when removing top	C&V
(Which hand is used) to hold a match	A, E
(Which hand is used) to unscrew the lid of a jar	A
(Which hand is used) to hold the top of a broom	A
(Which hand is used) to hold a spoon	E
(Which hand is used) when drawing	E

Notes: C&V, test for handedness, Crovitz and Zener (1962) A, Annett handedness Inventory (1970) E, Edinburgh handedness inventory, Oldfield (1971)

some researchers have employed hand skill measures as opposed to preference measures in order to gain a more valid measure of handedness.

In tasks such as the peg-moving task (see Figure 7.2) and the Purdue pegboard the participant has to move small pegs and place them into other holes as quickly as possible. In the Annett task, the pegs are placed in one row of holes and have to be moved individually across to the equivalent hole in the opposite row. Both hands will be assessed independently and their relative skill (typically a speed-versus-accuracy measure) will be assessed. Measures such as this allow the relative strength of each hand use to be identified; differences between hand skill efficiency are a measure of hand skill asymmetry (HSA). While Annett's handedness inventory is a handedness preference tool, her theory employs hand skill distributions (see Bishop 1990).

While handedness measures may reveal the presence of individual differences in human cognition, interpreting the causal factor(s) is more problematic; prenatal hormonal factors could be determining factors, though Annett (1970) and McManus (1984) would be likely to make an alternative explanation.

Methodological Issues

Annett (2000) discussed the importance of a genetic influence in her theoretical approach. The right shift (RS) theory essentially suggested that a random

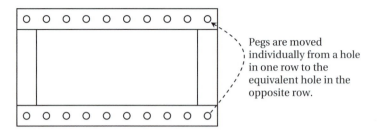

Figure 7.2   An example of peg-moving apparatus

process along with a RS factor determined the direction of handedness. According to Annett the RS$^+$ factor introduces a rightward bias into the distribution of handedness. Individuals with the RS$^+$/RS$^+$ genotype would be likely to possess a left-hemisphere advantage, for example with a left-hemisphere language locus. The hemispheric bias was considered to result from influences upon foetal growth. The number of RS$^+$ alleles an individual possessed thus determined the degree of bias. The RS$^+$/RS$^+$ combination was associated with strong dextrality in handedness, however an RS$^+$/RS$^-$ combination led to some slight sinistral tendencies. The RS$^-$/RS$^-$ combination led to the random distribution.

In addition, Annett's model suggested that men were slightly more likely to have a sinistral bias. Annett (1992) has suggested that individuals with the RS$^+$/RS$^-$ combination are more likely to be efficient at visuospatial processing. Casey (Pezaris and Casey 1991, discussed initially in Chapter 4) also adopted this approach when she observed spatial performance in an adolescent sample. The issue concerns how one would identify an individual as possessing the RS$^+$/RS$^-$ combination. Annett (1992) categorized participants on the basis of their right-hand use in particular subscale activities in her inventory.

Others such as Casey have employed *familial sinistrality* to the same effect. The assumption in Casey's measure of familial sinistrality is that an individual who displays dextrality on an inventory such as the Edinburgh handedness inventory, but has a close (first-degree) relative who would have a sinistral score on the inventory, is the individual who is likely to possess the RS$^+$/RS$^-$ combination. Notice that participants were asked to judge their relatives' handedness rather than recall actual measures of their relatives' handedness.

More recent research (Cerone and McKeever 1998) has questioned the usefulness of familial sinistrality (FS) as a predictor of spatial ability. Prior research by McKeever had not found the same pattern of results as Casey and Brabeck (1990), and in their 1998 study Cerone and McKeever attempted to replicate Casey's methodologies regarding FS measurement and the cognitive task employed. The authors found no relationships between their measure of FS with the participants' handedness scores or their mental rotation scores. Cerone and McKeever concluded:

> Finally, we come back to the basic question that prompted this and other studies concerned with FS and spatial ability – are they related? Present results suggest that they are not. (1998, p. 10)

McKeever *et al.* (2000) later suggested that FS was also not associated with hand skill asymmetry. The authors suggested this was further evidence for a lack of support for Annett's model. Alternatively it could be an indication of the ineffectiveness of FS as a measure of the RS$^+$/RS$^-$ combination (Halpern 1996). Research has subsequently attempted to identify the most appropriate measures of cerebral lateralization employing a variety of skill and preference measures (Corey *et al.* 2001; Elias *et al.* 1998; Reio *et al.* 2004).

There are clearly both conceptual and operational issues with handedness remaining to be resolved. The research to be discussed in the remainder of this chapter will focus upon the direct or indirect relationship of testosterone, T, upon cognitive processing efficacy. The use of finger digit ratio methodology below is based on a direct genetic explanation of individual differences in cerebral lateralization but its theoretical base also identifies a role for hormonal factors.

Finger Characteristics

Recent research has suggested that finger characteristics may be related to genetic characteristics associated with prenatal hormone activity (Manning *et al.* 1998; Sanders and Waters 2001). Manning *et al.* suggested that the ratio of the second-finger to fourth-finger length differed between men and women with the former having a significantly lower second-to-fourth digit ratio (see Figure 7.3). They went on to undertake hormonal assays in the men in the sample and found the second-to-fourth digit ratio was negatively correlated with T levels; thus within males (and presumably between sexes) higher levels of T are associated with lower second-to-fourth ratios. Research by Fink *et al.* (2004) identified the relationship between the 2D:4D ratio and behavioural measurements of handedness. Photocopies of the digit lengths were made in order to establish the ratio. Children were categorized as left- or right-hand-dominant; the girls had significantly greater right-hand dominance. More importantly, digit ratio was correlated with hand dominance (both overall measure and a task demanding dotting squares).

These studies suggest that there is a link between 2D:4D measurement and prenatal activity (mediated by handedness measures); however other research has questioned this. Buck *et al.* (2003) looked at the relationship between individuals who had experienced Congenital Adrenal Hyperplasia (CAH) in a sample of 77 men and 69 women. They employed an X-ray of the

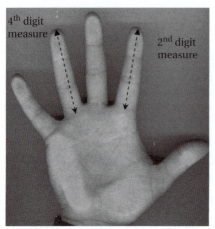

Measuring the 2D:4D ratio.

Callipers can be employed directly on the fingers, or photocopies of the hand or even X-ray scans of the digits. The author's hand (shown) has a 2D:4D ratio of about 0.949 which would be taken to indicate exposure to a relatively high level of prenatal T.

Figure 7.3   Measuring finger digit ratio

left hand and wrist with calliper measurement in order to identify the ratio of the second to the fourth digit. These authors were concerned about the accuracy of soft-tissue measurement of digit length. They found the typical sex difference, with the men displaying a lower ratio; more importantly they found that in the women there was no difference in 2D:4D ratio between the CAH and control groups, in contrast to earlier work.

Manning *et al.* (1998) developed a model whereby the Hox gene is responsible for the development of digits and testes. Testicular production of testosterone is presumed to affect the hormonal environment of the foetus, which will affect not only the development of the CNS but also the relative lengths of the second and fourth digits. In addition, Manning *et al.* suggested that dermatoglyphic characteristics (the patterns contributing to fingerprint identity) will also vary. Sanders and Waters (2001) have employed this latter characteristic in research.

Manning and his co-workers (Manning *et al.* 2003) later suggested that variation in the X-linked androgen receptor gene (AR) determines sensitivity to testosterone and that second-to-fourth digit ratio was a phenotypic correlate of AR structure. Manning has suggested that the digit ratio marker has important implications for a diverse range of medical/psychological phenomena (Fink *et al.* 2003, 2004; Manning *et al.* 2002; Robinson and Manning 2000; Sluming and Manning 2000). The diversity associated with the theory and the methodology is not unlike the complexity of the Geschwind and Galaburda hypotheses.

Research Findings

Prenatal Influences

Manning and Taylor (2001) employed the digit ratio measure as a somatic marker for prenatal testosterone, T. A low second-to-fourth digit (2D:4D) ratio was considered to indicate relatively high levels of prenatal T. Typically men have lower ratios than women (Manning *et al.* 1998). Manning and Taylor found a significant relationship between second-to-fourth digit ratio and (the Vandenberg and Kuse) mental rotation task performance. They concluded that the observed relationship could be a result of the prenatal influence of T upon right-hemisphere development and subsequent spatial ability. They also suggested, given their sample of sportsmen, that prenatal T could boost the developing vascular system, with implications for male fitness (Sluming and Manning 2000).

However, other research has failed to replicate this finding (Poulin *et al.* 2004). Poulin *et al.* found no evidence of a relationship between 2D:4D ratio and mental rotation task performance in both men and women. In a second task, object location, women outperformed men in object and object-to-location performance and the relationship with the 2D:4D ratio changed. In men there was no relationship, but in women the digit ratio was positively correlated with both object and object-to-location recall performance. This would suggest that a lower level of prenatal T is important in the development of these processes.

Recent research (Putz *et al.* 2004) has also failed to identify a relationship between digit ratio and MRT performance in men. However, in women there was a marginally significant positive correlative between the left-hand digit ratio and MRT and a marginally non-significant correlation in the right hand. This pattern would suggest that *low* prenatal T is associated with improved MRT performance. Further research by Burton *et al.* (2005) found significant correlations between second and fourth digit ratios in both men and women. However, the relationship was in opposite directions for women and men. Low-digit-ratio–high-prenatal-T was associated with high MRT performance in women. In men this pattern was reversed, with low digit ratio being associated with low MRT performance. These authors interpreted the results in the context of other observations of a curvilinear relationship between hormone level and cognition initially discussed above and also considered below.

Csatho *et al.* (2001) found in women a significant negative correlation between digit ratio and spatial location in a maze task. However, the findings when considering both sexes were inconsistent and suggest that if digit ratio is a valid marker of prenatal T then the prenatal influence must be complex, as Putz *et al.* (2004) suggest. Csatho *et al.* emphasized the relationship between the prenatal timing of T and the timing of 'sexually dimorphic trait differentiation'. Alternatively, given the process complexity of tasks such as MRT, it could be argued that it is the development of specific neural systems underlying discrete MRT processes that may be affected by fluctuating T levels.

The process approach is reflected in the MRT research by Hooven *et al.* (2004). This study employed stimuli based upon the original Shepard and Metzler (1971) study materials. They plotted RT and error rate as a function of angular disparity between the two block stimuli (see Figure 4.5 in Chapter 4).

Current T level was measured by saliva sample, presumed to be a measure of unbound testosterone which is related to free T levels considered to be biologically active. The level of T from this measure correlated with MRT performance. Closer inspection suggested that it was not the slope of the function which was related to T, but the intercept (intersection of function with the *y*-axis). The slope function is associated with the actual mental rotation of the stimuli in the task and thus T appears to be important for other aspects of the task, for example encoding, decision-making or decision processes.

Hooven *et al.* (2004) noted that the relationship with T was particularly apparent in trials where a 'different' decision and judgement was required, that is where successful mental rotation was impossible. High levels of T were associated with a lower intercept, prompting the authors to suggest that elevated levels of T may be associated with risk-taking in a novel context. (See Kerkman *et al.* 2000 in Chapter 4 for a consideration of these 'different' responses in MRT protocols.) Sanders and Waters (2001) employed a different somatic marker for prenatal hormonal activity: dermatoglyphics, the dermal ridges found on the palms and soles. According to Sanders and Waters the human fingerprint is established by the sixteenth foetal week. In both men and in women there is a higher finger ridge count in the right hand, with only a minority having the opposite pattern.

Sanders and Waters (2001) used this measure to identify within-sex groups and employed a range of cognitive tasks, some favouring women such as the controlled association task, where participants have to identify synonyms of four target words, and tasks favouring males such as mental rotation. The study found that participants (regardless of the participant's sex) with a greater number of ridges on the left performed the verbal tasks more efficiently, whereas the participants with a greater right-hand number had a significant tendency to perform the spatial tasks more effectively. While the authors concluded that a prenatal hormone (T or oestrogen) contributed to these effects, the important element of this research was that the impact was also a within-sex effect rather than merely a between-sex phenomenon.

Adult Research

Another methodology employed to indirectly measure dihydrotestosterone (DHT) is the use of hairline loss which Beech (2001) assumed was the result of cumulative DHT inhibiting the production of keratin, a constituent of hair. In a sample aged between 17 years and 55 years they found evidence of a nonlinear, inverted-U function between hair loss and the Shepard and Metzler (1971) mental rotation procedure. They took this as support for the findings of Moffat and Hampson (1996) who had found a similar inverted-U relationship of testosterone (T) with different spatial tasks (see below).

Perhaps a more direct way of considering the importance of hormonal influences upon cognition is to measure directly the hormonal level through assays. Moffat and Hampson (1996) used assays derived from saliva samples in order to identify levels of T in women and in men. Seven tasks were employed to assess measures of spatial ability, spatial visualization and spatial orientation, mental rotation and verbal fluency. Sex differences in favour of men were found in the spatial tasks but not in verbal fluency. In their analysis they collapsed the spatial task scores into a spatial composite, so information is not available for mental rotation separately. They found a significant nonlinear (inverted-U) function fit between the generic spatial ability measure and levels of T. In addition they noted a time-of-day impact associated with diurnal fluctuation in T. Thus in women the correlation was positive; in men the relationship was negative. This pattern was present only in participants assessed as right-handed with the Crovitz and Zener (1962) hand preference questionnaire.

McKeever and Deyo (1990) looked at T and DHT levels in a male college student sample. They measured spatial ability with two tasks, a conventional 3-D block recognition task requiring mental rotation and a spatial construction task requiring less mental rotation processing. T levels were not correlated with either spatial task; however, DHT was marginally ($p = 0.041$) related to the shape construction task. This supports the work of Hooven *et al.* (2004), which suggests that T influence may not be directly related to rotation processes. However, research by Neave *et al.* (1999) found a different pattern. They looked at the relationship of sexual orientation with cognitive task performance (spatial and verbal). They observed a nonlinear relationship between T levels (salivary samples) and mental rotation of the form observed by Moffat and Hampson (1996). Interestingly they found a linear relation with the water-level task, with higher levels of T associated with lower error rates. T levels were not related to the verbal fluency and synonym tasks.

Research by Yonker *et al.* (2003) looked at the relation of oestradiol with cognitive task performance. The sample of men and women were matched for oestradiol levels and age. Episodic memory was assessed in four contexts: verbal free recall, verbal cued recall, verbal recognition and face recognition. Typically women outperformed the men (though interestingly not in the verbal cued context). Given the matched levels of oestradiol the authors concluded that these sex differences could not be due to differences in oestradiol. The authors did note that within women (only) there was a significant correlation between oestradiol and face recognition. It should be noted though that with 18 participants, the power of the study is very low. They concluded that there is more to the impact of oestradiol than the level of circulating hormone, for example regional differences in oestrogen receptors may vary between the sexes.

A recent study of particular relevance of to the discussion of testosterone and cognitive task performance is the research of Josephs *et al.* (2003). They looked at the relationship between levels of T, stereotype threat and mathematics performance. Drawing from a literature that suggested that there is

a relationship between T level and perception of status, the authors predicted an interaction effect between sex, T level and stereotype threat condition. There are at least two interesting assumptions in this research:

- First, that high levels of T are associated with the social cognitions
  underpinning stereotype threat.

- Second, that a group of women with elevated levels of T relative to other
  women (a group which the research discussed above would suggest would
  have higher levels of spatial competencies) would be at most risk to
  impaired mathematics performance under stereotype threat conditions.

High T levels would therefore appear to be acting in different directions in
this mathematics context. The threat was activated by asking participants to
complete a pre-mathematics task questionnaire with items such as 'I feel
that some people feel I have less math ability because of my gender.' The
mathematics items were drawn from the quantitative section of the
Graduate Record Exam. The results suggested that women with high T levels
were more likely to have impaired mathematics performance; men with high
levels were more likely to have facilitated performance. This would suggest
that in this context the impact of T upon the social cognitions associated
with status is greater than its impact upon the spatial abilities underlying the
mathematics tasks.

This quasi-experimental design offers more control over the variables
being examined. Research by Postma *et al.* (2000) carried out an experimental study where the level of T was directly manipulated. In this study, healthy
young women were administered a single dose of testosterone and asked to
carry out an object location memory procedure (Postma *et al.* 1996, discussed in Chapter 3). The authors identified three discrete procedural elements: position location, object-to-location and combined processes. In
addition, an immediate and delayed (3-minute) condition was employed.
Generally T administration did not have an impact; however in the combined procedure there was an interaction between T administration and
time of recall, with a significant difference in performance between T and
no-T conditions in the 3-minute condition.

Activational Influences

A major methodological tool employed in the study of activational effects of
hormones has been to look at cognitive tasks across the menstrual cycle in
women where hormones fluctuate cyclically over about 30 days. The research
has tended to focus upon the variation in women in the level of two hormones, progesterone and oestradiol during the menstrual cycle. Note that
both hormones are relatively high during the luteal phase of the menstrual

cycle, during the menstrual phase they are relatively low. Research often compares the mid-luteal with the menstrual phase, a comparison of high with low levels of progesterone and oestradiol. However, this comparison would mean that the effect of these two hormones would be confounded, so some research has looked at the follicular-ovulation period where oestradiol is high and progesterone is low. Further, the pattern of events depicted above depends upon actual ovulation, and studies require assays as well as defined menstrual cycles in order to ensure that the pattern of hormonal levels is actually occurring as a result of ovulation.

Hampson and Kimura (1988) asked their participants to carry out a rod-and-frame task (spatial perception) and several motor tasks. They assumed that the former task typically favoured men while the speeded motor tasks typically favoured women. They observed that the spatial task was carried out more efficiently during the menstrual phase, whereas the motor tasks were more effectively carried out during the mid-luteal phase. They concluded: 'High levels of female hormones enhanced performance on tests at which females excel but were detrimental to performance on a task at which males excel' (1988, p. 458).

Hampson and Kimura's observation did not fully support other early studies investigating whether cognitive task performance may fluctuate over the menstrual cycle (Chiarello et al. 1989; Heister et al. 1989; Ho et al. 1986). Ho et al. (1986) found an effect on information processing rate in mental rotation during the ovulatory phase in contrast to the menstrual phase, but no change in spatial task error. In contrast Heister et al. (1989) found fluctuation in hemispheric advantage in cognitive task performance across four phases of the cycle: menstrual, follicular, luteal and pre-menstrual. In a lexical decision task no hemispheric changes or menstrual phase performance changes were noted. However, in a face recognition task (normal versus jumbled) a right-hemisphere advantage observed during the menstrual phase was reversed during the pre-menstrual phase. The response latencies were also significantly impaired during the pre-menstrual phase. In this task, typically associated with right-hemispheric function, response times were quickest during the follicular and luteal phases. What is not known is whether the advantage for RT is a perceptual-motor phenomenon or simply a motor phenomenon.

Chiarello et al. (1989) applied signal detection theory to tease apart changes in sensory processes and criterion responses across the cycle. Their results suggested that in a nonword/word discrimination task there was no change in sensory threshold but there was in the criterion response. In a line orientation task, there were significant changes across the menstrual cycle. This line orientation task typically evidences large sex differences in performance (see Chapter 3). Interestingly, line orientation judgement was better in the follicular phase than in the menstrual phase in the women. No visual field changes across the cycle were observed, though there was a tendency for right-hemispheric malleability through the cycle when undertaking the line orientation task.

Rode *et al.* (1995) also focused upon hemispheric function through the menstrual cycle. Participants carried out lexical and figural (>8-sided irregular polygon) matching tasks. The results compared luteal and menstrual phases and noted that there was no cycle effect associated with the lexical task, though there were effects for the figural task. In the menstrual phase RT slowed down for both left and right visual field presentations. However, the latency increase was significantly greater for the right visual field, indicating an advantage for the right hemisphere. The authors measured both the oestradiol and progesterone levels and found no association between these hormone levels and the patterns of results. They concluded that the observed malleability in right-hemisphere function was mediated by some process (or hormone) other than oestradiol and progesterone.

A later study by Hausmann *et al.* (2002) looked in detail at the hemispheric functioning across the menstrual cycle. Using tasks similar to those employed by Rode *et al.* (1995) they carried out assays to identify progesterone, oestradiol and testosterone levels. Their findings suggested a significant relationship between progesterone, left hemisphere and figural comparison (matching). The authors interpreted the findings as support for a hypothesis that suggests that progesterone activity effectively decouples collosum connectivity (Hausmann and Güntürkün 2000), producing a 'male-like' hemispheric dominance pattern during the menses but with less asymmetry during the mid-luteal phase.

Fluctuating spatial location memory processing has also been observed across the menstrual cycle (Postma *et al.* 1999). These authors decomposed the task into the components previously described in the Postma *et al.* (2000) study. In the latter, men showed an advantage for the positions-only condition, which requires a fine-grained coordinate memory for location (see Chapter 3). Menstrual cycle periodicity was established by self-report and the two cycle phases studied were the menstrual phase and a period 10 to 14 days after or prior to the menstrual phase. The study found that the only component process associated with the menstrual cycle phases was the position-only process, the one which exhibited sex differences. It is interesting that this finding contrasts with the findings by the same group discussed above (Postma *et al.* 2000), which indicated that T administration affected only the combined object-to-location process in spatial location working memory.

Another study has found a similar pattern of results where the particular spatial process showing menstrual cycle fluctuation is also the type of task evidencing the largest sex differences (Phillips and Silverman 1997). These authors asked participants to undertake a range of mental rotation procedures and a spatial relations task. The mental rotation varied from 2-D – card and flag rotation – to '3-D' – cube rotation (Shepard and Metzler 1971, block stimuli). The largest sex differences occurred in the 3-D mental rotation procedures (see Chapter 4). Another sample of women were then asked to undertake the tasks at either the menstrual or the mid-luteal phase. The authors found major effects with the three tasks – cube rotation, block rotation and spatial relations. This finding supports the notion above (Hampson 1995) that it is in visuospatial tasks where there are large sex differences that the impacts of hormonal influences are at their greatest, a conclusion partially supported by later research (Halpern and Tan 2001).

The research by Halpern and Tan also considered circalunary testosterone cycling in men; they predicted a 30-day cycle. Their results suggested that average T levels were related to mental rotation but in a different pattern in women and men. Higher T levels in women and lower levels in men were associated with better MRT performance (see above for a similar finding by Moffat and Hampson 1996). The authors reported (mirror-image) nonlinear trends for both men and women across 30-day cycles.

The research above indicates the importance of activational hormonal influences upon cognitive task performance. The cycle has typically been monthly or circalunar. However, there are diurnal and annual changes in T levels (Kimura 1999); thus Moffat and Hampson (1996) found changes in task performance through the day, dependent upon the time of day and the sex of the participant. Early in the morning when T levels are relatively elevated (in comparison with late morning) men performed relatively poorly and women relatively well in the Vandenberg and Kuse mental rotation procedure. The activational research, whether diurnal or circalunar, suggests that there is an optimum level of T for mental rotation performance.

Conclusions

This chapter has considered the influence of hormonal factors upon cognitive task performance. While this has been examined from a within-sex, individual-differences perspective, it should be noted that the impact of hormonal influences appears to differ between the sexes in certain situations.

The first section of the chapter considered theoretical orientations within the field: organizational and activational processes and theoretical models such as Geschwind and Galaburda (1987) and Nyborg (1990). The Geschwind and Galaburda model was complex in terms of its predictions; however, in relation to this chapter a key element was the putative role of testosterone in prenatal organizational processes. Testosterone was presumed to slow down the development of certain regions in the left hemisphere while facilitating analogous regions in the right hemisphere and adjacent left-hemispheric regions. A simple inference from this is that tasks recruiting these right-hemisphere structures would benefit from this influence. Given that male foetuses are more likely to be susceptible to testosterone (as they produce their own T), this is likely to result in their improved visuospatial task performance. The somatic marker most commonly employed to identify the influence of T is an indication of handedness tilted towards left-handedness or sinistrality. The *Brain and Cognition* (1994) special issue found no conclusive evidence linking sinistrality and visuospatial efficacy. Subsequent research has also found inconclusive patterns of results.

In many ways the equivocal nature of the research is not too surprising, considering that many visuospatial tasks recruit neural processes which may be right- and/or left-hemisphere-lateralized. Thus task performance will be dependent on which particular left- and right-hemispheric structures are influenced by prenatal T, and which lateralized structures are recruited by particular tasks. In addition, if the level of prenatal T fluctuates through the 9 months, the developmental trajectories of each of the cortical regions and related cognitive processes also need to be known (Putz *et al.* 2004). Further researchers such as Annett (1970) and McManus (1984) suggest that genetic factors may underlie the expression of handedness. There are also pragmatic issues associated with handedness measurement: for example should one employ hand skill or hand preference methodologies? Others such as Manning have employed the digit ratio measure as a more direct somatic marker of prenatal hormone action.

Manning's approach has been explicated within an evolutionary psychology perspective, and as such the second-to-fourth-digit ratio has been linked to an impressive range of behaviours as well as to cognitive task performance. Results have been equivocal and this may be due in part to the complexities of prenatal influence discussed above; in addition, task deconstruction may also be required in order to determine which cognitive processes, rather than tasks, are related to the second-to-fourth-digit ratio. A part of this process would involve identifying process commonalities between the research employing different somatic markers (the second-to-fourth-digit ratio, finger whirls and hair density).

The second major empirical section considered the impact of activational hormones – circalunar (monthly) and circadian (daily) in the main. Oestradiol, progesterone and testosterone appear to fluctuate systematically through the menstrual cycle. Extensive research has suggested that cognitive task efficacy fluctuates through the menstrual cycle. In addition there is evidence that hemispheric functioning itself may vary through the cycle. While there is some evidence that visuospatial task performance may be best during the menstrual week, when oestradiol and progesterone levels are relatively low in women, some findings do not support this (for example Chiarello *et al.* 1989).

One common factor that emerges from both the prenatal (organizational) and the activational research is that hormonal influences appear typically to be greatest with tasks that typically display sex differences (for example Hampson 1995; Phillips and Silverman 1997). Thus the within-sex influence of hormonal activity appears to be linked, in part, to putative hormonal factors mediating between-sex factors. A second common factor is seen in the work of Nyborg (1988, 1990) and Moffat and Hampson (1996), which suggests that there is an optimal level of hormonal activity for cognitive task performance. In Nyborg's exposition the important hormone is oestradiol whereas for Moffat and Hampson it is testosterone. In either case, women and men are typically at different points of the inverted-U function, so that an increasing level of the hormone will have a different effect on the two sexes. Thus if female foetuses are exposed to consistently increased levels of T (for example in CAH) then adult visuospatial cognitive task performance may benefit from these women having a more optimum level of testosterone. On the other hand, relatively high levels of testosterone in men (for example in the early morning) may shift men from a more optimum level and lead to relatively impaired task performance. Again though, this research needs to address the cognitive process *per se*, rather than limit the analysis to the task level.

Research to Do

Let us presume that the somatic markers, finger ratio, fingerprint patterns and handedness have a common core, a prenatal hormonal source. Should this be the case then one might expect their variation should be correlated. Persuade some enthusiastic psychology undergraduates to submit to having their hands photocopied then blackened and fingerprinted so that you may measure the digit ratios and finger whorls respectively. Consider how to measure the extent to which these discrete measures reflect the putative underlying causal factor, prenatal T levels. You could also consider how you could relate these multiple measures of prenatal T to the processes underlying mental rotation (Hooven *et al.* 2004).

8 Individual Differences Associated with Lifespan Development

Aim and Overview

The aim of this chapter is to discuss some of the theoretical approaches and the research findings of individual differences associated with lifespan development. The first component of the chapter considers differing theoretical perspectives in the study of cognitive development. The notions of *experience-expectant* and *experience-dependent* processes (Greenough *et al.* 1987) suggest the presence of discrete neural systems each with distinct developmental trajectories. The development of the nervous system occurs within a hormonal environment (see previous chapter) and is thus susceptible to hormonal influence through the lifespan. Thus prenatal, organizational influences will be considered upon both general behaviour and cognition in particular (Grimshaw *et al.* 1995; Hines *et al.* 2002). Later in the chapter the neuroprotective nature of oestrogen in adult ageing will also be considered (Resnick and Maki 2001). Speed-of-processing accounts of lifespan development will be discussed in relation to both child development (Fry and Hale 2000) and adult ageing (Salthouse 2000).

The neural development of children and adults will then be considered. The lay conception of neural development is one of increased mass of the brain as a result of increased neuron number. However, the research suggests that a key feature of child development is *pruning* – the reduction of numbers of synapses (Huttenlocher 1979). This is what Greenough *et al.* (1987) would predict for the experience-expectant neural processes as interaction refines the connections between neurons. Other research has also emphasized the importance of network development and the role of the prefrontal cortex in this process (Anderson 1998; Stuss & Anderson, 2004). This approach emphasizes the importance of the white matter underlying neural network development. Research into neural changes in adulthood also emphasizes an important role for the frontal lobes, an emphasis qualified by the research of Phillips and Della Sala (1998).

The cognitive research associated with lifespan development first considers cognition in childhood. The chapter considers perceptual, visuospatial and mnemonic processes. Young children have quite precocious perceptual processes, showing early competency in face recognition (Bartrip *et al.* 2001). However these early competencies may mask prolonged development in basic visual functioning, for example visual acuity, contrast sensitivity and configurational processing in face recognition. The research by Gathercole (Gathercole 1998; Gathercole *et al.* 2004) suggests that the structure of memory, in particular working memory, is present in younger children. In adulthood, many cognitive processes display a decrement in efficiency.

This decrement in the memory process appears to be present in young to middle adulthood. The observations of Schroeder and Salthouse (2004) suggest that between 20 and 50 years of age there is small but significant decline in many cognitive processes, including memory, reasoning and motor competency. It should be noted though that the cognitive decline in processes such as working memory is not necessarily homogeneous (Phillips and Hamilton 2001). In addition there is evidence for relatively intact social cognition and knowledge processes in older adults.

Theoretical Frameworks

Experience-Expectant and Experience-Dependent Processes

One of the most influential accounts of neural development, which embraces the suggestion of a major experiential impact upon the development of the nervous system, is the work of Greenough and co-workers (see Greenough *et al.* 1987). His research led him to consider that experience could act upon the development of the brain through two processes, *experience-expectant* and *experience-dependent* processes. An experience-expectant process is where the brain is primed to process and represent information which is likely to be experienced by all members of that species. According to Greenough (Greenough *et al.* 1987) this priming involves the generation of an excess of synaptic connections between neurons, the notion of *blooming*. Experience determines which connections will endure and which will be lost, the notion of *neural pruning*. One example of this process of neural pruning is the research by Huttenlocher (1979) on synaptic connections, to be discussed in detail in Chapter 11.

The implication from Greenough's work is that the impact of this experience is constrained in two ways: first, that the relevant experience must be present during a critical period of development, and, second, that though an absence of the appropriate experience will have an effect upon the number of synaptic connections its impact will be relatively small in relation to the impact upon *experience-dependent* processes. Figure 8.1 indicates the profile of synaptogenesis with experience-expectant processes.

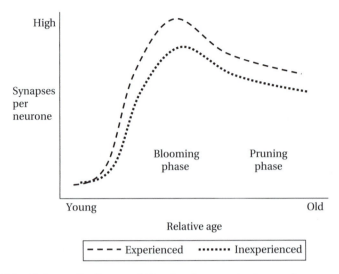

Figure 8.1   Schematic figure of the development of experience-expectant processes showing the phases of excessive synaptic overproduction (blooming) and synaptic reduction (pruning)

Greenough *et al.* discuss a visual example of this process: the development of ocular dominance columns in the visual cortex. These dominance columns are alternating areas of the visual cortex, which receive information from the left and right eye respectively (Hubel and Wiesel 1970). In the vast majority of humans and other species with binocularly overlapping visual fields, input from both eyes is normal and therefore the function is an ideal candidate for an experience-expectant process. However, in animal studies where one of the eyes is patched or sutured, afferent input from that eye is lost and the connections between the eye and the visual cortex appear to be impaired. This leads to a pattern of neural development where the ocular areas or stripes associated with the intact eye are relatively larger than the cortical areas associated with the occluded eye.

This atypical development is evidenced in humans who have experienced *form-deprivation amblyopia* and as a result suffer reduced visual acuity when using the affected eye. This can occur when neonates have cataracts over one of their eyes and therefore no patterned light is experienced through that eye. According to Greenough *et al.* (1987), competition exists between afferent inputs from the two eyes and if one eye is impaired then relatively excessive synaptic pruning will ultimately reduce its synaptic representation (see Figure 8.1 for a developmental profile which could occur as a result of 'deprived' or 'inexperienced' visual environment). Visual research also indicates that eye occlusion will have its maximum impact within a critical period early in development. The implication of this for human amblyopes is that remedial treatment needs to be carried out promptly once the diagnosis has been made.

A similar process may be observed in language development. Based upon the assumption that language acquisition and development is species-specific, research has shown that young infants show sophisticated discrimination of speech sounds or phonemes (Kuhl *et al.* 1992) not present in their own culture's speech.

Thus Japanese infants aged 2 to 3 months who have not been exposed to speech in the English language will discriminate between the two English words '*lob*' and '*rob*'. These two words differ only in their initial phoneme and therefore this implies that Japanese infants show phonemic discrimination in words they have not been previously exposed to. This suggests that human infants may possess a predetermined competence for phonemic discrimination for speech sounds in any language (Kuhl *et al.* 1992). However, if the Japanese infants are not continually exposed to these phonemic sounds in their subsequent development, they rapidly lose this ability. This loss of ability could be explained by Greenough's suggestion of synaptic pruning when afferent input is no longer present. Children not exposed to non-native speech sounds will be more likely to have the associated synaptic processes pruned. A parallel process is seen in the learning of a second language, where the younger the child is, the more effective is the learning (Johnson and Newport 1989).

The research discussed above indicates the importance of appropriate environmental interaction in order to produce the necessary afferent stimulation required in maintaining synaptic density. In the absence of such stimulation, particularly in early development, synaptic pruning will occur in these experience-expectant processes.

As a consequence of observing adult animals experiencing different levels of environmental complexity, Greenough and his colleagues posited the notion of *experience-dependent* processes. These processes arise from the idiosyncratic and unique interactions an individual may experience. These experiences will vary for individuals within and across cultures. An important aspect of these processes is that they are not so critically time-constrained in terms of their impact. Experiences throughout adulthood may continue to have an impact upon synaptic density and thus a loss of synapses with ageing may be counteracted by this new afferent activity. This may lead to the 'plateau phase' shown in Figure 8.2. Note also how deprivation or inexperience will lead to a major change in synaptic density in comparison with the impact of inexperience upon the experience-expectant processes.

The exposure of educational, vocational or of parenting demands made upon adults requires ongoing plasticity in the adult nervous system. Of course in some academics this may require a complete re-representation of their knowledge as ongoing evidence indicates that their models or thinking are entirely inappropriate!

A conceptualization of brain plasticity in this experience-dependent manner opens up the possibility that cultural influences, which may change over generations, will result in neural developmental processes that are cohort

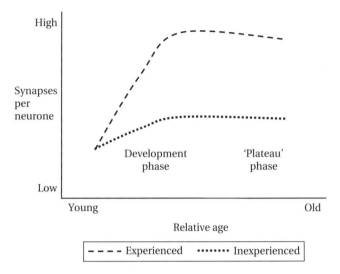

Figure 8.2   Schematic figure of the development of experience-dependent processes showing the phase of synaptic development and a 'plateau' phase present in adulthood

dependent. Such a perspective would have enabled Crawford and Chaffin (1997) to draw a more considered conclusion in response to the evidence that in many cognitive tasks the difference between men and women has been reducing in the past few decades (see Voyer *et al.* 1995). This observation led Crawford and Chaffin to suggest: 'Changes over the course of a few decades almost certainly reflect changes in the gender system rather than changes in biology' (p. 116).

There may certainly have been changes in the way Western culture has viewed the roles of men and women in the last 30 years. However, it could be suggested that this has afforded both women and men the opportunities for a greater range of experiences which through experience-dependent neural processes has meant that the neural organization of contemporary young adults may well be different from that of their parents 30 years earlier. Changes in a gendered culture may certainly have a sustained impact upon individuals within the culture, but only if the neural processes underlying the changed cognitions are sufficiently plastic or flexible enough. Figure 8.2 also indicates the potentially negative impact of constrained experiences within a gendered culture. The implementation of narrow sex role expectations is likely to deny diversity of experience and lead to a pattern of neural representation that is more akin to the 'inexperienced' profile shown in the figure.

Thus Greenough's conceptualization of experience-expectant and experience-dependent processes provides for an explanation of how both genetic and cultural factors may impact upon neural development and thus upon human cognition; see Johnston and Edwards (2002) and Rutter (2002) for a detailed account of the mechanisms by which genetic processes may be explicitly affected by experience.

Hormonal Influences

The paper by Garlick (2002) and the research programme of Casey and her co-workers (1990, 1992a, 1992b, 1996), to be discussed in detail in Chapter 11, both stress the importance of predisposed, genetic mechanisms in cognitive development. An alternative (but not necessarily independent) account discussed in the previous chapter stresses the influence of prenatal exposure to hormones such as testosterone, T (Geschwind and Galaburda 1987). It is possible that genetic factors contribute to this early environmental event, for example in the production of T in the mother, or in the foetus, or in the sensitivity of the androgen receptors in the foetus. Important predictions from this hypothesis are not only that neural mechanisms supporting spatial competence would be facilitated but also that early behaviours underpinning and reinforcing spatial mastery would be undertaken (Collaer and Hines 1995).

The review paper by Collaer and Hines found strong evidence for a link between prenatal hormonal influences and early gender-related behaviours in girls who had experienced CAH. However, there are research issues associated with employing participants with CAH (Hines *et al.* 2002). These authors cite issues such as the following:

- The altered external genitalia of the girl could alter the parents' perceptions and subsequent interactions with the baby.

- The condition requires extensive medical intervention and hospitalization, given that this group of girls are exposed to excessive levels of androgen.

- The relationship between prenatal androgen levels and subsequent behaviour may not hold over a 'normal' range of T levels.

Hines *et al.* (2002) investigated the relationship between maternal T and sex-hormone-binding globulin (SHBG) levels and gender-related behaviour in a sample of 679 children aged about 3.5 years. This study employed the Pre-School Activities Inventory, a gender role measure standardized in European countries and in the USA. Hines *et al.* noted that their measure of T levels varied with the phase of the pregnancy. Gender groups were identified on the basis of the inventory scores and the authors were able to establish groups of masculine, medium and feminine scores in both sexes. While no relationship between T, SHBG and behaviours was evident in the boys the authors found a significant relationship between T levels and masculine behaviour in the girls. Higher prenatal T scores were associated with higher masculine scores. This suggests that prenatal T may be associated with behavioural activities, which could facilitate the development of visuospatial competencies.

Later research by Knickmeyer (Knickmeyer *et al.* 2005) directly measured amniotic testosterone (aT) level in the foetus and related this to sex-typed behaviour in early childhood. These authors found large sex differences in play activity; however aT levels did not predict play activities, either in an overall regression analysis or in a within-sex analysis. In a stimulating discussion they identified putative explanations as to why no significant relationships were observed:

- Measuring amniotic fluid levels of testosterone may not accurately indicate the level of T exposure in the foetal CNS. However, the same research group has other findings (discussed below) which suggest that aT is a valid measure of prenatal T exposure in the foetal brain.

- It may be the case that aT will only have a marked effect upon play activity when it is present in atypically high levels, for example in girls with CAH (see previous Chapter).

- Prenatal T levels may impact differentially upon different psychological functions and cognitive processes. This statistical account considered whether a small sample size may not have been sensitive enough to detect a small relationship. The research by Hooven *et al.* (2004) discussed in the previous chapter also suggests that T may have a specific impact upon discrete cognitive processes.

- It may be the case that a different sampling period during foetal development might arise in a different pattern of results.

Grimshaw *et al.* (1995) in a longitudinal study initially measured amniotic T levels in a sample of boys and girls and then 7 years later assessed the children's performances in visuospatial tasks. They cited earlier research studies which had found equivocal findings, a negative correlation between prenatal T and block-building and a positive relationship between prenatal T and a task requiring mental rotation. In their study Grimshaw *et al.* employed a 2-D mental rotation procedure with a toy bear character stimulus. The Grimshaw *et al.* results suggested a significant linear relationship between MRT rate and the level of prenatal T in the small number of girls and boys in the study. However, the direction of the pattern was different for the boys and the girls.

These results are pertinent to the findings discussed in the previous chapter. Firstly, the results suggest that early prenatal influences within sexes may impact upon cognitive tasks only where sex differences are large and reliable (Hampson 1995). In addition the differential pattern of T upon rotation rate in the boys and the girls suggests that there is an optimum level of prenatal T for MRT competence. This observation is consistent with the suggestions of Nyborg (1990) and Moffat and Hampson (1996) in the previous chapter who also suggested a non-linear relationship between T and mental rotation performance. It is interesting to observe that the relationship is with the rate of mental rotation, the number of degrees rotated *per second*, a quite specific MRT component, rather than the more general component suggested by Hooven *et al.* (2004) in the previous chapter. Note though that the Hooven *et al.* study measured circulating T in undergraduates as opposed to exposure to prenatal T.

Speed of Processing Accounts

A major theoretical explanation of cognitive development both in childhood and in adulthood is the suggestion that a common process, speed of process-ing, underlies the changes in cognitive competencies observed in imagery, working memory and performance in fluid intelligence measures (Fry and Hale 1996, 2000; Salthouse 2000). Common measures of this construct are the digit symbol task initially identified in Chapter 5, and articulation rate, a meas-ure of speech rate. Fry and Hale found large relationships between age and pro-cessing speed, between processing speed and working memory and between working memory and fluid intelligence. The relationship between process-ing speed and working memory has received further support from Kail (1997), Chuah and Maybery (1999) and Hamilton *et al.* (2003). These studies have focused upon child development but a similar conceptualization has been put forward for changes in cognition associated with adult ageing. Deary (2001) put forward a similar representation, based upon the work of Salthouse (see Salthouse 2000) to describe general cognitive changes in adulthood.

The suggestion made by Salthouse was that age-associated changes observed in the primary abilities – reasoning, memory and so on – are effect-ively mediated by changes in processing speed. Thus Finkel and Pedersen (2004), in a twin study looking at ageing and cognition, suggested that in cross-sectional research up to 79 per cent of age-related variance can be accounted for by changes in speed of processing (though this is reduced in longitudinal research). The findings in their study again suggested that the influence of genetic factors on cognition in ageing was mediated primarily by processing speed. However, the influence of processing speed upon cog-nitive decline was less in the older (>65 years) participants in their study.

There is debate over the extent to which speed of processing measures are free of the contribution of cognitive or intellectual contributions (Anderson 1992). Even procedures that purport to measure simple reaction time may involve cognitive computations related to the speed/accuracy trade-off. The digit symbol substitution task, commonly employed as a measure of pro-cessing speed measure may have an LTM component, the association of digits with particular symbols, occurring in the task (Parkin and Java 2000).

Neural Development

Child Development

Epstein (2001) discussed the development of the CNS in relation to cognitive development, linking spurts in brain development to the observations of psychologists such as Vygotsky (1962) and Piaget (1967). Epstein, like Garlick (2002) and Greenough *et al.* (1987), emphasizes the importance of synpatic structures and communication (synaptogenesis) as the key element in brain development. Thus he argues that as new neurones are unlikely to be generated after the age of 4 years any further development is likely to reflect synaptic arborization (more diffuse and denser dendritic branching) and myelination. He suggests that brain development (indexed by brain mass) occurs in four-year cycles, with 2 to 4 years, 6 to 8 years, 10 to 12 years and 14 to 16 years evidencing the greatest change in weight (5 to 10 per cent).

Epstein (2001) also suggested (without citing evidence) that during the 10-to-12 age period girls displayed greater increases in brain mass than boys, a pattern reversed in the 14-to-16 period (see the cognitive work of Lynn *et al.* 2004 and Lynn and Tse-Chan, 2003 for a similar argument in Chapter 5). Epstein cited electrophysiological research evidence suggesting that there may be a final phase of development between 18 and 20 years. Epstein and others (for example Anderson 1998) have suggested a hierarchical development in the CNS, with posterior, sensory-based neural structures displaying relatively early maturity, and the anterior, prefrontal structures showing later maturation (though for counter-arguments see Johnson 2000 and Anderson 1998).

There are, though, difficulties in interpreting brain mass changes as the index of brain maturity. Brain development includes neural pruning processes, with programmed cell death, apoptosis (Caviness *et al.*1996; Huttenlocher 1979), which would act to reduce mass and potentially mask concurrent arborization processes. While refinement of synaptic interaction processes through synaptic pruning goes on extensively from the age of 8 through to adolescence, there is a suggestion that myelination continues throughout the second decade of life (for example see Paus *et al.* 2001). Thus this phase of neural development appears to come to a halt in the late teens, just as fluid processes reach their peak.

One consequence of the pruning process in later childhood and adolescence is that the extent of grey matter actually reduces (Van Petten *et al.* 2004). Thus there is a pattern of decreasing grey brain mass in child development occurring in the same time period as cognitive research indicates extensive cognitive improvement in performance. Van Petten *et al.* draw attention to the fact that this evidence casts doubts on the neural hypothesis, to be discussed in Chapter 9, that 'big is necessarily better'. An exception to this neurodevelopment pruning process may lie in children with autistic spectrum disorder (Waiter *et al.* 2004). These authors, in a structural neu-roimaging study, noted that in adolescents with autistic spectrum disorder (ASD) there were anomalous levels of grey matter in many parts of the cortex, including the prefrontal, the fusiform gyrus and the parietal/temporal lobes. Waiter *et al.* concluded:

> Normally, neurodevelopment processes produce a reduction in grey matter associated with apoptosis. Such processes could be abnormal in individuals with ASD, and if occurring in the areas identified may have particularly marked effects upon many aspects of social cognition, including imitation, face recognition, mental state attribution and joint attention. (p. 624)

Adult Development

Should fluid process efficacy reflect this neural refinement and development then one might presume that adulthood would see a loss of grey and white matter brain mass and this is what research has actually found. Thus Magnotta *et al.* (1999) investigated the effect of ageing upon gyrus and sulcus characteristics in a sample of healthy adults ranging in age from 18 to 82 years. They noted that gyrus characteristics became sharper and steeper and the sulcus characteristics became flattened. Cortical thickness was also reduced in the older age sample. The authors suggested that in the cortical thinning there was particular loss in grey matter, which was greater in men than in women. Research has suggested a trend indicating that men show a greater rate of brain atrophy; this was also found by Raz *et al.* (2004).

The research by Raz *et al.* suggests that the sex difference in atrophy may be greater for particular brain regions, for example the hippocampus and the frontal gyrus. These authors also found evidence that prefrontal regions showed the steepest atrophy function, in particular the dorsolateral pre-frontal cortex. This 'frontal' hypothesis of ageing has received some support but is contested by others (Phillips and Della Sala 1998). Phillips and Della Sala suggested that the concept of a generic frontal atrophy in ageing over-simplified the complex nature of prefrontal function. They suggested that one should consider the different functions associated with the dorsolateral and ventromedial prefrontal regions.

Research into crystallized processing in elderly adults does suggest a sus-tained competence well into old age (for example Finkel and Pedersen 2004). An example of social cognition competence in aged adults is the research directed at theory of mind performance (for example Happé *et al.* 1998). The issue of differential cognitive decline associated with the dorsolateral and ven-tromedial regions is evident in the work of Phillips and her colleagues (MacPherson *et al.* 2002; Phillips *et al.* 2002). These differential patterns of adult ageing appear to mimic the trajectories of the experience-expectant and experience-dependent processes displayed in Figures 8.1 and 8.2. (see Maylor *et al.* 2002 for a qualification of this conclusion in a theory-of-mind context).

Individual differences associated with age may not be the sole source of variation in these processes. Functional imaging research by Gur *et al.* (2002) suggested that while the prefrontal dorsolateral region was equivalent in volume for women and men, the orbitofrontal (ventromedial) region did reveal sex differences, with this region being larger in women. The sex difference in atrophy rate noted above (for example Raz *et al.* 2004) has led to the suggestion that neural ageing in women is protected by some aspect of their hormonal environment (see below).

Recent research by Van Petten *et al.* (2004) has found a linear relationship between grey matter mass and ageing, with the older participant in the sample evidencing smaller extents of grey matter. However, they also observed (after controlling for age and skull size) that the relationship between grey matter mass and memory was in a negative direction; smaller masses were associated with better memory task performance. A further review by Van Petten (2004) also found no evidence for the 'bigger-is-better' hypothesis when looking at hippocampus atrophy and memory performance.

Cognitive Development in Children and Adolescents

Foetal Development

Much in the hormonal accounts above emphasizes the importance of the prenatal, intrauterine environment. Hepper (2005) reviewed the developmental aspects of foetal behaviour which had emerged over the previous decade of research. This suggests that cognitive processes are exhibited across the gestation period and this affords the possibility identified above by Knickmeyer *et al.* (2005) that any influence of prenatal T levels may be dependent upon the period of development in which they are elevated. Hepper identified the following behavioural developmental sequence:

- The foetus will respond to touches around the mouth and cheeks at around 8 weeks. Later, at 14 weeks, the it will respond to the touching of its back and to the touching of the top of its head.

- The foetus begins to swallow amniotic fluid from about 12 weeks, thus it may potentially begin to experience flavours. By 16 weeks it will swallow more sweet fluid than bitter.

- The foetus begins to respond to sounds at about 6 months; in later pregnancy it demonstrates phonemic discrimination, for example discriminating the two speech sounds 'biba' and 'babi'.

- The foetal sensitivity appears to be greatest to frequencies of 125 to 150 Hz, which is the range in which the fundamental frequency of the mother's voice is likely to occur. The fundamental frequency is typically the lowest and most dominant frequency in an individual's speech.

Habituation, a technique typically employed to investigate infant perception, has been observed in foetus behaviour. Thus very early foetal research suggested that foetal responses to repeated car horn sound gradually reduce (habituated). This learning capability is also evidenced by the ability of the newborn to recognize the mother's voice and odour (a major potential confound in neonate studies of other perceptual processes!). Newborns also prefer music they have been exposed to prenatally. Interestingly this is preference which will disappear within 3 weeks if the newborn does not receive postnatal exposure to the music. This pattern of disappearance is evidence in the infant phonemic discrimination study by Kuhl *et al.* (1992) above and suggests synaptic pruning is occurring early in the neonate. In summary, these observations led Hepper to conclude that the foetus 'is continually active in and reactive to its environment' (p. 475).

Perceptual and Visuospatial Processes

The suggestion above of a hierarchical system of neural development suggests that one should expect a similar process of development in cognitive processes; for example if the posterior regions display relatively early maturation then one might expect to identify sophisticated perceptual processing in human infants. Nelson (2001) reviewed research into infant face perception where neonates show precocious face-processing competence. There is evidence that newborns prefer face-like configurations over similar non-face stimuli (Goren *et al.* 1975); an example of the stimuli employed is shown in Figure 8.3.

A stimulus with three blurred spots does not seem an ideal stimulus for newborns, far less one which they would actually prefer. However, a consideration of newborn spatial frequency sensitivity can provide some understanding of such research finding. Newborns and neonates have constrained spatial frequency or grating resolution and poor contrast sensitivity (see Figure 8.4) and thus when they perceive a face their visual cortex is capable

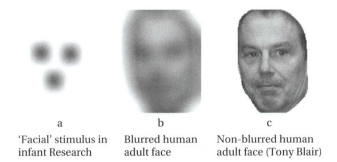

a	b	c
'Facial' stimulus in infant Research	Blurred human adult face	Non-blurred human adult face (Tony Blair)

Figure 8.3   Face stimuli with and without blurring (removal of high spatial frequencies)

of extracting only high-contrast and low-spatial-frequency information. Figure 8.3b shows a human face image that has had high-spatial-frequency information removed (in an imprecise manner!). This blurred image has greatest contrast around the two eye sockets and the mouth region; the spatial frequency and configuration characteristics are now more similar to those shown in Figure 8.3a.

This sophistication in newborns has led many researchers to consider that humans have a predisposition to recognize face-like stimuli. This competence would be a prime example of the experience-expectant processes discussed above and in Chapter 9. Johnson and Morton (1991) suggested that this newborn competence reflected a CONSPEC process, an innate ability to recognize others of the same species (conspecifics). This competency orients the newborn towards conspecifics but would not mediate recognition of particular conspecifics, that is the child's carers.

Would evolution have acted in a way which would have led to automatic recognition of particular faces such as Tony Blair's? This would probably require development of medium spatial frequency sensitivity in order for the finer idiosyncratic features to be resolved. There is evidence that low-spatial-frequency information in a mother's hairstyle facilitates recognition in young neonates. However, when a headscarf is worn so that it is only the facial features that have to be discriminated and recognized, newborns perform poorly. This competence comes later, perhaps at the age of about 1 month (Bartrip *et al.* 2001). Johnson and Morton (1991) would argue that at the point where idiosyncratic facial recognition occurs a new process is operating, a CONLERN process: the ability to recognize individual conspecific faces. This process is critically dependent upon particular experiences with the carer, and thus at this age face perception is more like an experience-dependent process.

A recent review of the research into general infant perception (Kovacs 2000) has suggested that neonates show high levels of competency in numerous perceptual processes including motion sensitivity, colour perception and in stereopsis or binocular vision. The importance of motion sensitivity in infants has been illustrated in recent research investigating visual search competencies of infants (Gerhardstein and Rovee-Collier 2002). This study employed reaction time slope as an index of the search type when locating feature and conjoint targets among sets of distracters. In 6- and 12-month-old infants, when the target was conjoint in nature, it had to have motion elements to be detected. At 18 months, when a static conjoint target could be detected, similar parallel and serial search functions to adults were present in the young children.

An important facilitation factor in the visual recognition of the face of a carer is the auditory cues from the carer. Infants are particularly sensitive to the speech of carers, benefiting from prenatal exposure to the carer's voice (see above). Infants are highly sensitive to a broader spectrum of sounds, being more sensitive to higher frequencies, than are older children and adults. Young infants under the age of 6 months exhibit the ability to discriminate phonemic contrasts in languages other than their native language (see above). This appears to be a consequence of language development rather than lack of experience of the sounds. When the speech sounds are isolated from a speech context, discrimination is possible. Another impressive aspect of newborn competence, cross-modal perception, has recently been demonstrated (Streri and Gentaz 2004). This research found that these infants are capable of matching tactile information (an object held in the hand) with visual information presented at another time. Cross-modal integration will be considered in further detail below.

The research evidence above indicates the precocious nature of infant perception; this supports the suggestion that posterior sensory/perceptual processes mature rapidly. However, other perceptual processes demand much more prolonged development. One such aspect was alluded to above: the need for spatial frequency and contrast sensitivity processes to develop. The development of these processes is illustrated in Figure 8.4.

Figure 8.4 indicates that the contrast sensitivity function of the newborn is remarkably limited; grating acuity is very much lower than adult levels but improves markedly over the first year, though it requires a further 5 years before adult levels of acuity are reached. Contrast sensitivity has not however reached adult levels and requires some 5 years more before reaching adult levels. Thus maturity of these processes follows a much more prolonged pathway. This is also indicated in other vision research (Crognale 2002), which found visual evoked potential (VEP) latencies reducing to a minimum only at 17 years of age. Evidence such as this is not so consistent with the suggestion of precocious development in the posterior cortex.

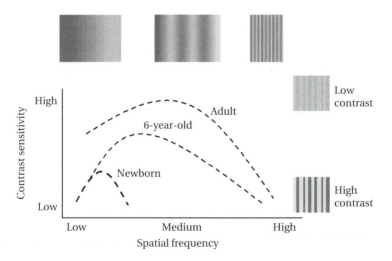

Figure 8.4 Development of spatial frequency resolution and contrast sensitivity

Face recognition processes, although competent in young children, for example when recognizing carers, still undergo extensive development. Early research suggested that children tend to employ external features when recognizing familiar and unfamiliar faces. In adults the typical findings have suggested that internal features (eye, nose, mouth details) are employed with familiar faces and external features (chin, ears and hairline details) for unfamiliar faces. However, recent child research has suggested that by the age of seven children may be beginning to make use of internal features for familiar faces (Bonner and Burton 2004). The authors suggest that it is between 5 and 7 years of age that children begin to allocate attention to the internal features. Other research suggests that children as young as 5 years old show similar patterns as adults in attending to the external features of unfamiliar faces (Want *et al.* 2003).

While this research indicates adult-like processing styles in 5- to 7-year-olds, other research findings suggest that yet other aspects of face-processing develop more slowly. One such area is in the use of featural (eyes, nose, mouth characteristics) versus configurational characteristics (metric distances and orientations between the features). This is exemplified by the findings of the research of Mondloch *et al.* (2002).

In this facial morphing study, Mondloch *et al.* varied configural, featural or global characteristics. While children were capable of detecting featural and global variations, they generated more errors than adults in the configural variants condition. In another experimental condition, though, children did display some rudimentary configural processing. This would suggest that the coordinate spatial relations underpinning the configural processes are still maturing in these children.

The research by Crognale (2002) above looked at VEP latencies across the lifespan and found that latencies began to increase over the age of 17 years; the greatest increase was for chromatic stimuli, however, indicating a more rapid decline in the parvocellular system. Sekuler and Sekuler (2000) in their review of vision and ageing indicated that contrast sensitivity detection in medium to high spatial frequencies (>3 c/deg) begins to decline after the age of 30, and visual acuity showed typical decline after 50. Sekuler and Sekuler attributed the decline to a mix of optical, retinal and 'low-level' visual processes. Binocular sensitivity also declines with age, particularly with high-spatial-frequency stimuli. They argued that perhaps the biggest decrement associated with ageing was evident in temporal resolution, a process where infant precocity was noticeable.

Visuospatial Processes

The early development of visuomotor integration has displayed individual differences associated with sex. Livesey and Inyili (1996) assessed the impacts of visual cues in a kinesthetic task involving passive movement by 4-year-olds.

Kinesthetic acuity was measured by moving the child's hands along trajectories which varied by about 22 degrees. A screening board hid the hand movement, and therefore the child had to employ kinesthetic feedback in order to judge the trajectory. In the basic procedure no sex differences were found; however when visual lines indicating potential trajectories were added to the screen, boys performed better than girls, more effectively matching the visual cues with their arm movements. This finding in children is similar to the adult observation of Chipman *et al.* (2002), which indicated sex differences on the differential reliance of visual information and information from the praxis system.

Livesey and Inyili also found a sex difference in a Lego block design task where children have to observe the construction of six blocks by the researcher then reconstruct the shape themselves. This observation replicated the earlier finding of McGuinness and Morley (1991) with pre-school children. In addition, Levine *et al.* (1999) found that in children aged between 4 and 7 years there was a consistent advantage for boys in spatial tasks demanding translation and rotation processes. Interestingly, the advantage for boys was equivalent in the two spatial processes. Research has also suggested that performance in tasks of field-independence at this age is linked to the gender role characteristics of the children (Chynn *et al.* 1991).

Recent research has considered the development of visuospatial competencies within more applied contexts. Joshi *et al.* (1999) looked at the development in spatial knowledge of the environment of children aged between 7 and 12 years. They had a particular interest in the impact upon spatial competencies of car travel to school as opposed to walking to school. They noted that in years 1970 to 1990 the proportion of 7-to-8-year-olds walking independently to school had dropped from 80 per cent to 10 per cent. They looked at three groups of children: those who went to school by car, those who walked with an adult and those who walked alone or with other children. The children undertook a large range of visuospatial tasks. Analysis by age indicated development in map orientation, mental rotation, block design, and map drawing utilizing landmarks or features. In regression analyses only accompaniment predicted spatial competence and this was significant only in the identification of landmarks on the map drawing. The children's perception of traffic danger was also associated with accompaniment.

The ability to orient to landmarks in the child's environment was assessed by Lehnung *et al.* (2003). They looked at children aged between 5 and 13 years. The children were positioned either around their kindergarten school or in their classroom. Their task was to point towards (unseen) landmarks on their campus. A large improvement in pointing direction was found between first-graders (about 7 years) and fifth-graders (about 12½ years). However, even kindergarten children were able to demonstrate rudimentary point accuracy (angular deviation error <32 degrees). The authors also noted that both sex and experience were significant predictors of task performance. At all ages boys were more accurate in their pointing than girls. Choi and

Silverman (2003) looked at the development of route-learning strategies in children aged between 8 and 17. The children carried out a variety of tasks, including mental rotation, object and location memory, water-level and map routes. In this study the effect sizes associated with sex showed a complex and interesting set of patterns in the 8-to-13 group of children:

- Girls were more accurate than boys in object memory performance at all of these ages.

- In location memory there was an increasing effect size, associated with age, favouring boys.

- There was an increasing effect size favouring boys in spatial relations task.

- There was a decreasing effect size favouring boys in the water-level task.

- However, in the route reconstruction it was not until the age of 13 that girls more systematically utilized landmarks, and boys more systematically employed Euclidean directions.

- In the older age range, 14 to 17 years, girls still continued to employ the landmark strategy more than boys, but in addition at 14, and to lesser extent at 17, girls employed relative direction cues rather than cardinal directions.

Choi and Silverman attempted to link many of the observed sex differences to the onset of puberty in both the girls and the boys. Implicit in this argument is the importance of hormonal surges during puberty. However, there are difficulties in interpreting the data in this study. A critique of the location memory procedure was given in Chapter 1 and Chapter 3: in their procedure the location memory process is confounded with object-to-location memory processes; in addition, there was an inconsistent relationship between sex differences and age. The girls' use of relative directions in the map task was observed at the age of 10 and 13 years but not at 11 and 12 years of age. Boys showed an advantage in spatial relations at 12, 13 and 15 years of age, but not at 14 years. In the water-level task, an advantage for boys at 9, 10 and 11 years disappeared at 12 to 15 years only to return at 16 and 17 years.

These inconsistent development patterns draw into question inferences about precisely when particular sex differences appear. However, even if sex differences did emerge at puberty this would not necessarily mean that hormonal action was the causal factor. Thus Newcombe and Dubas (1992) found that in girls aged 16 years, spatial ability (spatial relations and block design composite) was best predicted by gender personality characteristics rather than by puberty onset time. Yet other research has suggested differences in object location memory actually occurs later in development (Barnfield 1999).

The importance of timing of individual differences with age not only has implications for hormonal theories of sex differences. In visuospatial tasks of the type identified above where sex differences arise in young children, there is the possibility that the individual differences occur with the maturation of posterior cortical regions. Individual differences associated with the development of executive processes in prefrontal cortex would be expected to occur later in development when the prefrontal synaptic processes undergo systematic pruning,

Memory Processes

Tasks that make demands upon working memory (WM) processes (slave system processes in posterior cortex and/or executive processes which may draw upon prefrontal and posterior structures) are likely to demonstrate middle- to late-childhood development in task performance. While some research has investigated early childhood and noted age associated improvements (Simcock and Hayne 2003), most working memory research has looked at older age-groups. The emphasis upon visuospatial task performance would lead one to consider the importance of visuospatial working memory (VSWM) for individual differences.

Several studies have considered VSWM development (Hamilton *et al.* 2003; Orsini *et al.* 1987). Many researchers using the visual pattern task (VPT) have found that between the ages of 5 and 10 years, span level increases by more than a factor of 2. In Corsi block tasks, with either the original blocks or computerized derivatives, major age effects are observed but typically indicate less than a factor-of-2 improvement in span performance. The effect size associated with visuospatial task performance associated with age can be very large; thus the computerized VPT task reported by Phillips and Hamilton (2001) showed an effect size of $d = 1.66$, associated with the age change from children to adults. However, the difference in effect size associated with age and sex is quite different when one employs tasks which make less demand upon executive resources (for example see Dror and Kosslyn 1994). Thus in a visual memory task procedure devised to reduce executive demands the effect size associated with a change in age from child (7 years) to young adult was $d = 0.56$, with a performance improvement of less than 25 per cent (Phillips and Hamilton 2001).

Using tasks such as digit recall, word recall and nonword recall, Gathercole *et al.* (2004) identified the developmental trajectory of the phonological loop system in WM. The evidence they found (see their Figure 1, p. 181) suggests that these capacity measures show development until the age of 14 and 15 years. Again, the change in span performance is large, typically just under a factor of 2 improvement. Gathercole *et al.* also considered the development of verbal complex span tasks, backward digit, listening recall and counting recall (See Chapter 7). These tasks showed a remarkably similar trajectory to the verbal storage tasks, peaking at 14 to 15 years of age. These observations parallel those of Anderson (1998), who employed 'neuropsychological' measures of executive functions in children.

Anderson looked at planning, problem-solving, concept formation and mental flexibility. Planning as measured by the Rey Figure tasks showed steady improvement until the age of 12, the Tower of London task, taken as problem-solving task, displayed improvement in performance until 13. Other measures such as letter fluency showed development up to 12 years of age. Mental flexibility was measured by tasks such as the Wisconsin card sorting task and the Stroop test. In the Trails A format, children showed steady reduction in time taken through to the age of 13 years, with a factor of 2 improvement.

This research evidence suggests that executive task performance is typically reaching maturity between 12 and 14 years of age. This is slightly in advance of the neuropsychological research, which suggests prefrontal changes up to 15 and 16 years of age and perhaps beyond. However, it is interesting that while there is a temporary pause between 11 and 13 years of age in the visuospatial measures there is a suggestion in Gathercole *et al.*'s data that improvement of performance is still occurring between 14 and 15 years. This is consistent with the observations of some previous research (Isaacs and Vargha-Khadem 1989). Indeed some research has suggested improvement in young adults (De Luca *et al.* 2003). The findings related to sex differences in executive function have been rather equivocal (Warrick and Naglieri 1993).

While the pattern of individual differences associated with development in the conventional WM tasks appears relatively consistent, many issues remain as to the nature of actual cognitive development underpinning task improvement. What exactly happens in executive development? Is the improvement a result of an increase in executive resources, or a capacity improvement as suggested by Morra (1994). Alternative accounts emphasize speed of processing changes through child (and adult) development (Fry and Hale 2000). Yet another viewpoint considers improvements in a range of executive functions, including set-shifting, memory updating and inhibitory processes (Miyake *et al.* 2000).

Thus Bjorklund and Harnishfeger (1990) suggest that a crucial part of executive development is the increasingly accurate deployment of inhibitory processing of task-irrelevant information. This was also supported by Klenberg *et al.* (2001) (though see Pritchard and Neumann 2004 and MacPherson *et al.* 2003 for an alternative view). The nature of the executive – slave system interface during development has also come under scrutiny. While some research has suggested that phonological processes (Baddeley *et al.* 1998), for example phonological awareness, account for variance in vocabulary development, others have emphasized the importance of long-term memory (LTM) for phonological processing (Metsala 1999).

The contribution of LTM to the visuospatial working memory processes has also been an issue. The work of Hamilton *et al.* (2003) with children and adults suggests that the conventional task procedures recruit executive resources.

Consequently, change in VPT or Corsi block performance as a function of age may result from changes in how the executive interfaces the slave system. Thus apparent development in the slave system itself may well reflect executive development. This will be discussed in further detail below. (Note that McCafferty and Hamilton 2005 provide evidence for VSWM development in atypical development in the absence of executive support.)

Gathercole (1998) discussed the development of other aspects of memory such as autobiographical memory. She discussed the notion of 'childhood amnesia' where individuals find it difficult to retrieve experiences undergone earlier than at about 2 years. Research has suggested that typically the age of one's earliest memory is about 3.5 years, with a range of 2 to 8 years. Gathercole suggests that autobiographical memory, the recall of quite specific events, emerges at about 4 years. Although very young children may recall the events of a day, it has been argued (Nelson 1995) that rather than forming autobiographical events, these events are stored in an episodic memory which requires reinstatement of the event for successful retrieval at a later time.

Gathercole also provided an interesting example of the developmental aspect of autobiographical memory. She discussed research which had looked at autobiographical retrieval in children of an event which had occurred 7 years earlier. Children were either 3 or 4 years old when they had to evacuate their classrooms during a formal test as a result of a fire caused by popcorn in another part of the school building. Children who were 4 at the time of the fire could recall significantly more details of the event and were more likely to recall the room they were in. Gathercole's article also highlighted how ineffective children's eyewitness testimony could be (as can adult testimony!). However, an important point Gathercole makes is that there may be an underestimation of the child's memory capability as a consequence of the methodology employed, for example where testimony is requested by an unknown adult or where there is an attempt in the retrieval context to use dolls to represent the child's experience of the event.

Cognitive Development in Adulthood

Cognitive Changes

The process of neural development identified above suggests that if cognitive task performance depends upon underlying neural systems, then in adulthood one would expect a decline in (fluid) cognitive performance to match the atrophy evident in the CNS.

There is much evidence for a decline in performance in an elderly population; however recent research has shown that these changes in cognitive competency occur from young adulthood onwards (Schroeder and Salthouse 2004). Schroeder and Salthouse plotted the change in a range of competencies from memory and reasoning tasks through to auditory and motor competencies. The largest declines observed were in memory, at about 2.3 per cent per annum, and in spatial/reasoning capacity, about 1.8 per cent per annum. The tasks assumed to reflect more posterior neural structures, for example auditory processing, showed least decline. These memory and spatial/reasoning factors most likely reflect experience-expectant processes. However, the memory for sequences of tones showed little age-related loss. The authors found that the biggest age-related effect was an actual improvement in performance, in vocabulary, of about 5.2 per cent per annum. Vocabulary therefore is a prime example of an experience-dependent neural process.

This study indicates that decline in cognitive task performance is far from being homogeneous. In Chapter 2 a discussion of dynamic visual acuity (Ishigaki and Miyao 1994) reported an age-dependent sex difference but also noted that there was consistent decline in the process efficiency after the age of 20 years. This decline is also apparent in other visual functions, for example visual acuity and contrast sensitivity. However, some visual processing may be more resistant to the ageing process. Norman *et al.* (2003) observed the age-related change in movement perception in young (mean = 21.8 years) and older adults (mean = 72.6 years). The task involved the participants looking at two patterns of stimuli moving across the screen and judging whether the patterns were drifting at the same speed or not. The older group was impaired in their judgement on this task; they required about 5 per cent more difference in the drift rates in order to detect a difference. However, when the movement judgement had to be made in a background of visual noise the age difference in performance was no longer present. In this latter condition, there were individual differences associated with sex: in order to detect a difference older men required less percentage difference than did older women.

The summary of Philips and Hamilton (2001) suggests a significant association of working memory task performance and ageing; however, this is dependent upon the working memory process examined. Research by Maylor and her colleagues (Maylor *et al.* 2001; Reimers and Maylor 2005) does suggest that executive processes show a decline in efficiency; however, the decline is not equivalent across all cognitive processes investigated. Dror and Kosslyn (1994) also highlight a similar pattern of dissociation in visuospatial working memory process decline. Again it should be noted that hormones may act as a neuroprotective agent, slowing the decline in cognition in task performance in younger women aged up to 50 years (Kramer *et al.* 2003).

Hormonal Influences in Ageing

There has been considerable research looking at the relationship between hormonal activity and cognitive ageing in elderly age-groups. One immediate complication is the close pharmacological relationship between testosterone and oestradiol discussed in the previous chapter and illustrated in Figure 7.1.

Consequently, in many studies it is difficult to disentangle the impact of T and its derivative, oestradiol (Janowsky, *et al.* 2000). According to Janowsky *et al*, there are androgen receptors in the prefrontal, hippocampal and amygdala regions of the brain. Thus, in principal, cognitive processes related to memory, working memory and emotional processing could be susceptible to testosterone influence. In contrast to oestrogen activity in ageing women, the reduction of T in men as a function of age is relatively gradual. Thus healthy men in their seventies will have only 40 per cent less testosterone than equivalent men in their twenties.

Much of the research with oestradiol has addressed the extent to which this hormone can act as a neuroprotective agent, countering the deleterious affect of ageing upon cognition (see above). Thus Lebrun *et al.* (2005) observed that in postmenopausal women, those with higher levels of oestradiol were less likely to have cognitive impairment (dementia). These authors concluded that endogenous oestrogens may protect women against the typical decline of cognitive function seen in ageing. It has been argued that oestradiol has its impact through influence on cholinergic projections in the hippocampus and cortex (Gibbs and Aggarwal 1998). These findings are in contrast to an earlier study by Geerlings *et al.* (2003), who observed a positive relationship between oestradiol and dementia in an elderly sample of women.

A parallel study by Fonda *et al.* (2005) looked at the relationship between T and cognitive functioning in sample of about 1000 men. The study included measures of working memory (backward digit span), processing speed and visuospatial imagery. A large number of hormones were measured and considered in the analyses. Cognition was associated with ageing but hormonal activity did not mediate the age – cognition relationship. A similar conclusion was reached by Lessov-Schlaggar *et al.* (2005), who found no relationship between hormonal levels and cognition in elderly men. Thus the evidence for the importance of hormones upon cognition in the elderly from studies such as these is by no means unequivocal. Consequently, some research has considered the context in which hormonal treatment is given to patient groups.

Research by Resnick and Maki (2001) and Maki (2005) has investigated the impact of oestrogen replacement therapy upon cortical activity (indexed by PET measurement). The women observed in the Resnick and Maki study were aged over 55 years. Changes in blood flow were noted in posterior regions associated with memory function: the hippocampus, the entorhinal cortex and the middle temporal gyrus. In addition, prefrontal region changes were also noted with the oestrogen therapy regime. This observation is consistent with other findings studying the relationship between oestrogen and cognitive function (for example Smith *et al.* 1999). Later research by Anderer *et al.* (2005) looked at the impact of hormone replacement therapy in a group of postmenopausal women with an average age of 60. The electrophysiological index employed was the P300, an event-related potential component associated with high-level cognitive processing. This group of women displayed P300 components which were relatively slow and with smaller amplitudes. After treatment with an oestrogen – progestogen combination, the P300 latency was reduced. This indicates an improvement in cognitive efficiency post treatment.

A study by Aveleyra *et al.* (2005) considered the relative impact of an oestrogen versus oestrogen – progestogen therapy in a group of women who had recently begun the menopause. A range of visual, attentional and working memory measures were employed. Both therapeutic regimes led to cognitive improvement but across different tasks. The inconsistencies in the research findings discussed above may be partly explained by the timing of the intervention. Pinkerton and Henderson (2005) and Sherwin (2005) suggest that the timing of the intervention may be critical. The suggestion is that there is a window of opportunity shortly after the onset of the menopause where hormone therapy will have a positive effect upon cognition. Should the therapy timing be delayed then the positive effect may be lost and there may be a risk of induced dementia (Pinkerton and Henderson 2005).

Conclusions

The aim of this chapter has been to consider some of the individual differences associated with lifespan development. The chapter began with a consideration of several theoretical approaches to lifespan development. Experience-expectant and experience-dependent processes formed a major theoretical neural frame for the chapter. The developmental trajectories identified by Greenough *et al.* (1987) allow for the possibility that some cognitive processes may not inevitably show decline in adulthood, a pattern of heterogeneity which is present in the cognitive literature. The influence of hormones and speed of processing were also discussed.

While much of the hormonal research is directed towards prenatal, organizational, hormonal influences it is interesting to note that in adulthood the presence of hormones such as oestrogen may counteract (in women) the typical decline in some cognitive functions seen in men. Some are associated with a slowing in processing speed. Neural development is not always associated with increased number of neurons; the child developmental research indicates the importance of pruning in synaptic connections, emphasizing the importance of neural networks with frontal lobe structures in the network.

While infants show precocious face perception competencies, it is also clear that many aspects of face-processing and visual function require a prolonged period of development (Mondloch *et al.* 2002). Working memory processes, associated with prefrontal neural systems, appear to have sustained development well into adolescence despite the basic structures being present earlier in life (Gathercole 1998). Cognitive decline in adulthood is apparent, and this decline may begin to occur in early adulthood (Schroeder and Salthouse 2004). However, the decline is not homogeneous, either within the sexes or between the sexes. Thus it should be noted that some cognitive processes might display relatively weaker, less-age-associated changes (Dror and Kosslyn 1994; Phillips and Hamilton 2001). Extensive research has been carried out in order to identify the impact of hormones upon cognitive ageing. In general the results are equivocal, with issues of disentangling the separate impact of testosterone and oestradiol and in intervention studies identifying the time period where therapies may have a positive impact upon cognition.

Part IV
Theoretical Frameworks

9 Evolution, Brain and Cognition

Aim and Overview

The aim of the first chapter in this part of the book is to provide an account of the perspectives derived from evolutionary psychology and to discuss how these theories could explain the individual differences associated with sex in the architecture and functional architecture of the human brain. The premise in this chapter and throughout the textbook is that these neural processes underlie human cognitive functioning.

The first section of the chapter will consider the concept of natural selection and the critical interaction between environments (social and physical) and adaptation in the individual. This section will discuss theories emanating from evolutionary psychology which consider how the human brain and human cognition could arise from early hominid contexts. These include: social interactions within large groups, for example the motivation towards power and control; division of labour, for example women involved in foraging while men are involved in hunting; and sexual selection: how men and women might behave in order to ensure that their offspring will be likely to survive and breed in turn. These contexts have been advocated as the precursors of cognitive processes such as language, theory of mind, and visuo-spatial and mathematical competencies.

The subsequent section of this chapter will consider the extent to which sex differences in neuroanatomical structure are evidenced in humans. These architectural differences could occur at a global level, such as in overall brain mass, or at hemispheric level, that is in right versus left differences. Alternatively, the level of difference could be at a much more local level, for example in differences in particular structures such as the corpus collosum, the set of fibres (axons) connecting the two hemispheres. However, this section will emphasize the difficulties in attempting to relate human psychological function to the underlying architecture; it will be suggested that a rather more fruitful direction is to consider the relationship of psychological function to the functional architecture of the brain. The ongoing functioning of the brain can be monitored with techniques such as electrical stimulation, electrophysiology with recording electrodes and functional neuroimaging procedures such as PET and fMRI scanning. These functional investigations allow a stronger relationship to be identified between brain and cognition. The importance of these research observations for evolutionary hypotheses will be made explicit in the discussion.

Evolutionary Psychology

The Process of Natural Selection

According to Barrett *et al.* (2002) the process of natural selection is a relatively simple concept based upon three basic assumptions:

> Premise 1: All individuals of a particular species show variation in their behavioural, morphological and/or physiological traits – their *'phenotype'* … the Principle of Variation.
>
> Premise 2: A part of the variation between individuals is 'heritable': some of that variation will be passed on from one generation to the next … the Principle of Inheritance.
>
> Premise 3: There is competition among individuals for scarce resources such as food, mates and somewhere to live, and some of these variants will allow their bearers to compete more effectively … the Principle of Adaptation. (p. 3)

The principle of adaptation implies that in an environment where the individual has to compete for limited resources a particular adaptive characteristic may enable the individual to more successfully mate and have offspring. If the characteristic is inheritable and the environment remains the same, then the individual's offspring should be equally successful in turn in producing offspring. In this event the original individual is perceived as possessing *fitness*. In a relatively constant environment, this particular characteristic will be inherited by an increasing number of individuals and thus its frequency in subsequent generations within the population will increase.

Evolutionary psychology addresses the understanding of behaviour at several levels; the explanations given below are derived from Tinbergen (1963).

- What is the immediate or *proximate* cause of the behaviour? What specific stimulus context led to the behaviour?

- What factors in the individual's lifespan experience account for the behaviour? This is a developmental or *ontogenetic* level of explanation.

- What evolutionary context could account for the behaviour? This is the *phylogenetic* or historical cause.

- Why does the behaviour increase the individual's ability to survive and reproduce? This is a *functional* or *ultimate* explanation of behaviour.

Geary's 1998 Approach

According to Barrett *et al.* (2002) evolutionary psychology is particularly concerned with identifying the selection pressures that have shaped human
psychology over the course of evolutionary history. Thus evolutionary psychology looks at functional cortical architecture that indicates selection at
some point in early hominid evolution. Geary (1998) has suggested that the
fundamental human motivation is to exert control over the social, biological
and physical resources that support survival and reproduction. The relationship between emotion, cognition and motivation is presented in Figure 9.1.

The figure identifies many of the important features of Geary's (1998) account
of evolutionary influences upon human behaviour. He suggests that when early
hominids attempted to achieve control over the relevant resources they had to
develop competencies in their interaction with other individual hominids.
They also had to become competent within group encounters such as with
family or kin, or with in-group or out-group members; and finally they had to
gain an understanding of the important flora and fauna and to interact with and
attempt to control their ecological environment. Emotional processes were
viewed as crucial mediators in the interaction with others. At a general level joy
might be associated with positive evolutionary outcomes, for example finding a
mate. Negative emotions such as anger or sadness might be associated with loss
of resources or mates. In addition, the accurate perception of facial emotions is
an important element of the women-to-women interactions and the men-to-
men interactions discussed in more detail below. The nature and evolution of
the modules identified above are particularly important for this book and a
more detailed representation of the models is shown in Figure 9.2.

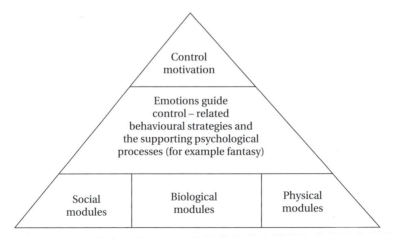

Figure 9.1   The motivation–emotion triangle (*Source*: Geary, D.C., *Male,
Female: The Evolution of Human Sex Differences,* Washington: American
Psychological Association, p. 160. With permission from the American
Psychological Association)

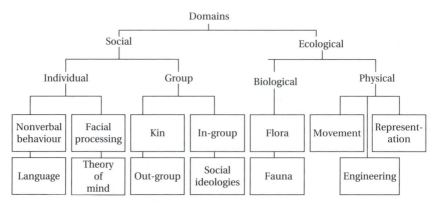

Figure 9.2 Evolved cognitive domains (*Source*: Geary, D.C., *Male, Female: The Evolution of Human Sex Differences*, Washington: American Psychological Association, p.160. With permission from the American Psychological Association)

Geary (1998) discusses the possibility that owing to the continuing presence of particular environmental events, the brain could develop pre-specified cognitive networks automatically triggered by these environmental stimuli. These 'domain-specific' modules would automatically encode and process information available from the environmental event, and are seen to be insular or encapsulated, that is not amenable to intrusion from other modules or more generic domain-general processes. The visual illusion phenomena discussed in Chapter 2 are taken as an example of such a module. Although viewers are aware they are experiencing a visual illusion, they cannot interfere with the process in order to achieve a veridical perception. Basic language-processing could also be taken as another such domain-specific insular process, although it has been argued recently that domain specificity in such a rigid form is not a necessary consequence of evolutionary processes (Cummins and Cummins 1999).

It is interesting to note the primacy given to social modules, or social cognition processes. The relationship between brain architecture and social complexity will be considered in more detail in the next section. Geary argued that in order to exert control over important resources such as other members of the same species, the individual would have to be sophisticated in their interpretation of signals from others, whether verbally or nonverbally communicated. In addition face-processing competencies would have to not only underpin facial recognition but also rapidly and effectively detect expressions of facial emotions.

The complexity of face-processing in humans is evidenced by research which indicates not just the recruitment of posterior cortical systems but also anterior ones, including the amygdala and prefrontal cortex, the circuit of Papez (Gur *et al.* 2002; Thomas *et al.* 2001). In addition, individuals displaying a lack of facial recognition, a condition labelled *prosopagnosia*, may still retain the ability to recognize facial expressions. While Geary further discusses in detail the importance of group contexts, perhaps the most important set of modules for the current discussion are the physical modules.

The movement module in Figure 9.2 directly mediates interaction within the environment particularly in contexts of prey capture and predator avoidance. In humans and other primates the important visuomotor or action-based pathway is the *dorsal pathway*, also discussed in detail in Chapter 2. In addition this pathway appears important in the anticipation of stimuli approaching the individual. This would be required in intra-sex competition for resources with men. The Watson and Kimura (1989–1991) research discussed in Chapter 2 showed an advantage for men in tasks which required sensory-motor action-based visual processing.

Another key element of these modules is the ability to represent the physical environment, for example the topography of surrounding areas. Many psychologists believe that the spatial abilities tapped in many modern psychometric measures derive from these early representational systems. Thus the Silverman and Eals (1992) and Eals and Silverman (1994) research, discussed in Chapter 4, attempted to account for the advantage for women in object location processing by a consideration of how they represented their environment when gathering fruit and so forth during the early hunter/gatherer cultures in hominid development.

Perhaps one of the most important features of the model set out by Geary and other evolutionary psychologists is the suggestion that these ancient precursors of modern cognition evolved within the social context of the early hominid cultures. Cognition is not viewed as a distinct psychological construct from motivational and social psychology; human cognition functions in order to enable individuals to gain control and power over other humans, which facilitates access to the relevant resources required to enhance reproductive fitness.

Alternative Accounts

While the discussion above identifies general principles of evolutionary psychology and natural selection, Geary (1998) adopts a sexual-selection hypothesis. Natural selection *per se* is less likely to lead to sex differences than sexual selection (Ecuyer-Dab and Robert 2004). According to Ecuyer-Dab and Robert, sexual differentiation in behaviour is likely to arise when: the reproductive rate is not same across the sexes; when one sex makes a greater parental investment than the other; and when one sex requires a longer time to complete the reproductive cycle. Consider the case in hominids where women have a longer reproductive cycle than men. Men could maximize their reproductive fitness by increasing their copulation frequency (a polygynous mating system). However, given the relative scarcity of ovulating women competition would exist between men to gain access to an ovulating woman. This could be achieved by men increasing their home range or by excluding other men by force or threat. In this context sexual selection would occur with the men with the most appropriate skills (navigation, strength, stamina and so on), showing greater fitness and consequently these particular skills would become more frequent in men. This suggests that particular spatial competencies may develop as a consequence of interaction within a larger home range.

Female hominids are biologically constrained by their requirement to ovulate, gestate and then breast-feed their offspring. Consequently, women would select mates on the basis of the potential to produce healthy children within a well-provided and resourced environment. Thus in this model, women would be less likely to require the physical and navigational skills of men to achieve successful mating. However, an alternative account of early hominid sex-differentiated behaviour has also been given (Eals and Silverman 1994; Silverman and Eals 1992). This approach employs the premise that women and men developed differing foraging acts: women specialized in gathering techniques while men hunted. The suggestion with this hypothesis is that men develop navigational and visuomotor skills in the tracking and trapping of animal prey.

These spatial competencies may substantially overlap with the skills which could arise from the intra-sex competition described above. However, an important consequence which does arise from the foraging hypothesis is that women could develop a discrete range of spatial skills. This hypothesis predicts that women will develop the ability to remember general locations of edible plants and precisely where the plants are located within this ambient vegetation and growth. This specific spatial competence has been explored with preliminary evidence suggesting that women are relatively competent in object location memory (Eals and Silverman 1994; Silverman and Eals 1992). This line of memory research was discussed and evaluated in detail in Chapter 3.

Ecuyer-Dab and Robert (2004) have suggested that a primary motivation for women with offspring is to ensure their own survival and consequently that of their offspring. They identified in one study the impact of parental bereavement upon infant mortality. While the death of a father led to a threefold increase in infant death, the death of the mother led to a fivefold increase. Thus a mother would increase her reproductive fitness by ensuring her own survival. In order to achieve this increase in survival Ecuyer-Dab and Robert have argued that hominid women would be more likely to eschew hunting and its increased mortality risk and instead undertake local food-gathering.

While it could be considered that much of evolutionary explanation is data-driven, observation of data patterns in contemporary psychology leads to a consideration of the context in which the initially adaptive behaviour emerged. However, many evolutionary theories generate novel hypothesis (Sherry and Hampson 1997), for example the female forager hypothesis would lead to the prediction that women might have competence in particular spatial competencies, in remembering the precise location of objects in an array. Thus this hypothesis can be subjected to empirical testing. Sherry and Hampson looked at a set of evolutionary hypotheses:

- foraging, where women might look for non-mobile food such as fruit and men hunt and track wild animals,

- sexual selection where men employed a larger range size for finding a mate,

- ispersal, where offspring move to other areas in order to avoid resource competition with parents,

- parental care, where reduced mobility of women may lead to more successful pregnancy and lactation.

Sherry and Hampson looked at the pattern of cognitive developmental observations in spatial competencies particularly in relation to hormonal activation at puberty.

Sherry and Hampson (1997) concluded that the sexual selection theories could best account for changes in spatial cognition at puberty. In addition they suggested that accounts such as Ecuyer-Dab and Robert's survival theory also explained well the impact of oestrogen upon women's spatial cognition. Wynn *et al.* (1996) reviewed relevant cognitive, neuroanatomical and archaeological evidence and evaluated a range of evolutionary hypotheses. They argued that the male hunting hypothesis context occurred too late in hominid evolution to account for spatial competencies. Archaeological evidence suggested the presence of mental rotation and spatial visualization skills prior to the findings of a hunting culture. They also concluded that the sexual selection hypotheses were relatively more consistent with the evidence.

Chapters 2, 3 and 4 discussed research pertinent to these hypotheses; however, there are other approaches which may provide evidence related to evolutionary explanations. One way a genetic contribution to cognitive competencies may be assessed is through the use of monozygotic and dizygotic twins (Bratko 1996). The study by Bratko found higher correlations in monozygotic twin pairs than in dizygotic pairs in verbal (for example fluency) and spatial (card rotation) tasks. Their estimate of heritability for these verbal and spatial measures ranged from 0.49 to 0.63. However, given that all participants lived at home, there is the concern that identical twins shared a more common environment than the same-sexed non-identical twins. An alternative source of evidence for genetic differences underlying sex differences lies in the research investigating neuroanatomical and functional architecture. This research will be considered in the next section.

Sex Differences in Neuroanatomy and Functional Architecture

Individual differences in brain neuroanatomy can be considered across a range of levels, from the global – overall brain mass, relative hemispheric mass – to local or regional size.

Global Level

Extensive research into individual differences at a global level has been carriedout by Rushton and his colleagues (Rushton & Ankney 1996, 2000; Rushton & Rushton, 2003). This research has been controversial because of the underlying assumptions and the subsequent inferences of the findings. Rushton and Ankney suggested that the finding that the brain is larger in men than in women has been recognized ever since the time of Broca in the mid nineteenth century. Given that brain size is related to body mass, and that men typically have larger bodies, this observation is not surprising. However, Rushton and Ankney went beyond this to suggest that when body mass is controlled, for example by matching body mass in men and women, men still possess a relatively larger brain volume (1442 ml versus 1332 ml, Rushton and Ankney 1996). This remaining difference in combination with the assumption that 'big is better' led Ankney (1995) to suggest that 'the sex difference in brain size relates to those intellectual abilities at which men excel, that is, spatial and mathematical abilities require more "brain power"' (p. 27).

Recent research continues to identify a relationship between brain size and intelligence scores (Akgun *et al.* 2003). However criticisms have been raised about how one proceeds to control for body mass when comparing brain size between groups or individuals (Peters *et al.* 1998). While a strong relationship may exist between height and brain size across ethnic groups, the relationship within groups or in different age-groups is poorer. These authors suggest that there no simple way to understand the relationship between body size and brain size. Thus a Japanese body may be typically smaller than a North European body, but it is not merely a scaled-down version of the European body. In addition, they have suggested the presence of errors or variability in brain size measurement itself, for example in the measurement procedure of magnetic resonance imaging.

Another issue raised by Peters *et al.* was the need to distinguish between brain volume associated with grey matter (neuronal material) and volume associated with white matter (axonal material). Their study noted that while sex differences in grey matter and white matter existed in their sample, when height was controlled for only the difference in white matter remained. More recent research has also suggested the largest difference in brain structure lies with the white matter rather than the neuronal mass *per se* (Allen *et al.* 2003).

This finding is in contrast to the finding of Gur *et al.* (1999) who suggested that women had a relatively higher grey-matter density.

Another study looking at global characteristics in women and men adopted a different assumption from Rushton and Ankney, presuming that smaller was better (Neubauer and Fink 2003). These authors suggested that focused cortical activity resulting in lower global cortical activation is typical of highly intelligent individuals. They labelled this the notion of *neural efficiency*. Using an EEG procedure to measure the power of alpha-wave activity during task completion, the authors observed that only in men did the expected pattern occur of higher performance with reduced global activation. The adoption of a completely opposite premise undermines the suggestion that big inevitably means better. Further evidence contravening this notion is presented below in the next section and in an earlier chapter (Chapter 8).

Another generic measure of cortical activity associated with white matter is conduction velocity of the axons themselves. A recent study has suggested that there are sex differences in conduction velocity (Reed *et al.* 2004). In this study a precise measurement of head length was recorded along with an early component of the visual evoked potential (VEP). The VEP typically measures visual cortex response to repeatedly presented stimuli. An early cortical response occurs with a latency of about 100 ms, the P100 component. In one of the stimulus conditions, the lowest spatial frequency condition (see Chapter 2), women displayed a P100 latency of about 98.06 ms while men had a mean latency of 99.27 ms. However, because the men had a longer head length, the calculated conduction velocity was greater for men: 1.94 m/s versus 1.87 m/s for women.

This suggestion of a fundamental difference in speed of processing between men and women has significant implications for cognitive performance, particularly in explanations of developmental changes in cognition (see Chapter 8 and the research of Fry and Hale 2000). However, others such as Garlick (2002) would suggest that speed of processing in neural networks is not as important as the pattern or weighting of synaptic interaction.

A final consideration of the functional implications of a large brain comes from evolutionary psychology itself (Barrett *et al.* 2002; Geary 1998) and was initially discussed above. This emphasis highlights the notion of a social brain or Machiavellian hypothesis. This suggests that brain size is strongly related to the number of individuals in the individual's social group. Across primate species as the number in the social group increases, a commensurate increase in cortical size is noted. The proposal being made is that in order for the individual to exert control over the pertinent resource needed to increase fitness, the individual must develop sophisticated social cognition skills in order to obtain power over the other individuals in the group. The greater the number in the group, the greater the complexity of social thinking demanded.

This argument by Barrett *et al.* (2002) would suggest that rather than brain size being related to abstract, fluid intelligence, it may be more likely to be related to social and emotional intelligences. Interestingly, when cranial size is controlled there are sex differences in the extent of grey matter in the prefrontal orbitoventral region, with adult women displaying a relatively greater extent than age-matched men (Gur *et al.* 2002). However, the complexities of interpretation of structural differences in the brain are exemplified in the Gur *et al.* (2002) paper. In their introduction the authors drew attention to the many observations that men performed better on a range of visuospatial tasks (see Chapters 2, 3 and 4 for some partial support for this suggestion). However, their own neuroimaging data suggest no difference in prefrontal dorsolateral regions, which presumably contribute to the sex differences in working memory discussed in Chapter 3. Thus the relationship between global architectural measures of the brain and cognitive functioning is currently far from being understood.

Hemispheric Level

While the discussion immediately above has focused upon sex differences at a global level, that is the whole brain, many researchers have looked at differences at the hemispheric level (Zilles *et al.* 1997). The majority view suggests that men have more lateralized representation than women, though the first model suggests the opposite. However, most of these early models typically made use of clinical observations where the brains of individuals who had evidenced cognitive dysfunction underwent investigation after death. Recent research discussed in earlier chapters has taken advantage of neuroimaging processes to provide strong evidence that there is evidence for bilateral representation of verbal and nonverbal processes in the human brain. However, lateralization does appear to be generally greater for verbal than nonverbal processes (Voyer 1996).

Kimura (1992, 1999) provided clinical evidence which suggested that women and men do not necessarily employ differential hemispheric demands when carrying out visuospatial tasks. Thus both women and men suffer most in mental rotation task performance when they experience right-hemisphere lesions. In a line orientation judgement task reported by Kimura (1999) she observed that with right-hemispheric damage 'women were, if anything, more affected' (Kimura 1999, p. 151). Her observations are supported by recent neuroimaging research on verbal analogies and line orientation (Gur *et al.* 2000). The general trend in this study was for greater activity in the left hemisphere for the analogies task and greater right-hemispheric activity for the line orientation. Interestingly though, men who performed the line orientation more accurately showed more bilateral activation. Thus in this visuospatial context, as Kimura noted earlier, men displayed less right-hemispheric dependence.

Kimura (1992, 1999) went on to suggest that the most interesting sex difference was intrahemispheric rather than interhemispheric. Again she employed clinical lesion data to suggest that difficulties associated with language (aphasia) and motor control (praxis) arose as a result of different regions in women and men. The patterns of left-hemispheric lesion associated with aphasia and dyspraxia differed between men and women. In both cases a greater percentage of women were disrupted by anterior lesions, with men disrupted more by posterior lesions.

The case for intrahemispheric differences is also evidenced in work by Mateer *et al.* (1982). This clinically based research arises from a context where patients who are fully conscious are about to undergo brain surgery. The surgeon needs to know in advance if surgical lesion will disrupt major psychological functions, so the patient is asked to carry out a task, for example articulation of sequential numbers, and simultaneously the surgeon electrically stimulates the brain regions which could be removed. (The brain itself has no pain receptors, so the patient does not experience pain with this procedure.)

Mateer *et al.* found that with a language task a greater area of left-hemispheric stimulation disrupted performance in male patients. This suggests that there are localized differences in neural language systems in men and women. Note however that this pattern is not fully congruent with the Kimura (1992) clinical data on aphasia. The evidence presented by Mateer *et al.* also has implications for the notion of 'big is better'. The evidence discussed above in Chapter 3, suggests that in many verbal-fluency tasks women outperform men. Yet their neural language representation appears much smaller in extent than that of men. This is further evidence to undermine a simplistic, 'big-is-better' notion.

Yet further research indicates sex differences in local as well as global architecture (Nopoulos *et al.* 2000). These authors, in a magnetic resonance imaging study, noted that while in the brain as whole, men evidenced a greater extent of grey matter, this depended upon the particular region of the brain. Thus they noted that the women possessed relatively more grey matter in their right parietal lobe than in their left. Allen *et al.* (2003) also found that while there was a sex difference in grey matter in the left parietal cortex in men (about 64 ml in men versus about 57 ml in women), no difference existed in the right parietal. It should be noted, though, that one of the largest sex differences ($d > 1.4$) existed in the extent of white matter in these same regions, with men having significantly more white matter.

Findings such as these have implications for theories which advocate hormonal impact upon developing parietal structures (Witelson 1991). Witelson has argued that sex hormones directly influence the occurrence of neural death and axonal pruning in the developing child. The results above suggest that any influence is more likely to be upon neural pruning of synapses and the white matter. The major emphasis by Witelson is upon prenatal and early postnatal influences of testosterone (see Chapter 8). However, it is likely that neuronal loss and synaptic pruning occurs most during middle to late childhood, thus a model needs to be generated which can link these early testosterone factors with later organizational changes in the brain.

A major issue with much of this research is that the emphasis is upon architectural differences between men and women. However, the presence of neuroanatomical differences itself does not necessitate the presence of performance or strategy differences in women and men. Research by Gur *et al.* (2000) attempted to bridge this (excessively) large gap between structure and function by employing functional architecture techniques, as did the Mateer *et al.* (1982) study. Studies which cannot simultaneously monitor brain activity and behaviour have major difficulties when extrapolating from one level of explanation to the other.

Consider the recent observations by Witelson *et al.* (1999a, 1999b) on the brain of Albert Einstein. Extensive differences were found between the parietal regions of Einstein's brain and a control sample. While Witelson acknowledged the difficulties in linking morphology or brain structure to psychological function, it did not prevent her from attempting to link these characteristics of Einstein's parietal cortex with his genius. She suggested that with regard to '[v]isuospatial cognition, mathematical thought and imagery of movement ... Einstein's exceptional intellect in these cognitive domains ... may be related to the atypical anatomy in his inferior parietal lobes' (Witelson 1999b, p. 2152).

Such post hoc rationale is evident in the early postmortem interpretations by individuals such as Broca and Dax in the nineteenth century. One could argue that it is much more appropriate to utilize functional techniques which reveal functional differences between the sexes, for example the Gur *et al.* (2000) study discussed above. Functional neuroimaging can be employed even when task performance between the sexes is equivalent; a difference in imaging pattern may reveal distinct strategy patterns underlying the equivalent performance. The particular advantage is that any neuroimaging differences cannot be attributed to performance differences. Thus Baxter *et al.* (2003) found in a semantic matching task (matching category and exemplar stimuli) that although women and men did not differ in task performance there were differences in the underlying functional architecture of the two sexes. Women showed a pattern of less diffuse activation in the left hemisphere and more bilateral activation than the men. Note that this pattern of activation supports the electrophysiological stimulation sex difference findings of Mateer *et al.* (1982).

As suggested in Chapter 1, interesting individual differences can occur in the absence of performance differences! In this task context, similar patterns of activation would suggest the deployment of similar strategies. Thus Frost *et al.* (1999) found that in a language task demanding semantic memory retrieval, where no performance difference was present, women and men showed similar interhemispheric and intrahemispheric activation.

Perhaps the major difficulty with research steeped in an architectural or functional architectural orientation is not in the identification of sex differences *per se*, as these differences appear prolific if not entirely unequiv-ocal. The difficulty lies with understanding how these sex differences occurred. An evolutionary account would suggest that these (functional) neuroanatomical differences, where they exist, could be accounted for by selection processes, for example sexual competition or hunter-gatherer-mediated, perhaps operationalized in humans by hormonal factors operating prenatally or in childhood. However, an alternative account of brain develop-ment, initially discussed in the previous chapter, by Greenough *et al.* (1987) has argued that action-based, experientially driven processes, can shape neural development and thus could be the catalyst for the neural sex differ-ences identified above.

In addition, both evolutionary pressures and lifespan experiences could contribute to brain development. This interactionist approach is evident in Geary's (1998) approach when he discusses the co-opting of physical mod-ules to develop contemporary skills in domains such as mathematics. It is also evident in other evolutionary work, for example that of Dellarosa Cummins *et al.* (1999), who suggested a process of *canalization* which biases neural development. However, these authors suggest that evolutionary processes can impact upon the flexibility of the process. Chapter 11 consid-ers these suggestions in more detail.

Conclusions

This chapter has considered the suggestion that the human brain and the associated human cognitions are a consequence of natural selection processes in early hominids. The mechanisms responsible for the evolution of the brain processes arise from an interaction between an individual's characteristics and the particular environmental demands. Individuals with favourable char-acteristics should be able to secure resources which ensure their ability to breed and also enable their offspring to be equally successful. Such individ-uals with relatively high fitness levels will therefore pass more of their genes onto successive generations, increasing the proportion of their genes in the overall gene pool. This selection process will continue for as long as the par-ticular heritable characteristics facilitate fitness. Should the environment change then these characteristics may no longer be selected for.

Geary (1998) discussed the development of a range of modules which have evolved in order to ensure a high level of fitness. These modules provide the individual with competencies ranging from social cognition through to physical and engineering modules required to represent and manipulate the environment. An important element of evolutionary accounts such as Geary's is the importance of social processes. Geary emphasized the impor-tance of sexual selection in the development of sex-specific competencies, for example if male competition forces an individual male to extend his home range in order to successfully mate then navigational skills will be likely to advantage this individual. Selection over generations will lead to male offspring developing competent 3-D representations of space, which Geary would argue underlie contemporary skills such as mathematics. Others such as Eals and Silverman (1994) emphasize selection arising from the different roles carried out by women and men in securing food resources – foraging and hunting respectively. Many evolutionary approaches emphasize the mediating role of hormones (Sherry and Hampson 1997).

One source of evidence for evolutionary accounts lies in research which has attempted to identify sex differences in neural architecture and functional architecture. This research has considered sex differences at global and local levels, from overall brain size through to the ratio of grey and white matter in different brain regions. While sex differences occur in the overall mass of the brain structure, it is difficult to discern the extent to which this is a mere consequence of the larger body mass of men or something in addition (Peters *et al.* 1998). The emphasis upon size differences in structure leads one to consider the implicit premise in such an approach, the 'big-is-better' assumption.

Throughout this section there is evidence provided which appears to undermine this simplistic approach of linking structure to function. Early models of sex differences in brain function emphasized interhemispheric differences. However, subsequent research has found patterns of results which suggest that in certain cognitive tasks men and women show similar hemispheric biases (Kimura 1999). Extensive research at the intrahemispheric level suggests the presence of sex differences in structure. However, if one is attempting to extrapolate from structure to cognitive function then functional research, monitoring underlying neural activity during task performance, is more likely to lead to a greater insight into the brain–behaviour relationship.

There is substantial evidence to suggest that at a more local level, structural and functional differences exist between women and men. However, a fundamental problem is in the interpretation of these neural differences. Evolutionary accounts would suggest that these individual differences arise from selection occurring in early hominid ancestry. However, others (Greenough *et al.* 1987) would suggest that experience-driven processes will also have an impact upon brain development. Thus the brain functional architecture observed in many of the studies above could be the result of an interaction between biological preparedness derived from early hominid selection *and* from life experiences. This is the focus of Chapter 11.

10 The Importance of the Socio-Cultural Environment

Aim and Overview

The previous chapter emphasized the importance of predetermined biological structures and processes in explaining differences in cognition between men and women. While this nativist approach most likely identifies important neural processes underlying these differences, a large body of theory and research has been directed towards establishing the importance of environmental factors in the cognitive task performance of men and women (see Fausto-Sterling, 1992). The aim of this chapter is to provide an account of the major theories of socialization which account for general differences in behaviour between women and men and in addition to discuss and evaluate the research literature associated with environmental explanations of these putative differences in cognition.

The first component of the chapter discusses a number of theoretical approaches: the psychoanalytic perspective, social learning theory, and the cognitive-developmental approach, including the notion of gender schema theory; the section concludes with a general discussion of feminist theories. The second section will discuss the research which strives to identify the more specific events which contribute to the differential life-experience pathways experienced by men and women in many cultures. This section will also evaluate the experimental research which employs training environments designed to facilitate the development of cognitive skills, particularly in visuospatial and mathematical domains. This research field is one which can provide direct evidence for the importance of environmental influences upon cognitive task performance.

Theoretical Explanations of the Socialization Processes in Women and Men

Psychoanalytic Theory

The original theory by Freud (1910) was directed towards an explanation of human personality drawn heavily from clinical observations. However,

Freud's theory has implications for differential experience in the socialization process of girls and boys. The approach has elicited criticism on its emphasis upon the male personality development, or androcentric approach. Freud's theory emphasizes a child's progress through a series of psychosexual stages: oral, anal, phallic, latent and genital. The presence of distinct and sequential stages reveals a significant biologically driven component to the theory; however the present discussion will focus upon the interpersonal aspects of the theory.

According to Freud human behaviour is dominated by two major drives: the *libido* (the sex drive) and *thanatos* (a death force). The libido focuses upon the regions of the body which provide sexual satisfaction, the erogenous zones, which vary in a manner dependent upon the age of the child. Initially the pleasure associated with feeding emphasizes the oral region of the body; however the child subsequently focuses upon the anal region (with potty training implications!). Importantly, by 5 or 6 years of age, boys and girls experience distinct processes during the phallic phase. At the core of this stage are the notions of the Oedipus complex and the Electra complex.

During this phase, according to Freud, a boy becomes interested in his penis, which has become a source of pleasure for him. Also at this age, the boy is presumed to have a strong attachment to his mother, which is associated with a sexual desire for the mother. The boy perceives his father as a rival for the mother but also recognizes that the father is a powerful competitor for his mother, and therefore the boy fears that the father will retaliate. In particular, the boy feels that the father will try to remove his penis and this results in the boy experiencing *castration anxiety*. As a consequence of this perception, the boy represses his feelings for his mother and identifies with his father, incorporating the father's characteristics. This *identification* process, according to Freud, underpins the boy's acquisitions of the (male) cultural values, leading to the development of a conscience or *superego*.

For a girl in the equivalent developmental phase, the experience is quite different according to Freud. A central feature is the girl's concern over a lack of a penis; feelings of deprivation lead to anxiety labelled *penis envy*. The girl's subsequent desire for her father is known as the Electra complex. However, this anxiety is never fully resolved and Freud's suggestion is that as a result the girl will develop an immature superego, continuing to be dependent upon her parents for the development of her value system. In addition the girl will develop characteristics such as passivity and masochism (Hyde 1996). Subsequent critiques of the Freudian theory have been critical of the *phallocentric* nature of the theory, the emphasis given to the penis and to the father in the process. Thus Horney (1924) suggested that there was in fact anxiety in the male over womb envy, while Chodorow (1976) emphasized the importance of the mother role in parenting (Lips 1993). This criticism of a theory of socialization being driven by a psychology of men will be revisited later in this chapter.

Social Learning Theory Approaches

The social-learning accounts of why women and men differ in their general behaviour (and cognition) emphasize the direct influence of socio-cultural factors in the socialization process. The extreme position would be that pertinent individuals in the child's life – parents, family, friends, teachers, work colleagues and so on – would entirely influence how the developing child would behave and think. This particular account would be labelled *cultural determinism* and could be considered as narrow an explanation of human behaviour as one drawn from a *biological deterministic* viewpoint. The basic principles of social learning theory are derived from early accounts of learning theory and have similar concepts such as *imitation* or *observational* learning and *reinforcement*.

In operant conditioning, reinforcement refers to an environmental event which typically occurs during or after behaviour and is likely to increase the likelihood that the particular behaviour will be repeated. Thus, in a *Skinner box*, a rat's random pressing of a particular lever may be reinforced by the delivery of a food pellet when the lever-pressing occurs. In a social learning theory context, a young girl would develop behaviours appropriate for females as a result of the selective reinforcement by others in her life. The key term here is *selective* reinforcement, whereby the girl receives reinforcement such as praise only when exhibiting behaviours appropriate for girls and/or women in that culture. Therefore, in order for differential reinforcement of girls and boys to occur, there must pre-exist some stereotypic perception of the different roles played by women and men in that culture which guides the nature of the reinforcement.

A second mechanism, which could lead to the development of different social roles in boys and girls, is the process of imitation. In this context, children learn appropriate behaviours by looking at the actions of others and then exhibiting the behaviour immediately or at a later time (observational learning). However, once again, one cannot presume that this could be an indiscriminate process, that is copying the behaviour of any pertinent person. In order to develop behaviour appropriate for girls, a young girl should only imitate the behaviours of other girls and/or women behaving in a culturally appropriate way. This suggests that the young girl must not only have some sense of gender identity, but also some general notion of stereotypic behaviours in that culture. This notion of *modelling* therefore implies that the child must possess some rudimentary social cognition in order to model the appropriate individual and behaviour. This particular aspect of differential role acquisition will be discussed in more detail later in this chapter.

An extreme cultural-deterministic view would leave little scope for the child to actively contribute to the process of socialization. However, the suggestions immediately above would suggest that the child's cognitive processes do influence the process. More recently, Bussey and Bandura (1999) have extended the social learning account in a social-cognitive theory of gender development.

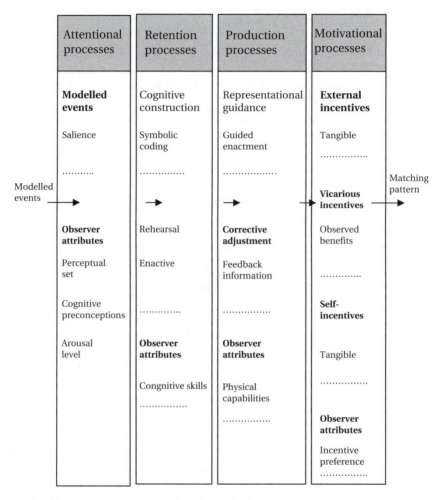

Figure 10.1 Processes underlying observational learning (*Source:* Bussey, K. and Bandura, A.L., Social cognitive theory of gender development and differentiation, *Psychological Review,* 106, 676–713. With permission from the American Psychological Association)

The more recent account has attempted to articulate the cognitive and social structures within which learning such as modelling occur. This theory emphasizes a range of human skills and characteristics – the capability for symbolization, the competencies underlying observational learning, self-regulation processes – and adopts a biological-potentialist approach and views. Consequently, these authors offer an integrative account of gender role development, offering a more precise understanding of the modelling process. The model underlying their theory is shown in Figure 10.1.

According to this model, children's perceptions and attention are guided by pre-existing cognitive knowledge; these preconceptions frame and make explicit what makes a stimulus salient. Thus, once children can differentiate men and women they will attend to the same biological sex model (Bussey and Bandura 1992). Factors such as arousal level will also impact upon the child's attention. Retention involves the memory for an event and is facilitated by the cognitive skills of the child, for example the ability to symbolically represent the information. Preconceptions and affective states will modify these representations. Children may be able to abstract rules of behaviour and consequently generate new symbolic representations. The next phase focuses upon the production of appropriate behaviour; this behaviour may be modified through comparison with knowledge representations relating to action in that particular situation.

The final component of the model deals with motivational factors; therefore, for example, children will be more likely to exhibit modelled behaviour if the reinforcement is direct and tangible. This model can therefore be seen to encompass physiological, affective, cognitive, social-cognitive and socio-cultural processes. Some other theoretical approaches, however, have placed significantly more emphasis upon the underlying cognitive processes (Bem 1981; Kohlberg 1966; Martin 1993; Martin and Halverson 1983; Martin *et al.* 2002).

Cognitive Developmental Theory

This approach to the process of socialization places the child at the centre of the process: how the child perceives, categorizes and attempts to interpret the social world. The perspective draws heavily on Piaget's consideration of child development where the child's actions and cognitions form the basis their subsequent development. This emphasis therefore stands in stark contrast to approaches that emphasize simple biological or cultural determinism.

A major cognitive development theorist is Kohlberg (1966), who contrasts his approach with the early social-learning approach using syllogisms:

A social learning syllogism:
'I want rewards.
I am rewarded for doing boy things.
Therefore, I want to be a boy.'

A cognitive developmental syllogism:
'I am a boy.
Therefore, I want to do boy things.
Therefore, the opportunity to do boy things (and to gain approval for doing them) is rewarding.'

This example is considered in Hargreaves and Colley (1986), p. 33.

Similar to Piagetian theory and Kohlberg's own conceptualization of moral development, this approach considers that children's thinking about gender progresses through a series of cognitive stages.

Initially, between the ages of 18 and 24 months children acquire the notion of *gender identity*: they know whether they are a girl or a boy: and can begin to label family members as women or men. However, the characteristics of a person (or self), which enables the child to label them (self) as a male or female, must possess some transient nature as the labelling is not seen as something which will necessarily endure as the example used by Kohlberg indicates:

(Jimmy has just turned four, his friend Johnny is four and a half)

JOHNNY: I'm going to be an airplane builder when I grow up.
JIMMY: When I grow up, I'll be a mommy.
JOHNNY: No, you can't be a mommy. You have to be a daddy.
JIMMY: No I am going to be a mommy
JOHNNY: No, you're not a girl, you can't be a mummy.
JIMMY: Yes I can. (Kohlberg 1966, p. 95)

Jimmy may know he is a boy but still considers that he could be a mother when older; he is lacking the concept of *gender constancy*. According to Kohlberg, an understanding of gender constancy provides the platform for the acquisition of gender roles. Thus his account suggests that after the age of 4 to 5 years, children will begin to acquire gender roles, gender stereotypes and accordingly begin to display differential behaviours.

However, extensive research has suggested that children exhibit stereotypic gender role behaviour at a much earlier age and consequently Kohlberg's assumptions have been questioned. A more detailed discussion of this issue will be undertaken later in this chapter. It is also interesting to note that Kohlberg's cognitive developmental account of moral development has come under criticism for its emphasis on men's experience during moral development (Murphy and Gilligan 1980).

Gender Schema Theory

A recent social cognition account of gender development emphasizes the role that a gender schema has in the child's thinking of a gendered world. A gender schema organizes the child's knowledge of the social world through a gender filter, that is people, behaviour and events may be understood within a gender framework. This knowledge structure can act to frame the child's perceptual, attentional and memory processes. Bem (1981) has argued that as the child learns the contents of the culture's stereotypic characteristics, the child will associate the appropriate characteristics with themselves and this leads to an integration of the self-schema with the gender schema. She suggested that:

the child also learns to evaluate his or her own adequacy as a person in terms of the gender schema, to match his or her preferences, attitudes, behaviours and personal attributes against the prototypes stored within it. The gender schema becomes a prescriptive standard or guide, and self esteem becomes its hostage. (p. 355)

Bem's account of a gender schema allows gender-schematic individuals to be identified through self-report inventories such as the Bem Sex Role Inventory (Bem 1974) and the Personal Attributes Questionnaire (Spence and Helmreich 1981). However, the conceptual basis for Bem's gender schema theory has been questioned by Spence and Helmreich (1981), Crane and Markus (1982), and Archer and co-workers in a series of studies. An important element of the research by Bem is that it enables characteristics, stereotypically associated with either males or females, to be possessed to varying degrees by individuals within one sex. The implications of this approach were discussed in detail in Chapter 6 and will be further considered below.

The work of Martin and co-workers (Martin and Halverson 1983; Martin 1993; Martin *et al.* 2002) has attempted to employ the gender schema as the explanatory mechanism underlying sex-role development. The fundamental structure of the model is the schema; according to Martin and Halverson, 'Schemas are naïve theories that guide information processing by structuring experiences, regulating behaviour and providing bases for making inferences and interpretations' (Martin and Halverson 1983, p. 1120). While Kohlberg (1966) identified gender constancy as the key cognitive platform for sex typing, Martin and Halverson suggested that in order to account for sex-typed behaviour at an earlier age, mere gender identity may be sufficient to drive a child's sex type behaviour. This particular issue, which emphasizes which cognitive structures are sufficient for sex-typed behaviour to occur, will be discussed in greater detail later in this chapter.

Feminist Psychology Considerations

Hyde (1996) identified a range of issues emphasized in feminist perspectives: status and power, sexuality, gender roles and socialization, consciousness-raising and so on. This section will emphasize the impact of status and power upon gender role socialization.

The accounts above of several of the theoretical perspectives depend upon the pre-existence of a gendered culture – one where adults' stereotype cognitions drive a differential interaction with children, dependent on whether the child is a girl or a boy. This pattern is the starting-point for these perspectives; however, for many feminists these socio-cultural structures are the products of a system which is organized around status and power. Thus a gendered society might act in order to discriminate against women, through lack of opportunities across a broad spectrum of careers and activities (see the section 'The Organizational Structure of Education' in Chapter 5). Most relevant for the present discussion is the suggestion that empirical observation and inference is not value-free, so that research that indicates a difference in performance between men and women could be taken as yet another device employed to sustain a gendered society where women are perceived in some inferior way.

The argument that we should consider a diverse range of explanations in differential gender role experience is stated well by Crawford and Chaffin (1997): 'To study ... sex differences in isolation from the social-structural and interactional factors that produce and maintain them is to participate uncritically in inequality within a gendered social order' (p. 122). Crawford and Chaffin are proposing that researchers working in an individual-differences context should be aware that their research activity and findings could contribute towards the stereotyped perceptions and putative inequalities associated with particular groups in a culture. The comment is directed at the researcher; however the section below considers the impact of these socio-cultural processes upon participants within a cognitive task context.

Socio-Cultural Influences in Cognitive Task Performance

How do socio-cultural processes present in a gendered society have an impact upon cognitive task performance? The majority of the perspectives discussed above placed gender role and stereotype constructs at the centre of their account as to why boys and girls acquire and exhibit different behaviours. The most pertinent question for this text is how social cognitions associated with gender role can lead to differences in cognitive task performance between men and women. An explanation of this impact may be derived from a theoretical model suggested by Deaux and Major (1987) which attempts to place the activation of gender-related behaviour within the social interaction context from which it emerges (see Figure 10.2).

This model attempts to account for the emergence of gender role behaviour within a social interaction context; however, many of its characteristics are pertinent to the cognitive task context.

In common with the models of Bussey and Bandura and Martin discussed above, this model assumes that the individual (the *perceiver* in the model) possesses a gender belief system, a gender schema, relating to gender-associated knowledge, knowledge that is not merely descriptive but prescriptive. Activation of the schema, according to Deaux and Major, is dependent on several major sources of influence; the gender schema is given priority in the individual's schema hierarchy, it is triggered by immediately preceding events and thoughts, it is elicited by the immediately observable general attributes of the *target*, and it is prompted by situations that are sex-linked. The early characteristics are similar to the conceptual characteristics in the theories above, though it is the last two sources which perhaps are of the most relevance to the present discussion. In this model, the characteristics of the target (another person) could be their sex, race or physical appearance. However, it is possible to argue that the characteristics of the task, for example its spatial appearance, could also trigger the schema, particularly when the task possesses sex-linked associations.

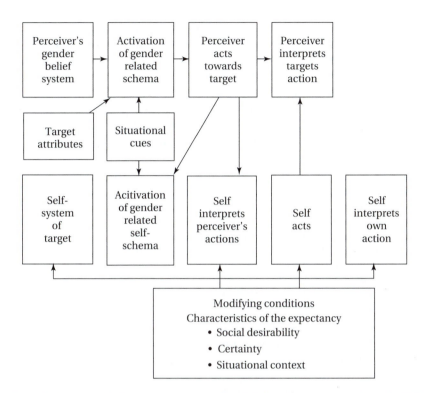

Figure 10.2 Social interaction context for gender schema activation (*Source*: Deaux, K. L and Major, B., 1987, Putting gender into context an interactive model of gender-related behaviour, *Psychological Review*, 94(3). With permission from the American Psychological Association)

This is emphasized under the characteristics of expectancy where Deaux and Major consider, in detail, the relevance of the situational context. Contexts likely to strongly evoke the gender schema 'provide salient cues to guide behaviour and have a fairly high degree of structure and definition' (Deaux and Major 1987, p. 379). In addition, through the process of self-verification (Bussey and Bandura's *corrective adjustment*) the individual will monitor their behaviour in relation to expectancies derived from their gender schema. Concerns over the matching of their behaviour with schematic expectancies may itself affect behaviour. As Deaux and Major suggest:

> Characteristics of situations that make them more public include a salient audience (particularly one that is evaluative), the potential for evaluation of behaviour by others, the expectation of future interaction with another, a camera, and personal identifiability. Under these conditions, behavior is more likely to conform to external standards of appropriateness. (p. 379)

The potential stress which may be associated with these cognitions, the concept of stereotype threat, was considered in earlier chapters.

Thus Durkin (1987) suggests that the social cognitions present in the task context can influence performance. He cites research by Hargreaves *et al.* (1985), which indicates that even in 10-to-11-year-old children task instructions impact upon performance. The salience of the task instruction set in activating gender schema cognitions was evidenced in research by Sharps *et al.* (1993, 1994). They employed the Vandenberg–Kuse mental rotation task (the task procedure is discussed in detail in Chapter 4; see Figure 4.5), a commonly employed task of spatial ability. Sharps *et al.* (1994) manipulated the content of the instructions:

Format 1 (Explicit spatial label)
The following is an evaluation of some of your spatial abilities, of your abilities to reason and solve problems regarding physical objects in space. Such abilities are involved in mechanical skills, and in navigation, map reading and work with tools. Please follow the instructions carefully.
Format 2 (Non-spatial instruction set)
The following is an evaluation of some of your mental abilities, of your abilities to reason and solve problems. Please follow the instructions carefully.

The authors would presume that the first instruction set wording activated a gender schema on the basis of much of its content, using terms such as 'spatial abilities', 'mechanical skills', 'map-reading' and so on. The second set is relatively constrained in its word use and is less likely to explicitly activate a gender schema. This study therefore is the precursor of the Massa *et al.* (2005) study discussed in Chapter 6. The difference between the studies is that Sharps *et al.* have adopted the Deaux and Major (1987) framework above which relates to the performance of women versus men, whereas Massa *et al.* looked at the impact upon women possessing different gender characteristics. The implication of this difference in research orientation will be discussed below.

Sharps *et al.* (1994) observed that with the first (spatial) instruction set, the conventional findings were obtained, with men obtaining a significantly higher score in the task. With the second (non-spatial) instruction set, no differences in performance were found between women and men. The authors concluded that non-cognitive processes could contribute to mental rotation task performance. Given the suggestions by Deaux and Major (1987) and Durkin (1987), one might presume that the explicit labelling of the spatial instructions more readily activated the gender schema of female participants and the ensuing self-evaluations led to impaired performance by the women in this experimental condition.

An interesting question arising from the findings of this study by Sharps *et al.* (1994) is the extent to which a task context must explicitly activate a gender schema before performance may be impaired. The instruction set employed in the experiment was not a verbatim replication of the Vandenberg – Kuse instructions, and the results did not entirely replicate the typical Vandenberg – Kuse findings. Consequently, more research is required in order to find out the extent to which explicit activation (Sharps *et al.*) versus implicit cues (original research) in the task instruction and procedure activate a gender schema.

It is interesting to note that there has been a recent approach to the consideration of the experience of being placed in a task context that activates a comparison of performance with membership of a stereotyped group. This concept has been labelled stereotype threat and has been investigated in several cognitive domains (Ashcraft and Kirk 2001); it was discussed earlier in Chapters 3, 5 and 7, in relation to social cognition and working memory and social cognition. The argument has taken the form that women in a mathematics or spatial task context have to contend with the stereotypic expectation that female participants perform relatively poorly in these domains in comparison with men. The pressure that arises from this contemplation may act to impair women's performance in these domains. This research was discussed in detail in the chapters which considered memory and mathematical performance in women and men, Chapters 3 and 5 respectively (see the section in Chapter 5 on stereotype threat and mathematics performance).

A critical assumption of the theory and the research discussed above is that the individual's gender belief system, the gender schema, accurately reflects the actual difference in task performance between men and women. While the determination of accuracy in social stereotypes may be problematic (Judd and Park 1993), research has suggested that there is a relationship between perceived stereotypic differences and actual differences between men and women across a range of behaviours (Swim 1994). Swim, in a United States sample, observed that for a range of behaviours – mathematics performance, verbal scholastic achievement test (SAT), leadership issues, susceptibility to influence and so on – participants either were accurate or in some cases underestimated the actual observed differences. Swim also noted, though, that some biases were present, for example in-group favouritism.

It is interesting to note that while much research has focused upon the construction of gender-stereotypic knowledge in children (for example Martin 1993) recent research has looked at the accuracy, variability and complexity in the child's gender schema (Blakemore 2003; Susskind 2003). The Blakemore study considered how rigorous the stereotyped perceptions were in children aged 3 to 11. Less-stereotypical dressing in girls was tolerated more than in boys; however less-stereotypical behaviour in girls was viewed more negatively than in boys. The study indicates that the relationship between gender-stereotypical knowledge and the resultant attitudes is quite complex.

The explicit assumption of the Deaux and Major (1987), Eccles (1987) and Geary (1996) models is that they should be employed in a consideration of how one understands differences in cognitive task performance between women and men. The one major exception to this is the approach of Bem (1981), whose gender schema model approach affords the opportunity for explaining within-sex differences in task performance. A key component in all of these models is the individual's conceptualization of the gender stereotyping in their particular culture. However, while the work of Martin (1993), Caldera *et al.* (1999) among others indicate that children can have well-established knowledge of gender stereotypes, this knowledge base becomes more sophisticated through its flexibility in older children (Martin 1993, p. 197). The findings of Bem (1974) and others discussed in detail in Chapter 6 indicate that in self-report measures the majority of undergraduate participants do not endorse a gender which is fully congruent with their own sex. According to Bem many individuals do not think of the world through a gender-schematic lens, and consequently all women (or all men) would not have similar motivations when completing cognitive tasks.

This is the difference between the Sharps *et al.* (1993, 1994) studies and the study by Massa *et al.* (2005) identified above and in Chapter 6. The Sharps studies presume that women will act in a homogeneous manner in the context of cognitive task demands or stereotype threat. The work of Massa *et al.* within a cognitive task instruction context and that of Schmader *et al.* (2004) within a stereotype threat context emphasize the importance of within-sex variability based upon gender.

The Importance of Differential Experiences for Cognition

Research has taken two broad approaches in attempting to identify the influence that experience may have upon human cognitive development. A non-experimental approach has been to assess the relevant experiences of the participants, typically through questionnaires, and assess whether this experience is associated with cognitive competence. Alternatively, some experimental research has exposed participants to some form of training in order to observe directly the direct impact of experience upon cognitive task performance. This final section of the chapter will consider these two approaches to the issue. Initially there will be a brief discussion of the research which has attempted to highlight some recent studies revealing the differential life experiences that boys and girls are exposed to in a gendered culture and how these may impact upon cognitive task performance.

Differential Experiences

One might consider that in the twenty-first century, the existence of differential stereotypic expectations for women and men or girls and boys might no longer exist in cultures such as those of North America and Europe. However, this does not appear to be the case. A recent study by Apparala *et al.* (2003) looked at a range of factors associated with egalitarian attitudes towards the participation of fathers and mothers in household and childcare activities.

The study considered factors at the individual level: age, social class, town location, religion; at the family level: size, age of children, mother's income; at the macro level: the proportion of women in the labour force and the post-materialistic nature of the culture. Their results suggested that younger partici-pants in the study held more egalitarian perceptions; in half of the European countries sampled, women held more egalitarian views. Individuals who had received a greater number of years of education also held more egalitar-ian views. These findings suggest that while many individuals have egalitar-ian attitudes there remain many individuals with conventional stereotypic attitudes towards household and childcare responsibilities.

More importantly for the present discussion is the possibility that the existence of gender stereotypes in adults will underpin the construction of differential opportunities afforded boys and girls and the development of differences in thinking and behaviour which may develop from these particu-lar life experiences (Tenenbaum and Leaper, 2003). These constructions may vary from the manipulation of the environment of babies – pink room and clothes colours and baby cards for girls, blue for boys (Pomerleau *et al.* 1990) – through to the choice of toys. Developmental Psychology textbooks have identified numerous differences in the early behaviours of boys and girls: gross motor skill deployment in kicking balls and rough-and-tumble play, doll play, outdoor play, same-sexed play patterns and so on.

It has been suggested (Wood *et al.* 2002) that many researchers consider toy selection and parental interaction in toy play to be important agents in the development of conventional gender role development. A consideration of some recent research investigating toy play in infants provides an insight into current understanding of parental interaction in infant play and also raises questions about the role that cognition plays in the development of toy play choices by infants.

The research by Wood *et al.* (2002) indicated that while parents and non-parental adults no longer so strongly categorized particular toys in a stereo-typical manner, there were still differences in the way toys were employed when the adults interacted with young children aged between 2 and 6 years. Thus while both mothers and fathers frequently employed stereotypically masculine toys with young girls and boys, there was a smaller range of toys employed with the boys, particularly in play with their mothers. Despite a shift in the stereotypic categorization of some toys it should be noted that, overall, stereotypically 'masculine' toys were perceived as more desirable for boys, 'feminine' toys for girls. Research by Laflamme *et al.* (2002) compared mother and father interaction during observed play contexts with children aged 9 to 15 months.

This Canadian study found a relatively high level of interaction of fathers in comparison with mothers. This level was also high in comparison to previ-ous observations of fathers in the USA. This pattern was attributed to either cultural differences or genuine differences arising in a shift towards egalitarian roles in the home. Mothers appeared to retain responsibility for basic care of the children. Another significant difference in behaviour related to the mothers' increased use of vocalization with the infants as well as the mothers' greater use of directives or requests. These studies suggest that while childcare practices in men and women may be changing, there may still remain differences in the ways adults interact with young children during activities with and without toys.

Wood *et al.* stressed the importance of child toy preference and use as a platform for gender role development. This critical relationship between toy preferences and gender role was explored by Campbell and her colleagues in a series of studies which observed infant preferences for toys (Campbell *et al.* 2000; Campbell *et al.* 2002). This research provided further evidence for infant preference for sex-congruent toys under the age of 16 months. The onset of the differential toy selection in female and male infants has important implications for the theories of gender role development identified earlier in the chapter.

The psychoanalytic perspective emphasizes the process of identification with the appropriate parent during the phallic period, from 4 to 6 years. Consequently, one would not expect to observe gender role behaviour in children younger than this age. The observations of such behaviours in younger children undermine the notion that some form of psychoanalytic identification process could mediate the initial flourishing of gendered behaviour. Likewise, Kohlberg's (1966) theory that places gender constancy at the core of gender thinking and behaviour, a competence typically seen in 4-to-5-year-olds, also has difficulty accounting for earlier gender role behaviour. The observations of gender role behaviour in younger children led Martin to consider that a gender schema could begin to be constructed from the period where the child developed some notion of gender identity, typically much earlier than 4 years of age. However, the observation by Campbell *et al.* found that boys displayed sex-congruent toy choices (by a visual preference technique) at 9 and 18 months.

This observation suggests that the sex difference is present even prior to the infant's ability to recognize themselves. Typically, this assessment is carried out with the *rouge test*. This procedure involves a patch of makeup being placed on the infant's face. A self-recognizing infant viewing themselves in a mirror will touch their own face as opposed to the mirror image. Campbell *et al.* concluded that their results 'suggested that sophisticated cognitive machinery, while it may enhance the expression of sex differences at later ages, is not necessary for their emergence' (Campbell *et al.* 2002, p. 214).

These authors postulated that these precocious toy preferences could arise from the presence of visual characteristics of the toys that made them more appealing to either girls or boys. In perceptual terms, these toys had different *affordances* for boys and girls. This explanation derived from an evolutionary explanation considered by Alexander (2003) whose suggestions of differences in perceptual processing in girls and boys were considered in more detail in Chapter 2. This account therefore undermines a gender schema approach, which has existing cognitive structures at its core. However, the Bussey and Bandura model in Figure 10.1 could accommodate these findings if one presumed that differential affordances could account for the differentially perceived salience in toys by girls and boys.

Another, perhaps more parsimonious, explanation of the results is that if the stereotypic toy stimuli employed in the Campbell *et al.* studies were also stereotypically used by the children's carers then infant visual preferences may be related merely to stimuli they have interacted with at home. Thus the observed results may have arisen from primitive (pre-cognitive) observational learning experiences. However, this would not account for the impact of other stimuli employed in the research. Whatever the ultimate explanations of the differences in infant preferences turn out to be, these observations by Campbell and her colleagues have provoked some stimulating reflections.

The Relationship Between Spatial Activity Experiences and Spatial Ability Competencies

Early research by Newcombe *et al.* (1983) employed an inventory of spatial activities and attempted to identify whether there was relationship between activity experience and spatial competence. A selection of the activities, gender-labelled, are shown in Table 10.1 below.

Newcombe *et al.* correlated the overall activity score with the Differential Aptitude Test, DAT, a visuospatial task (see Chapter 5). In a study with undergraduate students they observed a sex difference in the DAT performance; in addition men participated in more of the spatial activities labelled 'masculine', while women participated more in the 'feminine activities'. There was no sex difference in the neutral activities. Overall, there was a significant correlation between the activity measure and DAT performance ($r = +0.33$).

Table 10.1 Spatial activities and their gender association		
Masculine	**Neutral**	**Feminine**
Baseball	Bowling	Figure skating
Ice hockey	Pingpong	Gymnastics
Darts	Volleyball	Ballet
Skateboarding	Frisbee	Pottery
Car repair	Sculpting	Touch typing
Plumbing	Marching band	Interior-decorating

However, it should be noted that the relationship was only present in the women and not the male sample.

Caldera *et al.* (1999) in the introduction to their paper reviewed extensive research which had attempted to identify the relationship between toy play activities and visuospatial abilities, for example Tracy (1987). Caldera *et al.* looked specifically at the association of structured (child asked to copy a model block construction) and unstructured (child-led) block play with visuospatial competence. The pre-school children also undertook a block design task (see Chapter 5) and a children's embedded figures task (see the EFT procedure illustrated in Figure 2.7 in Chapter 2). They found that free block play and structured block play competencies were related to the block design task performance. In addition, elements of the structured block play (only) were related to the EFT performance; namely complexity and interest/involvement level. Cross-sectional research by Robert and Heroux (2004) noted that early childhood play was moderately related to performance in EFT and the water-level task (see Figure 2.8 in Chapter 2) at the ages of 9, 12 and 15 years.

Other research has focused upon the relationship between spatial experience (childhood or adulthood) and spatial ability in young adults (for example Flaherty 2005; Quaiser-Pohl and Lehmann 2002; Terlecki and Newcombe 2005; Voyer *et al.* 2000). All of these cited studies suggest that a relationship exists between earlier spatial experience and spatial ability in young adults. Thus Voyer *et al.* found that participants who had expressed preferences for spatial toys achieved higher scores on the 3-D mental rotation (MRT) and water-level tasks. However, an interesting aspect of their data was that a sex difference in the tasks was present only in those participants who had indicated a preference for spatial sports activities. Thus for mental rotation $d = 0.79$ in these participants, but for the participants who did not prefer spatial sports activities, a $d = 0.29$.

Quaiser-Pohl and Lehmann (2002) found that the sex difference in MRT was dependent upon the academic degree path of the participants. The largest effect size (favouring men) was in the arts, humanities and social sciences ($d = 1.92$). The smallest effect size was in computational visualistics, a computer-science-based degree, where $d = 0.27$. Thus, in this study, relevant degree experience was associated with the smallest effect size. The Terlecki and Newcombe (2005) study found that computer experience was associated with MRT performance. Path analyses by these authors suggested computer experience could account for the sex difference in the MRT procedure.

This sample of studies provides an indication of how non-cognitive task experiences may be related to cognitive task performance. However, as indicated in Chapter 1, these non-experimental observations preclude inferences about the direction of causality. Thus while one might wish to conclude that relevant experience led to an improvement in the cognitive task performance, it may be that the direction of the effect is in fact in the opposite direction. As Terlecki and Newcombe suggest, 'Our correlational study cannot rule out self-selection of video game and computer use by high spatial-ability individuals as an explanation of the data' (Terlecki and Newcombe 2005, p. 437).

An alternative account can be drawn for the notion of the 'bent-twig' concept discussed initially in Chapter 7 and to be discussed in detail in the next chapter. This explanation would suggest that girls and boys with predetermined competencies in visuospatial processing would actively seek out contexts, activities and tasks in which they would receive positive reinforcement from their success in these activities. This motivation would be predicted from elements of the models identified in Chapter 5 (Geary 1996, Figure, 5.5; Eccles 1987, Figure 5.6) and the Deaux and Major model identified above in Figure 10.2. Thus pre-school children with such competencies would be motivated to participate in a constructed block task; Caldera *et al.* (1999) noted that interest and motivation in the block play was one of the predictors of EFT performance in pre-school children. In addition should the process of activity and success be sustained (in the face of other stereotypic inhibitory processes) then it could be the case that such girls would choose to play with computers, pursue academically related courses such as mathematics and science and choose computer science as a degree to follow. This is the 'self-selection' concern of Terlecki and Newcombe (2005).

In order to overcome the problem of causality, some research has directly manipulated the relevant experience and measure the spatial task performance pre and post treatment. Baenninger and Newcombe (1989) investigated the relationship between the experimental manipulation of training context and the extent of improvement in women and men in the spatial task. The control group underwent a mere retaking of the task; in the specific training regime training was a particular task. In other conditions training was across a set of task formats. The most important observation lay in the relative improvement of women and men. While there appears to be a slightly large effect size in improvement with the women in the sample, analyses suggested this was not significant. Thus the benefits of visuospatial training were equivalent in women and men.

Baenninger and Newcombe argued that as asymptotic levels were not observed and both women and men were still improving at the end of the intervention it was difficult to come to any firm conclusion as to the nature of the relationship between training/experience and spatial competence. However, one conclusion is that both sexes may benefit from relevant experience. A more recent study by De Lisi and Wolford (2002) has incorporated the computer experience research into a training design study and looked at the impact upon girls and boys aged 8 to 9 years. The experimental group children were exposed to extensive play with a computer game called Tetris which requires rapid mental rotation of 2-D brick shapes on the screen in order to construct a wall shape. The control group children were allocated to a geographical piece of software. Over 5 hours of practice on these games was provided. The children were given a 2-D MRT task (see Figure 4.5) pre and post the computer treatment.

De Lisi and Wolford's results suggested that only the girls in the experimental group showed any benefit from the Tetris exposure, eliminating a pre-existing sex difference in the 2-D MRT procedure. The authors suggested that the girls may have developed a specific strategy during the Tetris exposure which was successfully applied to the 2-D MRT procedure. This focus upon an effective strategy within this group of girls would account for their small variability in the MRT performance in the post-treatment condition. The importance of strategy has also been emphasized by Bosco *et al.* (2004).

The De Lisi and Wolford research is a particularly interesting study which needs to be replicated and extended to other task formats, for example 3-D MRT performance. However, from the perspective of this text what is disappointing about the body of this research is the lack of orientation towards cognitive processes as opposed to task performance (for example see Law *et al.* 1995, for an exception to this). Thus it may be that what is learned is a set of procedures or strategies which are relevant for a specific cognitive task but which may not be generalized to other spatial task performances demanding different spatial processes. Should one of the aims of the research be to enable individuals to improve their competency in educational and career contexts (Keehner *et al.* 2004), then it is likely that a better understanding is required of the cognitive processes underlying cognitive task performance, the training regime and the applied context.

Conclusions

This chapter has considered theoretical models and empirical evidence stressing the importance of the socio-cultural environment upon the individual's social and cognitive development.

Theoretical approaches varied from Freud's psychodynamic model, emphasizing psychosexual proximal factors, through to gender-schematic accounts which emphasized the child's cognition in directing gender-related behaviour. Social learning theory and a more recent derivative, the social cognitive theory (Bussey and Bandura 1999), placed the child's cognition within a social context incorporating motivational factors. The social contextualization of the child's cognition is further emphasized in the model by Deaux and Major (1987). While this framing of cognition within the social context might be expected in a chapter emphasizing the socio-cultural environment, it should be stressed that Geary's (1998) evolutionary account discussed in Chapter 9 also places human cognition within a social context. The Deaux and Major model provides a framework for the content later in the chapter and in later chapters, which earlier considered the more immediate task social context and the associated social cognitions and their impact upon cognitive task performance.

Performance within the task context may be considered to be predominantly the consequence of the cognitive processes deployed within the task.

However the suggestions by Durkin (1987) as well as Deaux and Major (1987) suggest that the individual possesses not only cognitive processes pertinent to the task but also meta-cognitions associated with those competencies. Thus attitudes towards these competencies and the subsequent motivations will also impact upon task performance. The work of Sharps *et al.* (1994) on task-labelling suggests that activation of gender-related schemata related to task performance might impact upon performance. However, it was suggested that these models and research do not fully consider the impact of gender-schematic processing which will lead to significant within-sex differences.

The presence of these gender stereotypes reflects ongoing differential interaction with girls and boys in Western cultures. Toy play and selection which leads to different play experiences in young children is one example of the differential impact of parenting style. An interesting line of research by Campbell and her colleagues (Campbell *et al.* 2000, 2002) suggests that toy preference in girls and boys is prior to recognition of self. This observation is problematic for theoretical accounts that place cognition or social cognition at the centre or onset of sex-related behaviours. Recent social learning accounts of modelling (for example Bussey and Bandura 1992), gender schema accounts (for example Martin and Halverson 1983) and social cognition explanations (Deaux and Major 1987) all emphasize the child's cognitions in guiding behaviour. The work by Campbell suggests that such cognitions are not always necessary.

Research by Newcombe (Baenninger and Newcombe 1989; Newcombe *et al.* 1983) and others has suggested that spatial experiences associated with play and recreational activities are associated in a small but significant manner with cognitive task performance. Thus differential participation in these activities could contribute to individual differences in visuospatial competencies. However, a difficulty in interpreting this data is that the relationship between spatial activity and spatial competence could be mediated by a third factor, for example a biological predisposition. This will be the theme of the next chapter. However, in the Baenninger and Newcombe meta-analysis study, training effects were considered. These studies are more open to experimental control, and suggest that training can benefit cognitive task performance and that women and men benefit equally. However, research is required which emphasizes cognitive processes rather than task performance (e.g. Bosco *et al.* 2004).

11 An Interactionist Approach

Aim and Overview

The previous two chapters emphasized contrasting explanations for the presence of individual differences in human cognition, the polar arguments of the nature–nurture debate. Two recently published textbooks reflect these particular perspectives. Kimura's 1999 book *Sex and Cognition* focuses upon the evolutionary contribution to sex differences but offers relatively little discussion on the impact of environmental or socio-cultural factors. *Gender Differences in Human Cognition* by Caplan *et al.* (1997), in a critical consideration of individual-differences research, offers an alternative account emphasizing the socio-political context associated with gender difference research. Unfortunately, Caplan *et al.*'s consideration of evolutionary factors and neural processes is relatively constrained.

Rather than perceive human cognition in terms of *either* evolutionary *or* socio-cultural influences, the assumption in this book will be that both of these factors contribute to cognitive competencies and cognitive task performance. Therefore, the primary aim of this chapter will be to highlight how evolutionary processes may actually interact with socio-cultural influences in order to determine individual differences in cognitive task performance.

The initial component of the chapter is based upon the (reductionist) assumption that human cognition is dependent upon the underlying neural processes of the nervous system and that neural development is a consequence of the constant interplay between neural processes and environmental interactions (Anderson, 1998; Epstein 2001; Johnson, 2000; Johnston & Edwards, 2002). The aim of this section is to highlight the redundancy of an approach that emphasizes an 'either–or' perspective in individual differences. The following section highlights theoretical frameworks, which consider both evolutionary and environmental factors in cortical development. Greenough's (1987) suggestion of experience-expectant and experience-dependent processes and the 'biopsychosocial' model of Halpern (1992) will be discussed. The final section of the chapter will give the example of Casey's

(1996) approach to individual differences in spatial ability, a perspective which emphasizes the interaction between biologically programmed neural processes and particular facilitative environments.

Neural and Cognitive Development: A Comparative Approach

A distinctive feature of human development is the relatively long period of immaturity and dependency experienced in child development (Bjorklund and Pellegrini 2000). Thus Bjorklund suggests that in humans the period may last for 15 years yet is much reduced in other primates, e.g. chimpanzees for 8 years and macaques for 4 years. This behavioural development is accompanied by changes in the nature of the human brain. At birth, the weight of the human brain is approximately a third of that of the adult brain; however this proportion rapidly increases to 50 per cent by 6 months and is 90 per cent of adult size by the age of 5 years (Paus *et al.* 2001). This extensive period of postnatal growth is not seen in other primates such as chimpanzees and macaques (Bjorklund 1997). Beyond the age of 5 years the remaining 10 per cent increase in brain to adult weight masks the gross anatomical changes in brain structure in middle childhood.

Studies evaluating synaptic density (Huttenlocher 1979), grey matter and neuronal volume (Paus *et al.* 2001) suggest that there is a decrease in particular structures through this age period. Indeed the synaptic density at 2 years of age is a third greater than in adults (Huttenlocher 1979). However, other processes such as myelination may continue into the third decade (Paus *et al.* 2001). Mapped on to these events is a hierarchical developmental process where brain maturity is seen to occur earlier (prior to about 7 years of age) in the sensory regions of the brain, and later development, between 7 to 15 years, is seen in the prefrontal cortex in particular (Quartz 1999; Quartz and Sejnowski 1997). Anderson and co-workers, (1998, 2004) have drawn a parallel between the development of prefrontal cortical connections with posterior (parietal and temporal) regions of the brain and the developing competencies seen in children's performance of tasks demanding executive resources in working memory. Luciana and Nelson (1998) have emphasized the hierarchical development of working memory task performance with tasks demanding these posterior neural processes showing earlier competence.

The research discussed above indicates the developmental pathways underlying neural development and briefly how these developmental trajectories may be linked to cognitive functions such as executive processes. However, perhaps the most pertinent question here is: Why do the neural processes show prolonged developmental changes throughout childhood and indeed into adulthood (Kolb *et al.* 1998)? One possible answer could be that this prolonged brain development reflects a maturation process governed by some biologically predetermined, genetic factor. However, as Garlick (2002) points out there is a potential for 10^{15} connections between the neurones in the human adult brain and it is difficult to consider how predetermined processes could account for such a complex outcome. An alternative is to consider that the key factor in this brain maturity is the contribution made by diverse environmental interactions. Kolb was quite firm in his conclusion on this matter: 'Indeed it is now clear that experience alters the synaptic organization in species as diverse as fruit flies and humans' (p. 9).

As Bjorklund (1997) suggests

> Because brain growth continues well into adolescence, neuronal connections are created and modified long after they have become fixed in other species ... The result is a more 'flexible' brain (in terms of what neural connections can be made), which means more flexible thinking and behaviour. (p. 156)

This conclusion was shared by Quartz and Sejnowski (1997), whose computational model suggested that experience was at the heart of the process they labelled 'neural constructivism'.

When brain development is considered within this perspective, a consideration of neural function and cognition as deriving from either genetic or environmental (socio-cultural) factors appears rather simplistic and a more productive way forward would seem to be the consideration of genetic–environmental interaction processes (Johnston and Edwards, 2002; Rutter, 2002).

Interactionist Frameworks

Experience-Expectant and Experience-Dependent Processes

In Chapter 8 (see Figures 8.1 and 8.2) the concept of experience-expectant and experience-dependent neural processes (Greenough *et al.* 1987) was discussed. This is the suggestion that some neural developmental processes (experience-expectant) could be hard-wired because they were involved in processing information about stimuli invariably present in the environment, while other neural processes (experience-dependent) were dependent upon specific or idiosyncratic stimulation arising from a less predictable environment.

The hypotheses are shown in Figure 11.1a and b in a slightly modified form from Chapter 8. In Figure 11.1 the neural development processes have an emphasis on potential variability in development rather than on the shape of the developmental functions.

The figure illustrates the impact of the environmental experience of the individual upon the experience-expectant and experience-dependent processes. This is the consequence of activity-led development, and Greenough suggests that the experience-dependent processes, the crystallized processes,

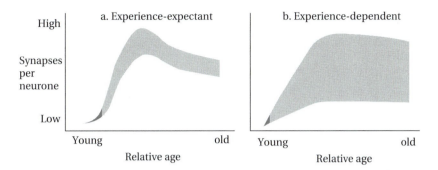

Figure 11.1 Variability in experience-expectant and experience-dependent neural processes as a function of activity-dependent development

by definition, are more susceptible to this influence. Thus variability in environmental experience leads to extensive variability in the development of these neural processes. By contrast, the experience-expectant, fluid processes show less sensitivity to these activity-driven factors. Johnson (2000) labels these latter processes as 'predetermined epigenesis', where there is a unidirectional casual path from genes, to neural structure and finally to functional neuroanatomy or psychological function. Johnson labelled processes dependent upon environmental activation 'probabilistic epigenesis'. This process allows for bidirectional influences in the interaction between genes, neuroanatomy and psychological function.

This latter approach reflects the neural constructivism approach identified by Quartz and Sejnowski (1997). Research such as Greenough *et al.* (1987) and the Quartz and Sejnowski paper emphasizes the importance of the activity experiences. However, Garlick (2002) emphasizes the contribution of individual differences to the neural plasticity process. One conceptualization of this emphasis is shown in Figure 11.2, which displays one potential representation of the source of variance in experience-dependent and -expectant processes due to individual differences. In this account, individual differences, the predetermined characteristics the individual possesses, have a greater impact upon the development of experience-expectant, fluid processes. This conceptualization of Garlick's emphasis is an alternative way of representing genetic and experiential influences in fluid and crystallized cognitive processes. Importantly it suggests that individuals do not possess equipotentiality for neural plasticity in development. Garlick (2002) suggested that some individuals are more efficient in adapting to their environment than others:

> [C]onsider the example of people whose brains are very good at adapting to the environment. They could then develop the appropriate neural circuits to comprehend and understand any phenomenon to which they are exposed. Therefore, these individuals would seem to be advanced for their age and would be considered to be 'bright' or 'gifted'. (p. 121)

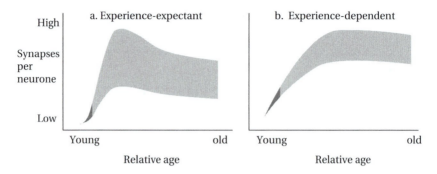

Figure 11.2   Variance in experience-expectant and experience-dependent neural processes as a function of individual differences

Garlick cited as evidence for his account the case of intervention studies that are targeted at children from relative impoverished socio-economic backgrounds. He argued that children in these programmes may have made temporary gains in intelligence task performance; however over a period of time, post-intervention, this relative gain would reduce to show no advantage. Garlick argued that this was a result of the non-intervention children within the normative population, with higher neural plasticity potential, showing more rapid neural development and eventually catching-up.

A recently constructed model of sex differences by Halpern (1992) indicates how an interaction explanation could account for cognitive differences between women and men. At the core of this model is cerebral organization, a key factor underpinning cognitive ability. This neural organization is influenced by both the genetic characteristics and the differential life experiences of the individual. The model therefore strongly advocates a consideration of interaction processes in neural development. However, one would have expected to see bidirectional arrows between differential life experiences and sex role stereotypes and expectations, as a strongly gendered culture might be expected to constrain an individual's life experience. More importantly the model really looks at cognitive abilities rather than cognitive processes such as perception, attention and memory. Thus it adopts the conventional approach to the explanation of individual differences between women and men; that is the model emphasizes similarities and differences in task performance or abilities rather than similarities and differences in cognitive processes.

An Example of Research Within an Interactionist Framework: The Work of Casey

In a review of her research programme Casey (1996) identified two theoretical developmental frameworks within which to consider nature–nurture issues in individual differences. Drawing from the earlier research Casey considered not only a biological–environmental interaction frame but also the notion of biological-environmental correlations. (See Lytton 2000 for an application of similar frameworks to development in general.) According to Casey a *passive gene correlation* occurs when a genetic influence is passed on to the child but in addition the carers of the child may provide an appropriate environment for the child to develop within. Thus a mother who inherits good spatial skills may well choose to provide an environment for her daughter, which will facilitate the development of similar skills in the daughter. Thus the mother could purchase the child some construction toys, which would afford rich spatial skill experience for the daughter.

In contrast a *reactive gene correlation* context occurs when individuals present in the environment react to the biological characteristics of the particular individual. Therefore a girl who inherits good spatial skills may be satisfied only with toys which stimulate these particular skills, and thus her carer may be forced to buy construction toys because the child does not choose to play with stereotypical feminine toys. In an *active gene correlation* context the child herself would actively seek out spatial toys. Thus in a preschool environment where a diverse range of play experiences may be offered, the girl who has acquired good spatial skills may seek out the large block area.

However, Casey's own approach emphasized a *biological–environmental interaction* frame where the interaction of genetic and experiential factors leads to an outcome not predicted from either factor alone. The genetic premise of Casey's model is derived from the work of Annett (1970; Annett 1985), which proposed that human neural organization, particularly cerebral lateralization, was under the influence of a right-shift gene (RS^+). The presence of this dominant gene would bias the left hemisphere towards both the representation of language and the control of the handedness. This latter implication afforded Annett the behavioural means to identify the presence or absence of this gene through the use of an inventory assessing handedness preferences.

Casey also assessed handedness in the participants but also the participants' relatives. This latter measure allowed Casey to identify right-handed participants with left-handed relatives (familial sinistrality). Casey considered that familial sinistrality in right-handed participants was a behavioural marker of the critical heterozygotic genotype pattern, (RS^+/RS^-), which Annett suggested would lead to high spatial ability. (In Chapter 7, the section entitled 'Methodological Issues' evaluated the measures of familial sinistrality.) Casey considered mathematics and science courses taken at high school to be a relevant spatial experience. The specific cognitive behaviour Casey focused upon was mental rotation. Although Casey was interested in accounting for differences between women and men her research programme was aimed specifically at identifying differences between different groups of women.

According to Casey high spatial competence can be achieved only by the appropriate combination of heterozygotic genotype (RS^+/RS^-) and mathematics/sciences school experience. Casey identified a subgroup of women who appeared to possess this particular combination of factors and whose mental rotation score was comparable with men's scores. This model has received criticism (Cerone and McKeever 1998; Halpern 1996) but most of the criticism has been directed not towards its conceptual assumptions of interaction effects but rather towards its methodologies. Other models of genetic action could have been considered and in addition Casey has also been criticized for the way she has attempted to identify the behavioural marker for a heterozygotic gene, that is the use of familial sinistrality as opposed to Annett's (1970) own strategy.

Casey and her colleagues identified the genotype through the measure of familial sinistrality. Girls following a mathematics/science major programme were consequently allocated to one of three categories: right-handed with at least one family member left-handed (RS^+/RS^-), right-handed with all right-handed relatives (RS^+/RS^+), and non-right-handed individuals (undetermined allele combination). The results of this study suggested that girls with RS^+/RS^- combination performed significantly better in an MRT procedure than girls in the other two groups. This RS^+/RS^- group performed equivalently to boys in MRT performance. In a sample of girls who were not taking mathematics/science majors, familial sinistrality status was not related to MRT performance. Interestingly, no such patterns were found when equivalent samples of boys were employed.

In the Pezaris and Casey (1991) study (initially discussed in the context of divided attention Chapter 3), adolescent girls and boys participated in a mental rotation procedure within a well-considered quasi-experimental format. The authors carried out an experimental manipulation involving dual-task conditions where the participants carried out the MRT procedure only, either while maintaining a pattern of dots (a demand upon visuospatial working memory) or while maintaining a sequence of digits (a demand upon verbal working memory). The aim of this study was to determine whether this target group of girls employed a distinct strategy from the girls in the other two groups.

Pezaris and Casey found that this RS^+/RS^- group suffered more disruption in MRT performance when concurrently maintaining the pattern of dots, a pattern similar to that observed for the boys in the study. The other two groups of girls were more susceptible to verbal interference. These findings suggest that this particular group of girls, with an appropriate combination of genotype and academic experience, are actually employing a strategy different from that of other girls undertaking the task, a strategy which may lead to more effective task performance under typical conditions.

Casey's account has at least two major implications:

- A proportion of girls, 50 per cent according to Casey, with the appropriate genotype and experience could achieve the visuospatial competencies of their male student counterparts. This would have implications for performance and assessments in any mathematics and science topics which depend upon competence in visuospatial processing. If Casey is correct then in a random sample of women one should expect to find a bimodal distribution of spatial task scores reflecting the different groups of women, rather than evidence of a normal distribution of scores.
- Her model suggests that the *only* way for right-handed women and girls to achieve this level of visuospatial competence is by this unique combination of genotype and experience. Any other combination would lead to low levels of competence (see Casey 1996, Figure 1); there appears to be no middle or mediocre level of performance achievable by girls possessing only one of the requisite factors.

Thus while appropriate educational experience may successfully intervene for the target group, what intervention is appropriate for the other 50 per cent of girls? This account becomes even more pessimistic if one accepts Annett's (2004) figures of 36 per cent for mixed handedness in the general population and actually slightly less in a female population. Thus Casey's approach would imply that the vast majority of girls and women would not be able to achieve high levels of spatial competency.

Conclusion

The aim of this chapter was to provide an alternative conceptualization for the importance of both the neural processes and the socio-cultural processes which underpin human cognition. Rather than accept that either genetic or cultural factors determine cognitive competency the chapter has suggested that a more productive approach would be to consider an interaction between these factors. Greenough's framework discusses experience-expectant and experience-dependent synaptic processes and indicates that, throughout the major part of the lifespan, experiences afforded by the individual's culture may continue to influence the synaptic patterning of the brain.

These interactive processes are made explicit in the Halpern (1992) model of sex differences where genetic influences upon hormonal systems and individual life experiences such as sex role expectations come together in order to determine the neural organization that underlies human cognition. A model such as this gives a more specific account of the processes involved in the interaction.

The chapter ended with a brief description of the research by Casey and her co-workers which has attempted to identify a subgroup of women with the appropriate combination of heterozygotic genotype for handedness and mathematics and science academic experience. This target group of women, according to Casey, would possess high spatial ability, specifically mental rotation competence. An interesting aspect of Casey's research is how she considered cognitive differences between men and women within a wider (within-sex) individual-differences framework. This is the perspective adopted throughout this book.

12 Synthesis

Aim and Overview

This concluding chapter will review the three major sections of the text: the individual differences associated with between-sex and within-sex cognitive processes, and the theoretical perspectives chapters. The chapter will conclude with a synthesis of the empirical findings and theoretical accounts, leading to some suggestions towards an agenda for future research.

The first major section of the chapter will discuss the extent to which the major theoretical approaches, the evolutionary approach and the social-constructivist approaches, are essentially discrete explanations of sex differences or whether there is some common ground. Informing this debate will be the research literature, which makes up the chapters in Part II: sensory, perceptual, attention, imagery and mnemonic processes. In addition the models and research findings in Chapter 5 on intelligence and educational achievement will also be considered. This component of the chapter will also discuss the importance of these theoretical approaches to the within-sex differences discussed in Part III.

The final section of the chapter will consider the limitations in the early conceptions of individual differences and highlights a more recent framework by Li (2003). This model emphasizes the dynamic interactive nature of phenotypic and socio-cultural influences upon behaviour throughout the lifespan of the individual. The section concludes with a consideration of how future research questions and designs may incorporate the perspectives advocated by Li.

Theoretical Accounts of Human Cognition

At first glance the theoretical accounts of human cognition in Chapters 9 and 10 present radically differing perspectives. In Chapter 9 the emphasis was on inherited characteristics which may contribute to cognitive competencies; in

Chapter 10 the emphasis was on the socio-cultural factors which influence the social cognitions brought to bear in the cognitive task context. However, there are elements in common in these two approaches. The socio-cultural approach emphasizes the importance of *situated cognition*, which according to Crawford and Chaffin (1997) is 'the ways in which the social and physical context of the activity affects the nature of the mental operations that people engage in and the mental abilities they develop' (p. 96).

An example of the process at work was provided by Crawford and Chaffin when describing research where individuals carried out mental arithmetic within an applied and relevant supermarket context or the same type of arithmetical processes were undertaken at home with one of the researchers. In the latter case, in the company of the researcher the participants' performance dropped. A whole range of situational factors could be envisaged, which could have contributed to this change in performance. For example, the individual participant's task expectations and motivations may have been affected by anxiety with the more explicit assessment context, or by the researcher's interaction with them and subsequently, according to Crawford and Chaffin (1997), the social cognitions of both the participant and of the researcher may be consequently shaped by such situational factors.

An example such as this indicates that task performance is not merely the simple deployment of cognitive processes free of other psychological factors such as social cognitions, motivation and arousal. However, evolutionary psychologists such as Geary (1998) do not deny the impact of these non-cognitive factors. In fact Geary emphasizes the importance of these factors when discussing the nature of adaptive behaviour. Figures 9.1 and 9.2 taken from Geary (1998) strongly embed the evolution of human cognition within motivational and social contexts, as Geary suggested: 'Human beings ... appear to be fundamentally designed to attempt to achieve some level of control over the social, biological, and physical resources that support survival and reproduction' (p. 161). He would thus argue that cognitions have evolved as a part of a complex psychological system with motivational, emotional and social cognition components. Therefore both Geary and Crawford and Chaffin (1997) emphasize cognition within a context; however, the context is separated in time, phylogenic versus ontogenic (see Li 2003).

In addition, both approaches emphasize that the more general behaviour of women and men may differ. Within a sexual selection context in early hominid ancestry, differential strategies by men and women would be required to lead to increased fitness in the two sexes. Thus men would be required to demonstrate more physical presence in either their threats or actual behaviour and develop greater competence in their understanding of the topography of their geographical environment. Consequently, these are the processes more likely to be selected in men. In a social constructivist account of human behaviour, the motivation for control argument discussed above is also relevant, but now within contemporary society.

Within a sexist culture men would strive to ensure than they exerted their control and power by constraining the opportunities of women within that culture (see Chapters 5 and 10). Thus in such a culture the roles carried out by men and women would be different, and the ensuing life experiences, stereotypes and social cognitions of women and men would also differ. (Note however that in a non-sexist culture, life experiences could not necessarily contribute to sex differences.) However, evolutionary and socio-cultural approaches do account for individual differences in human cognition in fundamentally different ways.

Evolutionary accounts suggest that sex differences in human cognition in contemporary society are the result of selected (adapted) characteristics in men and women. These inherited characteristics then shape the development of the child through its experience, leading to differential cognitive competencies in girls and women and in boys and men. Important agents in this process are the organizational and activational influences of testosterone, T, which occur prenatally and throughout post-adolescence and young adulthood. The operationalization of these inherited characteristics may be better understood within a development framework (Bjorklund and Pellegrini 2000). A socio-cultural account would also emphasize a developmental perspective in explaining individual differences in cognition. However, at the heart of the social cognition models discussed in Chapters 5 and 10 (Eccles 1987; Fennema and Peterson 1985) is the relationship between the contemporary socio-cultural factors, the child's perception of these characteristics and their consequent cognitive task expectations. The child's acquisition of these social cognitions is made explicit in the work of Bem (1981).

Thus while both perspectives suggest an impact upon the development of the individual, the mechanisms by which the impact is mediated are on a different time scale. Socio-cultural accounts place emphasis upon the cultural context in which the individual actually develops. Evolutionary accounts place an emphasis upon the cultural contexts in early hominid history which over time have shaped adaptive cognitive processes in humans. Perhaps the most important difference between the approaches is in the implications for intervention. If cognition is genetically driven then intervention is quite problematic owing to technological constraints. However, if the development of cognitive competencies is driven by social structures then processes such as education and politics can act as agents for change.

The mechanisms by which these two accounts impact upon human cognition also lead to different predictions about which type of individual differences are likely to occur. An evolutionary account based upon sexual selection suggests that as a result of the different strategies employed by women and men in mate selection, the inheritable characteristics will be different for women and men. Consequently, evolutionary psychology would emphasize between-sex differences. While hunter-gatherer accounts may perhaps afford more opportunity for within-sex variability, it is common for the term *sexually dimorphic characteristics* to feature in evolutionary research manuscripts indicating a strong emphasis on between-sex differences. Note though that should hormones be the proximal mechanism for selected structures in human cognition, then their cyclical activity will provide sources of variance in within-sex cognition performance (see also McCarthy and Konkle 2005).

At the centre of social constructivist approaches are the developing social cognitions of the child within the *social milieu*. While this approach might imply a social-deterministic view this could occur only if the child demonstrates little agency in the process. Where the child is active in their construction of their representation of the social world then potentially the more potent factor in the generation of social cognitions in the task context is not the sex of the child or adult but the possession and utilization of gender schemata. It is women with feminine gender characteristics and men with masculine characteristics who will be most likely to adopt the social cognitions (discussed in the models in previous chapters) in response to the stereotypic labels associated with particular tasks. The activation of gender-related social cognitions will vary within the sexes as well as between them and thus will readily account for within-sex as well as between-sex individual differences. A research example, identified briefly in Chapter 6, that supports this suggestion is the study by Schmader *et al.* (2004).

In this study the authors attempted to identify the impact of gender schema (belief) characteristics upon self-perceived mathematics competency and in a second study the impact of these gender schemata upon stereotype threat activated within a mathematics task context. Women, who endorsed gender-stereotyped views, that is those who were more likely to judge that men possessed higher levels of mathematics competencies, were more likely to report negative self-perceptions of mathematics competency. More importantly, these same women were more likely to have impaired mathematics performance with explicit stereotype threat manipulation. Thus a social-constructivist approach that places the activation of gender schemata at the centre of task performance is in a position to account extensively for these within-sex individual differences. It is for this reason that Chapter 6, 'Individual Differences Associated with Gender', began the section which shifted the orientation of the text from between-sex differences to within-sex individual differences.

These two major theoretical perspectives do share some elements in common but also possess fundamental differences in how they account for individual differences in human cognition. However, despite the fact that they do have different explanations of human cognition these theoretical approaches are not necessarily mutually exclusive in their accounts of cognitive performance. Cognitive task performance may well result from an interaction between inherited (cognitive) characteristics and the participant's social cognitions. This is the view advocated by Halpern (1992, 2000) and the view put forward in Chapter 11 of this text.

The starting point for the suggestion that brain development cannot be solely dependent upon inherited characteristics is the consideration of the complexity of putative neurodevelopment. With the potential for 10^{15} synaptic connections it is difficult to see how this development could be pre-programmed (Garlick 2002). The alternative explanation would be that the direction of some components of neural development is activity-led; this is the notion of neural constructivism identified in Chapter 11 (Quartz and Sejnowski 1997). This principle underlies the concept of experience-dependent processes suggested by Greenough *et al.* (1987) and discussed in Chapters 8 and 11. The concept of activity-led processes suggests that the constrained opportunities for women within a sexist culture will result in a neural organization different from any that could otherwise have been realized.

Consequently, the adult human brain is likely to be some product of prede-termined and experientially driven factors. Therefore, concurrent socio-cul-tural influences could impact upon cognitive processes in two ways: facilitating or constraining the development of experience-dependent neural processes associated with cognitive processes, and influencing the neural processes associated with the social cognition processes recruited in task contexts.

While the concept of experience-dependent processes affords the possibility that socio-cultural factors could impact upon the neural processes underlying cognitive development, recent research has suggested that neural plasticity may itself be constrained (see the Chapter 11 discussion by Garlick 2002). An example of such a constraint is in the bent-twig approach adopted by Casey (1996), which suggests that high visuospatial ability (e.g. in mental rotation) may result only from the appropriate combination of genetic (RS^+/RS^-) and experience (mathematics and science majors at college). The quite rigorous constraint explicit in this proposal is that women who may well have experi-enced relevant mathematics or science majors or courses at college will still not develop high spatial abilities if they do not possess the appropriate geno-type. These observations would suggest that while there is a potential for experience-led processes to shape neural development, the potential might be constrained by individual differences that are actually inherited.

A Process-Oriented Approach to Individual Differences

One of the major theoretical and organizational frameworks of this book has been the focus upon cognitive processes deployed within cognitive task con-texts. This process-oriented approach to individual differences and in par-ticular sex differences has been strongly advocated by Halpern (1992, 1996, 2004). Halpern and Wright (1996) were critical of the approach to individual differences which emphasized the task content: the notion of verbal, quanti-tative and visuospatial abilities. They suggested that an emphasis upon the underlying cognitive processes would lead to a greater understanding of the sources of sex differences. In the conventional psychometric approach, for instance the selective use of strategies by participants in task completion, would not be the focus of the study; rather it would be considered a problematic issue.

Voyer *et al.* (1995) in their meta-analysis on spatial abilities also discussed difficulties in adopting a process-oriented approach. They suggested that if participants could deploy different strategies during a task, then:

> a classification of spatial tests based on the underlying processes could lead to classifying the same test in several different categories. This approach does not represent a practical way to distinguish among spatial tasks. (pp. 251–2)

However, in agreement with Halpern, this book presumes that the consideration of the underlying cognitive processes, such as strategy use, is a more effective approach to understanding individual differences in cognition. There are extensive research findings identified in Chapters 2, 3 and 4, ranging from odour perception through to the memory for location of objects, which suggest that verbal working memory and long-term memory cognitive processes may scaffold task performance. This appears to be particularly the case for women. Should tasks like these really be labelled non-verbal if performance is mediated by verbal semantic and retrieval processes?

It could also be argued that the psychometric emphasis upon *task* performance places the study of human cognition within an artificial ecological context. Advantage in a specific paper-and-pen cognitive task could surely not have emerged from this task competency being selected in early hominid ancestry. Equally, these particular task competencies could not have derived from socio-cultural experiences, as no child would have endured (one hopes) an upbringing where such cognitive task completion was a daily event. Successful verbal analogies task performance or mental rotation task performance must, more likely, derive from particular selected cognitive processes, and/or cognitive resources arising from the activities of the child.

According to some critics (e.g. Holloway 1994) the deployment of psychometric procedures was a part of the state's attempt to govern and regulate the population. The critical factor pertinent to the current discussion is that within a patriarchal context the presence of sex differences would be taken to indicate women's inferiority in these tasks. This text has attempted to identify differences favouring women or men without placing any implicit value on the observed difference. However, in a process-oriented approach, *task* performance need not display individual differences for the study to have interest for the psychologist. As identified in Chapter 1 and in Chapter 9, in some circumstances it may be simpler to understand more effectively the individual differences in the underlying cognitive processes when task performance is equivalent between the groups of interest. Thus in this scenario the identification of individual differences is much less likely to raise issues such as the socio-political implications raised by Holloway (1994). In this context the individual differences are of most consequence to cognitive psychologists rather than social-science commentators.

However, a cognitive process approach is certainly not without its difficulties. While it is easy for textbooks such as this one to parcel the processes of perception, attention and memory neatly into discrete chapters, in reality these cognitive processes function in an intimately interactive manner and actual separation may be problematic. Thus attention is considered a process not merely discrete in its own right but also one contributing to perceptual phenomena (see Rinsink 2002) and a process intimately bound to working memory and executive processes in particular (Kane *et al.* 2001). An ultimate aim therefore of a cognitive process orientation is not merely to identify the importance of a particular cognitive process for individual differences, but also to consider how this process interacts with other cognitive processes in order to mediate a particular task performance. This added complexity is emphasized when one considers the content of Chapter 5: performance in intelligence and educational contexts. This chapter places cognitive processes within the framework of social cognition and motivation and indicates the complex and more generic psychological nature of task performance. When considering the research into the contribution of cognitive processes, these are considerations to bear in mind.

The Sources of Individual Differences in Human Cognition

The research discussed in Chapter 2 examined the presence of sex differences in auditory and visual perception. In many cases there was evidence for individual differences associated with sex in sensory processes. The weight of the research evidence suggested that where differences in auditory sensitivity lay, they generally favoured women. Sex differences appear to exist from low-level auditory processing through to phonemic processes (Majeres 1999). These sex differences in auditory sensory processes are congruent with the suggestions of sex differences in speech articulation (Kimura 1999).

In visual sensory processing the findings are more equivocal. Early research suggested that men exhibit greater acuity to both static and dynamic stimuli. However, recent research has suggested that with grating acuity, a form of static acuity, there are no sex differences (Solberg and Brown 2002). There does appear to be more systematic evidence for sex differences in the processing of colour or wavelength information. This has led some such as Alexander (2003) to suggest that retinal and visual pathway differences are the result of selection arising from the gatherer/hunter roles of women and men. Alexander went on to suggest that these visual differences could account for toy preference in infants at an age which precedes the cognitive processes association with sex identity (Campbell *et al.* 2002).

Research into visual functioning in the ventral and dorsal pathways has also suggested the presence of sex differences. Visuomotor tasks, presumably drawing upon the dorsal system, indicate advantages for men. An advantage for men in dynamic visual acuity would also suggest that men are more efficient in some ventral processes. The research discussed in Chapter 8 indicates that there are also extensive individual differences associated with age in both sensory and perceptual processes in the visual system. Visual acuity improves through childhood then declines in later adulthood, as does contrast sensitivity.

In the field of visual illusions, where more complex perceptual processes are at work, the results are equivocal. Although McGuinness (1985) has argued that women will perform more effectively in illusory tasks with angled line stimuli, later research with the Ponzo illusion did not provide support for this (Miller 2001). In complex tasks such as the water-level task and the line orientation judgement task, men typically achieved higher scores. Yet explanations of these sex differences appeared to suggest that the advantage for men may actually come from the priority of attentional allocation to the contextual information. Men may give low priority to the frame of the glass in the water-level protocol, but utilize the frame of the paper in the line orientation procedure. Should this be the case, then attention processes, in addition to perceptual processes, may account for performance differences. At this level of task complexity, a better understanding of the underlying cognitive processes will come from an appreciation of the separate contribution of attention, imagery and working-memory processes (e.g. Miyake *et al.* 2001).

Chapter 3 reviewed research into attention and memory, and it became apparent in this chapter that multiple cognitive processes act in concert with one another. Thus dual-task research protocols looking at divided attention which recruit executive resources in working memory and visual imagery procedures are likely to place demands upon visuospatial working memory in general. Attentional differences are predicted from evolutionary accounts of hunter/gatherer roles. Klein (2000) made the explicit prediction that if early in human ancestry women were predominantly fruit/food-gatherers then they would have developed better visual search skills and in particular show greater evidence for inhibition of return (IOR). Unfortunately, there appear to be few studies looking directly at IOR, though several studies have employed protocols which demand allocation of attention across arrays. These studies are generally understood to demand location memory competence and were discussed later in Chapter 3; however, a part of the performance could be dependent upon the attentional competencies discussed above (McGivern *et al.* 1997).

This chapter considered the extent to which the research literature suggested sex differences in working memory and long-term memory processes. There appears to be substantial research indicating individual differences in working memory efficacy. In particular, complex tasks, demanding verbally based executive processes, typically suggest that women perform the tasks more effectively. There is some evidence which suggests, that in the performance of particular visuospatial working memory (VSWM) procedures, men exhibit more effective processing. However, an important factor that emerges from some of these studies is that verbal (working) memory may scaffold perform-ance in tasks purporting to assess VSWM efficacy, particularly in women. It may also be the case that verbal working memory efficacy in women results from the verbal LTM scaffolding of these task processes.

The chapter reviewed extensive research suggesting that in verbal LTM, women evidenced significantly more efficient memory processing. This super-iority in verbal LTM processes may contribute to the observation that in long-term visual memory tasks, such as navigation and map tasks, women are more likely to employ landmark representations which could be verbally mediated. Men tend to employ survey (Euclidean) cues which may be disrupted by con-current visuospatial processing (Saucier *et al.* 2003). This chapter consequently provided strong evidence for extensive and diverse individual differences in memory processes associated with the sex of the participant. Chapter 11 high-lighted within-sex individual differences associated with working memory and LTM. However, age effects in working memory may be dependent upon the extent to which tasks make demands upon executive resources (Phillips and Hamilton 2001).

However, Chapter 3 also identified numerous issues which potentially confound and constrain the inferences which may be made from the research findings. The problem of process differentiation in task performance was raised initially in connection with the section dealing with cognitive processes, more precisely the difficulty of separating imagery processes from mnemonic processes. However, the issue of cognitive process separation pervades most of the chapter. Thus verbal LTM processes may scaffold verbal working memory performance, and in turn verbal processes may help support per-formance in tasks which appear on the surface to demand visuospatial pro-cessing in visuospatial working memory and long-term visual memory processes. In addition, this chapter explicitly recognizes, through the process of stereotype threat, the contribution of social-cognition and social-affective factors in cognitive task performance. This is genuinely a situated cognition context where cognitive processes function together alongside social cogni-tion and affective processes. While at present this may make more difficult the extraction of a combined and unique contribution to task performance by a particular cognitive process, it should not however be allowed to inhibit future research which may attempt to disentangle such influences.

Perhaps the most extensive research area in individual differences associated with sex is in the field of visual imagery, the topic for Chapter 4. Richardson (1999) noted that sex differences were apparent not just in tasks such as mental rotation but also in the reports of vividness of imagery. Sex differences in mental rotation are among the largest observed in individual-differences research, though many of the factors in task performance are still not fully understood and continue to be controversial. Task factors such as stimulus format (paper versus computer) and stimulus complexity (2-D versus 3-D) act to mediate differences in the effect size associated with the sex of the participant. The importance of performance factors such as the impact of timed protocols is still eliciting debate (Voyer *et al.* 2004). Voyer *et al.* found a consistent effect of sex across a range of timed procedures; however they also found that guessing by women varied according to the time demands. They suggested that their findings 'supported an interpretation by which performance factors and the level of spatial ability jointly affect gender differences on the MRT' (Voyer *et al.* 2004, p. 81).

The research by Sharps and her colleagues (Sharps *et al.* 1993, 1994) also suggests that factors such as task instruction may also have an impact upon the performance of women. These performance factors may well reflect an impact upon the social cognitions which participants bring to and deploy within the MRT task context. Given that mental imagery processes recruit working memory resources, it may be difficult to locate where within the cortical architecture the impact of social cognitions is located. The subsequent chapter on memory, Chapter 4, identified research which had attempted to relate the impact upon working memory of stereotype threat elicited in task contexts.

Nowhere in the book is the complex nature of the psychological processes underlying task performance made more evident than in Chapter 5 where performance in intelligence tasks and educational assessments is considered. The chapter begins with a process-orientated approach, with the suggestion that cognitive processes such as working memory contribute to performance in intelligence tests and scholastic achievement. Indeed, some researchers suggest that working memory and g are almost isomorphic constructs (Colom *et al.* 2004). However, extensive research also suggests that social cognition processes impact upon both working memory and mathematics performance (Schmader 2002; Schmader and Johns 2003). Consequently, an understanding of performance within contexts such as intelligence-testing (Dutke and Stober 2001) and educational assessment requires a consideration of a wider range of contributory factors.

Perhaps the most articulated theoretical frames are those of Geary (1996) and Eccles (Eccles 1987; Eccles and Wigfield 2002). While the former emphasizes evolutionary processes mediated by neural processes, the latter focuses upon the importance of socio-cultural influences mediated by the task-contextualized social cognitions of the individual. The chapter also discussed the suggestion that the education process itself could contribute to individual differences in educational achievement. This influence could act directly for instance in the form of teacher–student interaction (Fennema *et al.* 1990; Rustemeyer 1999) and the nature of scholastic assessment (Lynn and Mau, 2001) or could act indirectly through the structure and organization of faculty staff sex profiles. Thus the evidence reviewed in the chapter suggests that the proportion of women in higher education is at its greatest at first-degree level and at its lowest in the proportion of the 'highest' status level of the faculty.

The presence of sex differences in educational attainment depends upon the subject of the curriculum and the age of the individual. The discussion in Chapter 5 indicates that in international studies of educational achievement, 15-year-old girls achieved consistently higher levels in reading-related school subjects. While the same data suggested an advantage in many countries for boys in mathematics, the educational data discussed in the chapter suggests that sex differences in mathematics may be age-dependent (Geary 1998). Recent examination results in the UK and other countries suggest that across a range of subject areas girls are outperforming boys. However, as Skelton (2001) suggests, a more pertinent consideration would be to focus on within-sex differences and in particular on the variability of performance with boys. This emphasis of within-sex achievement is represented and discussed in several of the tables in Chapter 5. An emphasis on within-sex variability was the motivation for the final part of the book where individual differences associated with gender, hormonal influences and development were discussed.

In Part III, the initial chapter, Chapter 6, reviewed the literature associated with cognitive task performance in individuals with varying gender characteristics. While the conventional thinking views the possession and display of gender characteristics as a social construction, some research does suggest that early hormonal factors may contribute to the process (Baucom *et al.* 1985; Csatho *et al.* 2003; Hines *et al.* 2002b). Perhaps the major issue highlighted in the theorizing of gender is the extent to which gender is a multifaceted phenomenon. Researchers such as Bem (Bem 1981, 1985) consider that the identification of self-reported gender characteristics is sufficient to predict other gender-related characteristics in the individual, such as gender-schematic processing. Others (Archer 1991; Archer and Lloyd 2002; Archer *et al.* 1995; Spence 1985, 1991) would strongly dispute the suggestion that gender could be effectively assessed by a self-report inventory. There is research indicating that individual differences are associated with gender (Hamilton 1995; Signorella and Jamison 1986); however, much of research in the field appears to suffer from this lack of the coherent conceptualization of gender. Consequently, the importance of gender characteristics for within-sex variability in cognitive processing may remain underestimated while the research field lacks sophisticated conceptualization.

Chapter 7 considered within-sex differences associated with hormonal influences, both organizational and activational. Methodological issues associated with identifying prenatal testosterone were discussed with a variety of putative somatic markers identified: handedness, footedness, finger digit ratio, fingerprint whorls and hair density. While hormonal influences are central to many evolutionary accounts of sex differences (Hampson 1995), the chapter's emphasis was upon within-sex variability associated with hormones. Research with CAH samples exemplified the organizational research while menstrual cycle research exemplified the activational research. An interesting point that emerged in both the organizational and the activational research was that hormonal influences on task performance in within-sex contexts typically occurred with tasks which tended to display large sex differences. This suggests that causal factors associated with within-sex individual differences need not be fully independent of some of the factors mediating between-sex differences.

Chapter 8, the final empirical chapter, discussed individual differences associated with age and development. The theoretical discussion focused primarily upon experience-expectant and experience-dependent neural processes in human development. A particularly important suggestion was that that neural plasticity in humans may be constrained by individual differences which are genetically driven (Garlick 2002). This constraint was emphasized by Casey's research (Casey 1996) whereby high levels of spatial ability could develop only when individuals possessed the appropriate geno-type (RS⁺/RS⁺). Large effect sizes associated with development were identified but in addition some cognitive processes showed little change in perform-ance from middle childhood to middle adulthood.

A key feature in age-related change in working memory appears to be associated with executive functioning (Hamilton *et al.* 2003). However, other accounts of age-related cognitive change may depend upon changes in speed of processing (Fry and Hale 2000). While in the past the emphasis in develop-mental psychology has been upon child development, what is clear from more recent research is that neural plasticity is present in adults, even in processes such as working memory (De Luca *et al.* 2003). This change in emphasis has led to more research investigating individual differences with young-to-middle-aged adults (Schroeder and Salthouse 2004). This complements the extensive research that has typically compared younger adults with much older adults.

The findings discussed in Chapters 6, 7 and 8 suggest that there are extensive individual differences associated with within-sex cognitive performance. This research not only complements between-sex research, but may also inform our understanding of between-sex individual differences. Much of this research has emphasized the underlying cognitive processes, for example working memory processes or speed of processing. However, as with the sex difference research there is a need for more research which is process-oriented. The final section of this chapter concludes with possible ways forward for research investigating individual differences in cognition.

Some Ways Forward

This text has discussed several theoretical models relating to cognitive task processing: models emphasizing evolutionary accounts of individual differ-ences (for example for example Geary 1998), models emphasizing socio-cultural factors (for example Eccles 1987) and models which incorporate both evolutionary and socio-cultural explanations (for example Halpern 1992). The approach of this textbook is most sympathetic with the eclectic approach posited by Halpern (1992), which urges the need to be inclusive when attempting to identify the factors underlying the complex nature of human cognition. However, there are shortcomings in Halpern's model which are addressed only partially in her later account (Halpern 2000). The first lies with an emphasis upon cognitive abilities rather than cognitive processes. Despite advocating a process-oriented approach the book (Halpern 1992) emphasizes cognitive abilities: verbal, spatial and quantitative. Her textbook content/organization also emphasizes abilities rather than cognitive processes *per se*. Thus any model orientation should be directed towards the array of cognitive processes, where Halpern and this author believe the locus of individual differences lies.

In addition most of the models identified above provide a rather constrained and 'flat' account of the interaction between various factors and cognitive efficacy. They tend not to make fully explicit the dynamic nature of the interaction of these factors throughout the development of the individual (though Halpern 1992, 2000 does refer to such considerations they are not fully explicit in the model). Perhaps a more effective illustration of the dynamic interaction between phylogeny and culture is the theoretical framework suggested by Li (2003).

Li (2003) highlights the dynamic nature of the interaction between individual, culture and human phylogeny. The model emphasized the parallel and sequential lifespan or ontogenic influences upon the individual. Culture is viewed as acting upon human evolutionary processes, upon the developmental context of the individual and, thirdly, directly upon moment to moment activities. An example of the long-range effect of culture upon human evolutionary history is the development of dairy-farming. Thus in cultures where dairy-farming has long been practised, over 90 per cent of the individuals in the culture are lactose-absorbers, suggesting that lactose absorption has been selected for.

An example given by Li of mid-term effects on lifespan development would be the style of schooling and the metacognitive styles developed by the children. Direct cultural influences acting from moment to moment are varied, Li citing as a research example the impact of postal codes upon how individuals process digits. Perhaps the most important element of the model is its emphasis on the concurrent and ongoing influences of phylogeny and culture which impact throughout the lifespan of the individual from prenatal influence through to impacts in late adulthood.

While the emphasis is upon cultural factors, the model affords an understanding of how cultural, individual and neural processes interact dynamically through the lifespan of the individual. For example, cultural practices in early hominid history, for example hunting and gathering roles or sex selection differences, would lead to phenotypic differences, perhaps mediated by hormonal factors. This may lead to early behavioural differences, for example rough-and-tumble play, which if culturally sanctioned could lead to further cognitive and neural changes in the development of the individual. Thus throughout the ontogeny of the individual, neural, social, cognitive and experiential or situational events act in concert as the platform facilitating the development of the individual.

A model such as this makes entirely redundant those accounts from within a constrained perspective, as Li (2003) suggests:

> Although there have been attempts to study the nature–nurture and mind–brain interactions by different strands of developmental and life sciences, studying them separately misses the dynamic gestalt of the open developmental system cutting across multiple levels … A unique contribution of the current framework is that it highlights how interactive processes and developmental plasticity at different levels are closely connected to each other and unfold across different time scales. (p. 172)

Note that Li's account of individual differences is as relevant to within-sex individual differences as to between-sex differences.

How can future research work within such a framework? Li (2003) insists that research which adopts a relatively narrow theoretical stance will fail to appreciate the developmental dynamic of interacting neural, cognitive and socio-cultural factors. Does this mean that future research should adopt only a multidisciplinary approach to the research? It is unlikely that many researchers could acquire the necessary resources to employ cognitive, neuroimaging and general behavioural measures concurrently in their research. However it is more feasible that researchers should be able to frame their research questions within an interdisciplinary context. Thus Josephs *et al.* (2003) considered the impact of stereotype threat (social cognition) and how it interacted with individuals with differing T levels (evolutionary) when carrying out a cognitive task. Likewise Tracy (1987) reviewed research relating toy experience, gender role, spatial ability and subsequent educational achievement. In reality, though, most research is unlikely to generate research questions which cut across the differing or multiple levels, but will ask questions which are predominantly either cognitive in nature, addressed at social cognition issues or targeted towards neural or hormonal systems. For these researchers the framework suggested by Li may have a different impact, namely an impact upon research design. Consider the following example.

In a task context where performance outcome may differ between individuals the researcher could consider the following issues in the construction of the research design. The task instructions should, where appropriate, explicitly aim to decontextualize the research context and make use of strategies aimed at reducing the impact of stereotype threat (Good *et al.* 2003; Marx and Roman 2002). The assessment context itself, regardless of subject content, may generate anxieties (Aronson *et al.* 1999) which require different considerations in task instructions. Gender schema possession could be measured. Further biographical information on the participant can be collated in order to afford controlled or matched comparisons. This information could include: handedness, finger digit ratio, time of day when individual participants carry out the task, and menstrual phase details. Biographical information such as this explicitly recognizes the contribution that neural and hormonal factors play in task performance.

Above all, this text has argued that the research design should strive towards a clearer description of the cognitive process of interest. Research such as Loring-Meier and Halpern (1999) aims to deconstruct the cognitive processes underlying task performance, and thus individual differences can be associated with delineated cognitive processes. The work of Postma and his colleagues (Postma and De Haan 1996; Postma *et al.* 1998, 1999, 2004) is another example of research which adopts a componential approach to task appraisal. However, where the research adopts a conventional protocol and employs an established task, and the task is known to make complex demands upon cognitive systems, the research question should be embedded in this broader cognitive framework. In addition the inference made from the findings should be necessarily constrained in order not to invite confounding of the interpretation.

Finally, a process-oriented research approach does not require individual differences at the task performance level for the research to be interesting and informative. In some contexts, a lack of individual differences at this level is preferable when one is really interested in the underlying functional processes of the task. Research such as this is much more likely to be informative to the cognitive psychologist than to a wider audience. In summary, the advice given above essentially states that research should be explicitly cognizant of the broader theoretical frames within which the specific research question is constructed. This framework should form an important component of the conceptual context underpinning the research and should also provide a wider psychological forum for the discussion of the findings.

References

Abad, F. J., Colom, R., Rebollo, I., & Escorial, S. (2004). Sex differential item functioning in the Raven's Advanced progressive Matrices: evidence for bias. *Personality and Individual Differences, 36*(6), 1459–70.

Adams, J. W., & Snowling, M. J. (2001). Executive function and reading impairments in children reported by their teachers as 'hyperactive'. *British Journal of Developmental Psychology, 19*(2), 293–306.

Aglioti, S., & Tomaiuolo, F. (2000). Spatial stimulus-response compatibility and coding of tactile motor events: Influence of distance between stimulated and responding body parts, spatial complexity of the task and sex of subject. *Perceptual and Motor Skills, 91*(1), 3–14.

Akgun, A., Okuyan, M., Baytan, S. H., & Topbas, M. (2003). Relationship between nonverbal IQ and brain size in right and left-handed men and women. *International Journal of Neuroscience, 113*(7), 893–902.

Alexander, G. M. (2003). An evolutionary perspective of sex-typed toy preferences: Pink, blue, and the brain. *Archives of Sexual Behavior, 32*(1), 7–14.

Alivisatos, B., & Petrides, M. (1997). Functional activation of the human brain during mental rotation. *Neuropsychologia, 35*(2), 111–18.

Allen, J. S., Damasio, H., Grabowski, T. J., Bruss, J., & Zhang, W. (2003). Sexual dimorphism and asymmetries in the gray-white composition of the human cerebrum. *Neuroimage, 18*(4), 880–94.

Amunts, K., Jancke, L., Mohlberg, H., Steinmetz, H., & Zilles, K. (2000). Interhemispheric asymmetry of the human motor cortex related to handedness and gender. *Neuropsychologia, 38*(3), 304–12.

Anderer, P., Saletu, B., Gruber, D., Linzmayer, L., Semlitsch, H. V., Saletu-Zyhlarz, G., *et al.* (2005). Age-related cognitive decline in the menopause: effects of hormone replacement therapy on cognitive event-related potentials. *Maturitas, 51*(3), 254–69.

Anderson, M. (1992). *Intelligence and Development.* Cambridge, MA: Blackwell Publishers.

Anderson, V. (1998). Assessing Executive Functions in Children: Biological, Psychological and Developmental Considerations. *Neuropsychological Rehabilitation, 8*(3), 319–49.

Ankney, C. D. (1995). Sex-Differences in Brain Size and Mental Abilities – Comments. *Personality and Individual Differences, 18*(3), 423–4.

Annett, M. (1970). A classification of hand preference by association. *British Journal of Psychology, 61*(3), 303–21.

Annett, M. (1985). *Left, Right, Hand and Brain: The Right Shift Theory.* Hove: Lawrence Earlbaum Associates.

Annett, M. (1992). Spatial Ability in subgroups of left- and right-handers. *British Journal of Psychology, 83*(4), 493–515.

Annett, M. (1994). Geschwind's Legacy. *Brain and Cognition, 26*(2), 236–42.

Annett, M. (1999). Handedness and lexical skills in undergraduates. *Cortex, 35*(3), 357–72.

Annett, M. (2000). Predicting Combinations of Left And right Asymmetries. *Cortex, 36*(36), 485–505.

Annett, M. (2004). Hand preference observed in large healthy samples: Classification, norms and interpretations of increased non-right-handedness by the right shift theory. *British Journal of Psychology, 95*(3), 339–53.

Apparala, M. L., Reifman, A., & Munsch, J. (2003). Cross-national comparison of attitudes toward fathers' and mothers' participation in household tasks and childcare. *Sex Roles, 48*(5–6), 189–203.

Archer, J. (1991). A methodological commentary on gender schema research. *British Journal of Social Psychology, 30*(2), 185–8.

Archer, J., & Lloyd, B. (2002). *Sex and Gender* (2nd ed.). Cambridge: Cambridge University Press.

Archer, J., Smith, J., & Kilpatrick, G. (1995). The Association between Gender Scale Measures and Gender Clustering in Recall. *Sex Roles, 33*(3–4), 299–308.

Aronson, J., Lustina, M. J., Good, C., Keough, K., & Steele, C. M. (1999). When white men can't do math: Necessary and sufficient factors in stereotype threat. *Journal of Experimental Social Psychology, 35*(1), 29–46.

Ashcraft, M. H. (2002). Math anxiety: Personal, educational, and cognitive consequences. *Current Directions in Psychological Science, 11*(5), 181–5.

Ashcraft, M. H., & Kirk, E. P. (2001). The relationships among working memory, math anxiety, and performance. *Journal of Experimental Psychology-General, 130*(2), 224–37.

Astur, R. S., Ortiz, M. L., & Sutherland, R. J. (1998). A characterisation of performance by men and women in a virtual Morris water task: A large and reliable sex difference. *Behavioural Brain Research, 93* (185–90).

Auster, C. J., & Ohm, S. C. (2000). Masculinity and femininity in contemporary American Society: A re-evaluation using the Bem Sex-Role Inventory. *Sex Roles, 43*(7/8), 499–528.

Aveleyra, E., Carranza-Lira, S., Ulloa-Aguirre, A., & Ostrosky-Solis, F. (2005). Cognitive effects of hormone therapy in early postmenopausal women. *International Journal of Psychology, 40*(5), 314–23.

Awh, E., Anllo-Vento, L., & Hillyard, S. A. (2000). The role of spatial selective attention in working memory for locations: Evidence from event-related potentials. *Journal of Cognitive Neuroscience, 12*(5), 840–7.

Awh, E., & Jonides, J. (2001). Overlapping mechanisms of attention and spatial working memory. *Trends in Cognitive Sciences, 5*(3), 119–26.

Awh, E., Jonides, J., & Reuter-Lorenz, P. A. (1998). Rehearsal in spatial working memory. *Journal of Experimental Psychology-Human Perception and Performance, 24*(3), 780–90.

Ayalon, H. (2003). Women and men go to university: Mathematical background and gender differences in choice of field in higher education. *Sex Roles, 48*(5–6), 277–90.

Baddeley, A., Gathercole, S., & Papagno, C. (1998). The Phonological Loop as a Language Learning Device. *Psychological Review, 105*(1), 158–73.

Baddeley, A. (1996). Exploring the central executive. *Quarterly Journal of Experimental Psychology, 49A*(1), 5–28.

Baddeley, A. D. (1986). *Working Memory*. Oxford: Oxford University Press.

Baddeley, A. D. (1997). *Human memory: theory and practice.* Hove: Pyschology Press.

Baddeley, A. D., & Hitch, G. (1974). Working memory. In G. A. Bower (Ed.), *Recent advances in learning and motivation* (Vol. 8, pp. 47–90). New York: Academic Press.

Baenninger, M., & Newcombe, N. (1989). The Role of Experience in Spatial Test-Performance – a Meta-Analysis. *Sex Roles, 20*(5–6), 327–44.

Baker, M. A. (Ed.). (1987). *Sex differences in human performance*: Chichester, UK: John Wiley and Sons, Ltd.

Balistreri, E., & Busch-Rossnagel, N. A. (1989). Field Independence as a Function of Sex, Sex-Roles, and the Sex-Role Appropriateness of the Task. *Pereceptual and Motor Skills, 68*(1), 115–21.

Baloğlu, M. (2003). Individual differences in statistics anxiety among college students. *Personality and Individual Differences, 34*(5), 855–65.

Bandura, A., Barbaranelli, C., Caprara, G. V., & Pastorelli, C. (1996). Multifaceted impact of self-efficacy beliefs on academic functioning. *Child Development, 67*(3), 1206–22.

Barnfield, A. M. C. (1999). Development of sex differences in spatial memory. *Perceptual and Motor Skills, 89*(1), 339–50.

Baron-Cohen, S. (2002). The extreme male brain theory of autism. *Trends in Cognitive Sciences, 6*(6), 248–55.

Barrett, L., Dunbar, R., & Lycett, J. (2002). *Human Evolutionary Pyschology.* New York: Palgrave.

Bartrip, J., Morton, J., & de Schonen, S. (2001). Responses to mother's face in 3-week to 5-month-old infants. *British Journal of Developmental Psychology, 19*(2), 219–32.

Basow, S. A., & Medcalf, K. L. (1988). Academic-Achievement and Attributions among College-Students – Effects of Gender and Sex Typing. *Sex Roles, 19*(9–10), 555–67.

Baucom, D. H., Besch, P. K., & Callahan, S. (1985). Relation Between Testosterone Concentration, Sex-Role Identity, and Personality Among Females. *Personality Processes and Individual Differences, 48*(5), 1218–26.

Bauer, B., & Jolicoeur, P. (1996). Stimulus dimensionality effects in mental rotation. *Journal of Experimental Psychology-Human Perception and Performance, 22*(1), 82–94.

Baxter, L. C., Saykin, A. J., Flashman, L. A., Johnson, S. C., Guerin, S. J., Babcock, D. R., *et al.* (2003). Sex differences in semantic language processing: A functional MRI study. *Brain and Cognition, 84*(2), 264–72.

Bayliss, A. P., di Pellegrino, G., & Tipper, S. P. (2005). Sex differences in eye gaze and symbolic cueing of attention. *Quarterly Journal of Experimental Psychology, 58A*(4), 631–50.

Beech, J. R. (2001). A curvilinear relationship between hair loss and mental rotation and neuroticism: a possible influence of sustained dihydrotestosterone production. *Personality and Individual Differences, 31*(2), 185–92.

Bem, S. L. (1974). The measurement of psychological androgyny. *Journal of Consulting and Clinical Psychology, 42*(2), 155–62.

Bem, S. L. (1981). Gender schema theory: a cognitive account of sex-typing. *Psychological Review, 88*(4), 354–64.

Bem, S. L. (Ed.). (1985). *Androgyny and gender schema theory: A conceptual and empirical integration.* Lincoln: University of Nebraska Press.

Bengtsson, S., Berglund, H., Gulyas, B., Cohen, E., & Savic, I. (2001). Brain activation during odor perception in males and females. *Neuroreport, 12*(9), 2027–33.

Bernard, M. E., Boyle, G. J., & Jackling, B. F. (1990). Sex-Role Identity And Mental Ability. *Personality and Individual Differences, 11*(3), 213–17.

Bishop, D. V. M. (1990). *Handedness and Developmental Disorder.* Hove: LEA.

Bjorklund, D. F. (1997). The role of immaturity in human development. *Psychological Bulletin, 122*(2), 153–69.

Bjorklund, D. F., & Harnishfeger, K. K. (1990). The Resources Construct in Cognitive Development: Diverse Sources of Evidence and a Theory of Inefficient Inhibition. *10*(48–71).

Bjorklund, D. F., & Pellegrini, A. D. (2000). Child development and evolutionary psychology. *Child Development, 71*(6), 1687–708.

Blakemore, J. E. O. (2003). Children's beliefs about violating gender norms: Boys shouldn't look like girls, and girls shouldn't act like boys. *Sex Roles, 48*(9–10), 411–19.

Block, R. A., Arnott, D. P., Quigley, B., & Lynch, W. C. (1989). Unilateral nostril breathing influences lateralised cognitive performance. *Brain and Cognition, 9*(2), 181–90.

Bonner, L., & Burton, M. (2004). 7–11-year-old children show an advantage for matching and recognizing the internal features of familiar faces: Evidence against a developmental shift. *Quarterly Journal of Experimental Psychology Section a-Human Experimental Psychology, 57*(6), 1019–29.

Bosco, A., Longoni, A. M., & Vecchi, T. (2004). Gender effects in spatial orientation: Cognitive profiles and mental strategies. *Applied Cognitive Psychology, 18*(5), 519–32.

Brabyn, L. B., & McGuinness, D. (1979). Gender Differences in Response to Spatial-Frequency and Stimulus Orientation. *Perception & Psychophysics, 26*(4), 319–24.

Brand, G., & Millot, J.-M. (2001). Sex differences in human olfaction: Between evidence and enigma. *Quarterly Journal of Experimental Psychology, 54b*(3), 259–70.

Bratko, D. (1996). Twin study of verbal and spatial abilities. *Personality and Individual Differences., 21*(4), 621 –4.

Broadbent, D. E. (1958). *Perception and communication.* London: Pergamon.

Brosnan, M. J. (1998). The implications for academic attainment of perceived gender-appropriateness upon spatial task performance. *British Journal of Educational Psychology, 68*(2), 203–15.

Bruce, V., Green, P. R., & Georgeson, M. A. (1996). *Visual perception: physiology, pyschology and ecology* (3rd ed.). Hove: Psychology Press.

Bruce, V., Green, P. R., & Georgeson, M. A. (2003). *Visual perception: physiology, pyschology and ecology* (4th ed.). Hove: Pyschology Press.

Bruyer, R., & Scailquin, J. C. (1998). The visuospatial sketchpad for mental images: Testing the multicomponent model of working memory. *Acta Psychologica, 98*(1), 17–36.

Bryden, M. P., McManus, I. C., & Bulman-Fleming, M. B. (1994a). Evaluating the Empirical Support for the Geschwind-Behan-Galaburda Model of Cerebral Lateralization. *Brain and Cognition, 26*(2), 103–67.

Bryden, M. P., McManus, I. C., & Bulman-Fleming, M. B. (1994b). Gbg, Bmb, R-and-L, X-and-Y – Reply to Commentaries. *Brain and Cognition, 26*(2), 312–26.

Buck, J. J., Williams, R. M., Hughes, I. A., & Acerini, C. L. (2003). In-utero androgen exposure and 2nd to 4th digit length ratio – comparisons between healthy controls and females with classical congenital adrenal hyperplasia. *Human Reproduction, 18*(5), 976–9.

Bull, R., & Scerif, G. (2001). Executive functioning as a predictor of children's mathematics ability: Inhibition, switching, and working memory. *Developmental Neuropsychology, 19*(3), 273–93.

Burnett, P. C. (2002). Teacher Praise and Feedback and Students' Perceptions of the Classroom Environment. *Educational Psychology, 22*(1), 5–16.

Burton, L. A., Henninger, D., & Hafetz, J. (2005). Gender differences in relations of mental rotation, verbal fluency, and SAT scores to finger length ratios as hormonal indexes. *Developmental Neuropsychology, 28*(1), 493–505.

Bussey, K., & Bandura, A. (1992). Self-Regulatory Mechanisms Governing Gender Development. *Child Development, 63*(5), 1236–50.

Bussey, K., & Bandura, A. (1999). Social cognitive theory of gender development and differentiation. *Psychological Review, 106*(4), 676–713.

Cahill, L. (2003a). Sex- and hemisphere-related influences on the neurobiology of emotionally influenced memory. *Progress in Neuro-Psychopharmacology & Biological Psychiatry, 27*(8), 1235–41.

Cahill, L. (2003b). Sex-related influences on the neurobiology of emotionally influenced memory. *Amygdala in Brain Function: Basic and Clinical Approaches,* Vol. 985, pp. 163–73.

Cahill, L., Haier, R. J., White, N. S., Fallon, J., Kilpatrick, L., Lawrence, C., *et al.* (2001). Sex-related difference in amygdala activity during emotionally influenced memory storage. *Neurobiology of Learning and Memory, 75*(1), 1–9.

Cahill, L., & van Stegeren, A. (2003). Sex-related impairment of memory for emotional events with beta-adrenergic blockade. *Neurobiology of Learning and Memory, 79*(1), 81–8.

Caldera, Y. M., Culp, A. M., O'Brien, M., Truglio, R. T., Alvarez, M., & Huston, A. C. (1999). Children's play preferences, construction play with blocks, and visual-spatial skills: Are they related? *International Journal of Behavioral Development, 23*(4), 855–72.

Campbell, A., Shirley, L., & Caygill, L. (2002). Sex-typed preferences in three domains: Do two-year-olds need cognitive variables? *British Journal of Psychology, 93*(2), 203–17.

Campbell, A., Shirley, L., Heywood, C., & Crook, C. (2000). Infants' visual preference for sex-congruent babies, children, toys and activities: A longitudinal study. *British Journal of Developmental Psychology, 18*(4), 479–98.

Campbell, R., Elgar, K., Kuntsi, J., Akers, R., Terstegge, J., Coleman, M., *et al.* (2002). The classification of 'fear' from faces is associated with face recognition skill in women. *Neuropsychologia, 40*(6), 575–84.

Capitani, E., Laiacona, M., & Ciceri, E. (1991). Sex-Differences in Spatial Memory – a Reanalysis of Block Tapping Long-Term-Memory According to the Short-Term-Memory Level. *Italian Journal of Neurological Sciences, 12*(5), 461–6.

Caplan, P. J., & Caplan, J. B. (1997a). Do Sex-Related Cognitive Differences Exist, and Why Do People Seek Them Out? In P. J. Caplan, M. Crawford, J. S. Hyde & J. T. E. Richardson (Eds), *Gender Differences in Human Cognition.* Oxford: Oxford University Press.

Caplan, P. J., & Caplan, J. B. (1997b). Gender Differences in Cognition: Results from Meta-Analyses. In P. J. Caplan, M. Crawford, J. S. Hyde & J. T. E. Richardson (Eds), *Gender Differences in Human Cognition* (pp. 52–80). Oxford: Oxford University Press.

Caplan, P. J., Crawford, M., Hyde, J. S., & Richardson, J. T. E. (Eds). (1997). *Gender Differences in Human Cognition.* Oxford: Oxford University Press.

Carpenter, P. A., Just, M. A., Keller, T. A., Eddy, W., & Thulborn, K. (1999). Graded functional activation in the visuospatial system with the amount of task demand. *Journal of Cognitive Neuroscience, 11*(1), 9–24.

Carroll, J. B. (1993). *Human Cognitive Abilities: A Survey of Factor-Analytic Studies.* Cambridge: Cambridge University Press.

Casey, M. B. (1996). Understanding Individual Differences in Spatial Ability within females: A Nature/Nurture Interactionist Framework. *Developmental Review, 16*(3), 241–60.

Casey, M. B., & Brabeck, M. M. (1990). Women who excel on a spatial task: Proposed genetic and environmental factors. *Brain and Cognition, 12*(1), 73–84.

Casey, M. B., Colon, D., & Goris, Y. (1992a). Family Handedness as a Predictor of Mental Rotation Ability among Minority Girls in a Math Science Training-Program. *Brain and Cognition, 18*(1), 88–96.

Casey, M. B., Nuttall, R., & Benbow, C. P. (1995). The Influence of Spatial Ability on Gender Differences in Mathematics College Entrance Test-Scores across Diverse Samples. *Developmental Psychology, 31*(4), 697–705.

Casey, M. B., Nuttall, R. L., & Pezaris, E. (1997). Mediators of gender differences in mathematics college entrance test scores: A comparison of spatial skills with internalized beliefs and anxieties. *Developmental Psychology, 33*(4), 669–80.

Casey, M. B., Nuttall, R. L., & Pezaris, E. (2001). Spatial-mechanical reasoning skills versus mathematics self-confidence as mediators of gender differences on mathematics subtests using cross-national gender-based items. *Journal for Research in Mathematics Education, 32*(1), 28–57.

Casey, M. B., Pezaris, E., & Nuttall, R. (1992b). Spatial Ability As A Predictor Of Math Achievement: The Importance Of Sex And Handedness Patterns. *Neuropsychologia, 30*(1), 35–45.

Castel, A. D., Pratt, J., & Craik, F. I. M. (2003). The role of spatial working memory in inhibition of return: Evidence from divided attention tasks. *Perception & Psychophysics, 65*(6), 970–81.

Caviness, V. S., Kennedy, D. N., Richelme, C., Rademacher, J., & Filipek, P. A. (1996). The human brain age 7–11 years: A volumetric analysis based on magnetic resonance images. *Cerebral Cortex, 6*(5), 726–36.

Cerone, L. J., & McKeever, W. F. (1998). Mental rotation test performances and familial sinistrality in dextrals, with special reference to the bent twig theory. *Learning and Individual Differences, 10*(1), 1–12.

Chan, R. C. K. (2001). A further study on the sustained attention response to task (SART): the effect of age, gender and education. *Brain Injury, 15*(9), 819–29.

Chanquoy, L., & Alamargot, D. (2002). Working memory and writing: Evolution of models and assessment of research. *Annee Psychologique, 102*(2), 363–98.

Cherney, I. D., & Ryalls, B. O. (1999). Gender-Linked Differences in the Incidental Memory of Children and Adults. *Journal of Experimental Child Psychology, 72*(4), 305–28.

Chiarello, C., McMahon, M. A., & Schaefer, K. (1989). Visual Cerebral Lateralization over Phases of the Menstrual-Cycle – a Preliminary Investigation. *Brain and Cognition, 11*(1), 18–36.

Chipman, K., Hampson, E., & Kimura, D. (2002). A sex difference in reliance on vision during manual sequencing tasks. *Neuropschologia, 40*(7), 910–16.

Chipman, K., & Kimura, D. (1998). An investigation of sex differences on incidental memory for verbal and pictorial material. *Learning and Individual Differences, 10*(4), 259–72.

Chodorow, N. (1976). Oedipal Asymmetries and Heterosexual Knots. *Social Problems, 23*(4), 454–68.

Choi, J., & L'Hirondelle, N. (2005). Object location memory: A direct test of the verbal memory hypothesis. *Learning and Individual Differences, 15*(3), 237–45.

Choi, J., & Silverman, I. (2003). Processes underlying sex differences in route-learning strategies in children and adolescents. *Personality and Individual Differences, 34*(7), 1153–66.

Christensen, L. B. (1988). *Experimental Methodology* (4th ed.). Newton, MA: Allyn and Bacon, Inc.

Chuah, Y. M. L., & Maybery, M. T. (1999). Verbal and spatial short-term memory: Common sources of developmental change? *Journal of Experimental Child Psychology, 73*(1), 7–44.

Chynn, E. W., Garrod, A., Demick, J., & Devos, E. (1991). Correlations among Field Dependence-Independence, Sex, Sex-Role Stereotype, and Age of Preschoolers. *Perceptual and Motor Skills, 73*(3), 747–56.

Cocchini, G., Logie, R. H., Della Sala, S., MacPherson, S. E., & Baddeley, A. (2002). Concurrent performance of two memory tasks: Evidence for domain-specific working memory systems. *Memory and Cognition, 30*(7), 1086–95.

Cohen, M. S., Kosslyn, S. M., Breiter, H. C., DiGirolamo, G. J., Thompson, W. L., Anderson, A. K., *et al.* (1996). Changes in cortical activity during mental rotation – A mapping study using functional MRI. *Brain, 119*(1), 89–100.

Collaer, M. L., & Hines, M. (1995). Human Behavioral Sex-Differences – a Role for Gonadal-Hormones During Early Development. *Psychological Bulletin, 118*(1), 55–107.

Collaer, M. L., & Nelson, J. D. (2002). Large visuospatial sex difference in line judgment: Possible role of attentional factors. *Brain and Cognition, 49*(1), 1–12.

Colley, A., Ball, J., Kirby, N., Harvey, R., & Vingelen, I. (2002). Gender-linked differences in everyday memory performance: Effort makes the difference. *Sex Roles, 47*(11–12), 577–82.

Collins, D. W., & Kimura, D. (1997). A large sex difference on a two-dimensional mental rotation task. *Behavioral Neuroscience, 111*(4), 845–9.

Colom, R., Contreras, J., Arend, I., Leal, O. G., & Santacreu, J. (2004). Sex differences in verbal reasoning are mediated by sex differences in spatial ability. *Psychological Record, 54*(3), 365–72.

Colom, R., Flores-Mendoza, C., & Rebollo, I. (2003). Working memory and intelligence. *Personality and Individual Differences, 34*(1), 33–9.

Colom, R., & Garcia-Lopez, O. (2002). Sex differences in fluid intelligence among high school graduates. *Personality and Individual Differences, 32*(3), 445–51.

Colom, R., & Lynn, R. (2004). Testing the developmental theory of sex differences in intelligence on 12-18 year olds. *Personality and Individual Differences, 36*(1), 75–82.

Colom, R., Quiroga, M. A., & Juan-Espinosa, M. (1999). Are cognitive sex differences disappearing? Evidence from Spanish populations. *Personality and Individual Differences, 27*(6), 1189–95.

Colom, R., Rebollo, I., Palacios, A., Juan-Espinosa, M., & Kyllonen, P. C. (2004). Working memory is (almost) perfectly predicted by g. *Intelligence, 32*(3), 277–96.

Coney, J., & Fitzgerald, J. (2000). Gender differences in the recognition of laterally presented affective nouns. *Cognition and Emotion, 14*(3), 325–39.

Conway, A. R. A., Kane, M. J., & Engle, R. W. (2003). Working memory capacity and its relation to general intelligence. *Trends in Cognitive Sciences, 7*(12), 547–52.

Corballis, M. C. (1997). Mental rotation and the right hemisphere. *Brain and Language, 57*(1), 100–21.

Coren, S. (1994). Methodological Problems in Determining the Relationship between Handedness and Immune-System Function. *Brain and Cognition, 26*(2), 168–73.

Corey, D. M., Hurley, M. M., & Foundas, A. L. (2001). Right and left handedness defined – A multivariate approach using hand preference and hand performance measures. *Neuropsychiatry Neuropsychology and Behavioral Neurology, 14*(3), 144–52.

Cornoldi, C., & Vecchi, T. (2003). *Visuo-Spatial Working Memory and Individual Differences.* Hove: Psychology Press.

Cowan, R. L., Frederick, B. D., Rainey, M., Levin, J. M., Maas, L. C., Bang, J., *et al.* (2000). Sex differences in response to red and blue light in human primary visual cortex: a bold fMRI study. *Psychiatry Research-Neuroimaging, 100*(3), 129–38.

Crane, M., & Markus, H. (1982). Gender Identity – the Benefits of a Self-Schema Approach. *Journal of Personality and Social Psychology, 43*(6), 1195–7.

Crawford, M., & Chaffin, R. (1997). The Meanings of Difference: Cognition in Social and Cultural Context. In P. J. Caplan, M. Crawford, J. S. Hyde & J. T. E. Richardson (Eds), *Gender Differences in Human Cognition* (pp. 81–130). Oxford: Oxford University Press.

Crognale, M. A. (2002). Development, maturation and aging of chromatic visual pathways: VEP results. *Journal of Vision, 2*(6), 438–50.

Crovitz, H. F., & Zener, K. (1962). A group-test for assessing hand- and eye-dominance. *American Journal of Psychology, 75*(2), 271–6.

Crucian, G. P., & Berenbaum, S. A. (1998). Sex Differences in Right Hemisphere Tasks. *Brain and Cognition, 36*(3), 377–89.

Csatho, A., Osvath, A., Bicsak, E., Karadi, K., Manning, J., & Kallai, J. (2003). Sex role identity related to the ratio of second to fourth digit length in women. *Biological Psychology, 62*(2), 147–56.

Csatho, A., Osvath, A., Karadi, K., Bicsak, T., Manning, J., & Kallai, J. (2001). Spatial navigation related to the ratio of second to fourth digit length in women. *Learning and Individual Differences, 13*(3), 239–49.

Cummins, D. D., & Cummins, R. (1999). Biological preparedness and evolutionary explanation. *Cognition, 73*(3), B37–B53.

Dabbs Jr, J. M., Chang, E. L., Strong, R. A., & Milun, R. (1998). Spatial Ability, Navigation Strategy, and Geographic Knowldege Among Men and Women. *Evolution and Human Behavior, 19*(2), 89–98.

Daneman, M., & Carpenter, P. A. (1980). Individual Differences in working memory and reading. *Journal of Verbal Learning and Verbal Behavior, 19*(4), 450–66.

Davis, P. J. (1999). Gender differences in autobiographical memory for child-hood emotional experiences. *Journal of Personality and Social Psychology, 76*(3), 498–510.

De Beni, R., & Palladino, P. (2000). Intrusion errors in working memory tasks – Are they related to reading comprehension ability? *Learning and Individual Differences, 12*(2), 131–43.

De Lisi, R., & Wolford, J. L. (2002). Improving children's mental rotation accuracy with computer game playing. *Journal of Genetic Psychology, 163*(3), 272–82.

De Luca, C. R., Wood, S. J., Anderson, V., Buchanan, J. A., Proffitt, T. M., Mahony, K., *et al.* (2003). Normative data from the Cantab. I: Development of executive function over the lifespan. *Journal of Clinical and Experimental Neuropsychology, 25*(2), 242–54.

Deary, I. J. (2001). *Intelligence: A very short introduction.* New York: Oxford University Press.

Deaux, K., & Major, B. (1987). Putting Gender into Context – an Inter-active Model of Gender-Related Behavior. *Psychological Review, 94*(3), 369–89.

Declerck, C., & De Brabander, B. (2002). Sex differences in susceptibility to the Poggendorff illusion. *Perceptual and Motor Skills, 94*(1), 3–8.

deJonge, P., & deJong, P. F. (1996). Working memory, intelligence and reading ability in children. *Personality and Individual Differences, 21*(6), 1007–20.

Delgado, A. R., & Prieto, G. (1996). Sex differences in visuospatial ability: Do performance factors play such an important role? *Memory & Cognition, 24*(4), 504–10.

Delgado, A. R., & Prieto, G. (2003). Cognitive mediators and sex-related differences in mathematics. *Intelligence, 32*(1), 25–32.

Della Sala, S., Gray, C., Baddeley, A., Allamano, N., & Wilson, L. (1999). Pattern span: a tool for unwelding visuo-spatial memory. *Neuropsychologia, 37*(10), 1189–99.

Demont, E., & Botzung, A. (2003). The contribution of phonological awareness and working memory to reading disabilities: A longitudinal study of dyslexics and beginning readers. *Annee Psychologique, 103*(3), 377–409.

Department for Education and Skills (1999) (Data File) Available from the DfES statistics website retrieved June 2, 2006 from http://www.dfes.gov.uk/

Department for Education and Skills (2001) (Data File) Available from the DfES statistics website retrieved June 2, 2006 from http://www.dfes.gov.uk/

Department for Education and Skills (2002) (Data File) Available from the DfES statistics website retrieved June 4, 2006 from http://www.dfes.gov.uk/

Deregowski, J. B., Shepherd, J. W., & Slaven, G. A. (1997). Sex differences on Bartel's task: An investigation into perception of real and depicted distances. *British Journal of Psychology, 88*(4), 637–51.

Dest, D. o. E., Science and Training, Australia. (2005). Selected higher education staff statistics, 2003 (Publication no http://www.dest.gov.au/sectors/higher_education/publications_resources/profiles/staff_2003_selected_higher_education_statistics.htm). Retrieved August 20, 2005.

DeStefano, D., & LeFevre, J. A. (2004). The role of working memory in mental arithmetic. *European Journal of Cognitive Psychology, 16*(3), 353–86.

Deutsch, G., Bourbon, W. T., Papanicolaou, A. C., & Eisenberg, H. M. (1988). Visuospatial Tasks Compared Via Activation of Regional Cerebral Blood-Flow. *Neuropsychologia, 26*(3), 445–52.

Dittmar, M. L., Warm, J. S., Dember, W. N., & Ricks, D. F. (1993). Sex-Differences in Vigilance Performance and Perceived Workload. *Journal of General Psychology, 120*(3), 309–22.

Dror, I. E., & Kosslyn, S. M. (1994). Mental-Imagery and Aging. *Psychology and Aging, 9*(1), 90–102.

Ducommun, C. Y., Murray, M. M., Thut, G., Bellmann, A., Viaud-Delmon, I., Clarke, S., *et al.* (2002). Segregated processing of auditory motion and auditory location: An ERP mapping study. *Neuroimage, 16*(1), 76–88.

Duff, S. C., & Logie, R. H. (2001). Processing and storage in working memory span. *The Quarterly Journal of Experimental Psychology, 54A*(1), 31–48.

Duff, S. J., & Hampson, E. (2001). A sex difference on a novel spatial working memory task in humans. *Brain and Cognition, 47*(3), 470–93.

Durkin, K. (1987). Social Cognition and Social Context in the Construction of Sex Differences. In M. A. Baker (Ed.), *Sex Differences in Human Performance* (pp. 141–70). Chichester: John Wiley & Sons, Ltd.

Dutke, S., & Stober, J. (2001). Test anxiety, working memory, and cognitive performance: Supportive effects of sequential demands. *Cognition & Emotion, 15*(3), 381–9.

Eals, M., & Silverman, I. (1994). The hunter-gatherer theory of spatial sex differences: Proximate factors mediating the female advantage in recall of object arrays. *Ethology and Sociobiology, 15*(2), 95–105.

Eccles, J. S. (1987). Gender-Roles and Womens Achievement-Related Decisions. *Psychology of Women Quarterly, 11*(2), 135–71.

Eccles, J. S., & Wigfield, A. (2002). Motivation, beliefs, values and goals. *Annual Review of Psychology, 53*, 109–32.

Ecuyer-Dab, I., & Robert, M. (2004). Have sex differences in spatial ability evolved from male competition for mating and female concern for survival? *Cognition, 91*(3), 221–57.

Edwards, R., & Hamilton, M. A. (2004). You Need to Understand My Gender Role: An Empirical Test of Tannen's Model of Gender and Communication. *Sex Roles, 50*(7/8), 491–504.

Elias, L. J., Bryden, M. P., & Bulman-Fleming, M. B. (1998). Footedness is a better predictor than is handedness of emotional lateralization. *Neuropsychologia, 36*(1), 37–43.

Ellis, L., & Ficek, C. (2001). Color preferences according to gender and sexual orientation. *Personality and Individual Differences, 31*(8), 1375–9.

Embretson, S. E. (1995). The Role of Working-Memory Capacity and General Control Processes in Intelligence. *Intelligence, 20*(2), 169–89.

Engle, R. W., Tuholski, S. W., Laughlin, J. E., & Conway, A. R. A. (1999). Working memory, short term memory, and general fluid intelligence: A latent-variable approach. *Journal of Experimental Psychology: General, 128*(3), 309–331.

Epstein, H. T. (2001). An Outline of the Role of Brain in Human Cognitive Development. *Brain and Cognition, 45*(1), 44–51.

Epting, L. K., & Overman, W. H. (1998). Sex-sensitive tasks in men and women: A search for performance fluctuations across the menstrual cycle. *Behavioral Neuroscience, 112*(6), 1304–17.

Eysenck, M. W. (1994). *Individual differences: Normal and abnormal*. Hove: Lawrence Erlbaum Associates Ltd.

Eysenck, M. W., & Calvo, M. G. (1992). Anxiety and performance: The processing efficiency theory. *Cognition & Emotion, 6*(6), 409–34.

Farsides, T., & Woodfield, R. (2003). Individual Differences and undergraduate academic success: the roles of personality, intelligence and application. *Personality and Individual Differences, 34*(7), 1225–43.

Fausto-Sterling, A. (1992). *Myths of Gender*. New York: Basic Books.

Feingold, A. (1988). Cognitive Gender Differences are Disappearing. *American Psychologist, 43*(2), 95–103.

Fennema, E., & Peterson, P. (1985). Autonomous Learning Behavior: A Possible Explanation of Gender-Related Differences in Mathematics. In L. C. Wilkinson & C. B. Marrett (Eds), *Gender Influences in Classroom Interactions* (pp. 17–35): Academic Press.

Fennema, E., Peterson, P. L., Carpenter, T. P., & Lubinski, C. A. (1990). Teachers' attribution and beliefs about girls, boys and mathematics. *Educational Studies in Mathematics, 21*(1), 55–69.

Ferrini-Mundy, J. (1987). Spatial Training For Calculus Students: Sex Differences in Achievement and in Visualization Ability. *Journal for Research in Mathematics Education, 18*(2), 126–40.

Fink, B., Manning, J. T., Neave, N., & Grammer, K. (2004). Second to fourth digit ratio and facial asymmetry. *Evolution and Human Behavior, 25*(2), 125–32.

Fink, B., Neave, N., & Manning, J. T. (2003). Second to fourth digit ratio, body mass index, waist-to-hip ratio, and waist-to-chest ratio: their relationships in heterosexual men and women. *Annals of Human Biology, 30*(6), 728–38.

Finkel, D., & Pedersen, N. L. (2004). Processing speed and longitudinal trajectories of change for cognitive abilities: The Swedish Adoption/Twin Study of Aging. *Aging Neuropsychology and Cognition, 11*(2–3), 325–45.

Fisk, J. E., & Sharp, C. A. (2003). The role of the executive system in visuospatial memory functioning. *Brain and Cognition, 52*(3), 364–81.

Flaherty, M. (2005). Gender differences in mental rotation ability in three cultures: Ireland, Ecuador and Japan. *Psychologia, 48*(1), 31–8.

Floyd, R. G., Evans, J. J., & McGrew, K. S. (2003). Relations between measures of Cattell-Horn-Carroll (CHC) cognitive abilities and mathematics achievement across the school-age years. *Psychology in the Schools, 40*(2), 155–71.

Fonda, S. J., Bertrand, R., O'Donnell, A., Longcope, C., & McKinlay, J. B. (2005). Age, hormones, and cognitive functioning among middle-aged and elderly men: Cross-sectional evidence from the Massachusetts male aging study. *Journals of Gerontology Series A: Biological Sciences and Medical Sciences, 60*(3), 385–90.

Forget, H., & Cohen, H. (1994). Life after Birth – the Influence of Steroid-Hormones on Cerebral Structure and Function Is Not Fixed Prenatally. *Brain and Cognition, 26*(2), 243–8.

Freud, S. (1910). The origin and development of psychoanalysis. *American Journal of Psychology, 21*, 181–96.

Friedman, L. (1995). The Space Factor in Mathematics – Gender Differences. *Review of Educational Research, 65*(1), 22–50.

Frost, J. A., Binder, J. R., Springer, J. A., Hammeke, T. A., Bellgowan, P. S. F., Rao, S. M., *et al.* (1999). Language processing is strongly left lateralized in both sexes – Evidence from functional MRI. *Brain, 122*(2), 199–208.

Fry, A. F., & Hale, S. (1996). Processing speed, working memory, and fluid intelligence: Evidence for a developmental cascade. *Psychological Science, 7*(4), 237–41.

Fry, A. F., & Hale, S. (2000). Relationships among processing speed, working memory, and fluid intelligence in children. *Biological Psychology, 54*(1), 1–34.

Furst, A. J., & Hitch, G. J. (2000). Separate roles for executive and phonological components of working memory in mental arithmetic. *Memory & Cognition, 28*(5), 774–82.

Galea, L. A. M., & Kimura, D. (1993). Sex differences in route learning. *Personality and Individual Differences, 14*(1), 53–65.

Gallagher, A. M., De Lisi, R., Holst, P. C., Morely, M., & Cahalan, M. (2000). Gender Differences in Advanced Mathematical Problem Solving. *Journal of Experimental Child Psychology, 75*(3), 165–90.

Gandour, J., Xu, Y. S., Wong, D., Dzemidzic, M., Lowe, M., Li, X. J., *et al.* (2003). Neural correlates of segmental and tonal information in speech perception. *Human Brain Mapping, 20*(4), 185–200.

Garden, S., Cornoldi, C., & Logie, R. H. (2002). Visuo-Spatial Working Memory in Navigation. *Applied Cognitive Psychology, 16*(1), 35–50.

Garlick, D. (2002). Understanding the nature of the general factor of intelligence: the role of individual differences in neural plasticity as an explanatory mechanism. *Psychological Review, 109*(1), 116–36.

Gathercole, S., & Pickering, S. J. (2000). Working memory deficits in children with low achievements in the national curriculum at 7 years of age. *British Journal of Educational Psychology, 70*(2), 177–94.

Gathercole, S. E. (1998). The development of memory. *Journal of Child Psychology and Psychiatry, 39*(1), 3–27.

Gathercole, S. E., Brown, L., & Pickering, S. J. (2003). Working memory assessments at school entry as longitudinal predictors of National Curriculum attainment levels. *Educational and Child Psychology, 20*(3), 109–22.

Gathercole, S. E., & Pickering, S. J. (2000). Assessment of working memory in six- and seven-year-old children. *Journal of Educational Psychology, 92*(2), 377–90.

Gathercole, S. E., Pickering, S. J., Ambridge, B., & Wearing, H. (2004). The structure of working memory from 4 to 15 years of age. *Developmental Psychology, 40*(2), 177–90.

Geary, D. C. (1995). Sexual selection and sex differences in spatial cognition. *Learning and Individual Differences, 7*(4), 53–65.

Geary, D. C. (1996). Sexual selection and sex differences in mathematical abilities. *Behavioral and Brain Sciences, 19*(2), 229–84.

Geary, D. C. (1998). *Male, Female, The Evolution of Human Sex Differences.* Washington: American Psychological Association.

Geary, D. C. (2004). Mathematics and learning disabilities. *Journal of Learning Disabilities, 37*(1), 4–15.

Geary, D. C., Saults, S. J., Liu, F., & Hoard, M. K. (2000). Sex Differences in Spatial Cognition, Computational Fluency, and Arithmetical Reasoning. *Journal of Experimental Child Psychology, 77*(4), 337–53.

Geerlings, M. I., Launer, L. J., de Jong, F. H., Ruitenberg, A., Stijnen, T., van Swieten, J. C., *et al.* (2003). Endogenous estradiol and risk of dementia in women and men: The Rotterdam Study. *Annals of Neurology, 53*(5), 607–15.

Geffen, G., Rosa, V., & Luciano, M. (2000). Sex differences in the perception of tactile simultaneity. *Cortex, 36*(3), 323–35.

George, Y. S. (2002). *Gender, Science and Technology in Higher Education and Research in Sweden: Five Years after National Policies Implementation.* American Association for the Advancement of Science.

Gerhardstein, P., & Rovee-Collier, C. (2002). The Development of Visual Search in Infants and Very Young Children. *Journal of Experimental Child Psychology, 81*(2), 194–215.

Geschwind, N., & Behan, P. (1984). Laterality, hormones and immunity. In N. Geschwind & Galaburda, A.M. (Eds), *Cerebral Dominance: the Biological Foundations* (pp. 211–24). Cambridge, MA: Harvard University Press.

Geschwind, N., & Galaburda, A. M. (1985a). Cerebral Lateralization – Biological Mechanisms, Associations, and Pathology 1. A Hypothesis and a Program for Research. *Archives of Neurology, 42*(5), 428–59.

Geschwind, N., & Galaburda, A. M. (1985b). Cerebral Lateralization – Biological Mechanisms, Associations, and Pathology 2. A Hypothesis and a Program for Research. *Archives of Neurology, 42*(6), 521–52.

Geschwind, N., & Galaburda, A. M. (1987). *Cerebral Lateralization: Biological Mechanisms, Pathologies and Associations.* Cambridge, MA: MIT Press.

Giambra, L. M., & Quilter, R. E. (1989). Sex-Differences in Sustained Attention across the Adult Life-Span. *Journal of Applied Psychology, 74*(1), 91–5.

Gibbs, R. B., & Aggarwal, P. (1998). Estrogen and basal forebrain cholinergic neurons: Implications for brain aging and Alzheimer's disease-related cognitive decline. *Hormones and Behavior, 34*(2), 98–111.

Ginn, S. R., & Stiehl, S. (1999). Effects of sex, gender schema, and gender-related activities on mental rotation. *Perceptual and Motor Skills, 88*(1), 342–50.

Goddard, L., Dritschel, B., & Burton, A. (1998). Gender differences in the dual-task effects on autobiographical memory retrieval during social problem solving. *British Journal of Psychology, 89*(4), 611–27.

Goldstein, D., Haldane, D., & Mitchell, C. (1990). Sex differences in visual-spatial ability: The role of performance factors. *Memory and Cognition, 18*(5), 546–50.

Goldstein, E. B. (2002). *Sensation and Perception* (6th ed.). Pacific Grove: Wadsworth.

Good, C., Aronson, J., & Inzlicht, M. (2003). Improving adolescents' standardized test performance: An intervention to reduce the effects of stereotype threat. *Journal of Applied Developmental Psychology, 24*(6), 645–62.

Goren, C. C., Sarty, M., & Wu, P. Y. K. (1975). Visual Following and Pattern-Discrimination of Face-Like Stimuli by Newborn-Infants. *Pediatrics, 56*(4), 544–9.

Grabowska, A., Nowicka, A., & Szymanska, O. (1999). Sex related effect of unilateral brain lesions on the perception of the Mueller-Lyer illusion. *Cortex, 35*(2), 231–41.

Greenough, W. T., Black, J. E., & Wallace, C. S. (1987). Experience and Brain-Development. *Child Development, 58*(3), 539–59.

Grimshaw, G. M., Sitarenios, G., & Finegan, J.-A. K. (1995). Mental Rotation at 7 Years: Relations with Prenatal Testosterone Levels and Spatial Play Experiences. *Brain and Cognition, 29*(1), 85–100.

Gron, G., Wunderlick, A. P., Spitzer, M., Tomczak, R., & Riepe, M. (2000). Brain activation during human navigation: gender-different neural networks as substrate of performance. *Nature Neuroscience, 3*(4), 404–7.

Gur, R. C., Alsop, D., Glahn, D., Petty, R., Swanson, C. L., Maldjian, J. A., *et al.* (2000). An fMRI study of sex differences in regional activation to a verbal and a spatial task. *Brain and Language, 74*(2), 157–70.

Gur, R. C., Gunning-Dixon, F., Bilker, W. B., & Gur, R. E. (2002). Sex differences in temporo-limbic and frontal brain volumes of healthy adults. *Cerebral Cortex, 12*(9), 998–1003.

Gur, R. C., Turetsky, B. I., Matsui, M., Yan, M., Bilker, W., Hughett, P., *et al.* (1999). Sex differences in brain gray and white matter in healthy young adults: Correlations with cognitive performance. *Journal of Neuroscience, 19*(10), 4065–72.

Hale, J. B., Fiorello, C. A., Bertin, M., & Sherman, R. (2003). Predicting math achievement through neuropsychological interpretation of WISC-III variance components. *Journal of Psychoeducational Assessment, 21*(4), 358–80.

Halpern, D. F. (1992). *Sex Differences in Cognitive Abilities* (2nd ed.). Hove: Lawrence Earlbaum.

Halpern, D. F. (1994). Evaluating Support for the Geschwind-Behan-Galaburda Model – with a Rubber Ruler and a Thumb on the Scale. *Brain and Cognition, 26*(2), 185–90.

Halpern, D. F. (1996). Sex, Brains, Hands and Spatial Cognition. *Developmental Review, 16*(3), 261–70.

Halpern, D. F. (2000). *Sex Differences in Cognitive Abilities* (3rd ed.). London: Lawrence Earlbaum.

Halpern, D. F. (2004). A cognitive-process taxonomy for sex differences in cognitive abilities. *Current Directions in Psychological Science, 13*(4), 135–9.

Halpern, D. F., & LaMay, M. L. (2000). The smarter sex: A critical review of sex differences in intelligence. *Educational Psychology Review, 12*(2), 229–46.

Halpern, D. F., & Tan, U. (2001). Stereotypes and steroids: Using a psychobiosocial model to understand cognitive sex differences. *Brain and Cognition, 45*(3), 392–414.

Halpern, D. F., & Wright, T. M. (1996). A process-oriented model of cognitive sex differences. *Learning and Individual Differences, 8*(1), 3–24.

Hamilton, C. J. (1995). Beyond sex differences in visuo-spatial processing: The impact of gender trait possession. *British Journal of Psychology, 86*(1), 1–20.

Hamilton, C. J., Coates, R. O., & Heffernan, T. (2003). What develops in visuo-spatial working memory development? *European Journal of Cognitive Psychology, 15*(1), 43–69.

Hamilton, C. J., Moss, M., Case, G., Kennedy, D., & Little, L. (2002). *Is the validity of the Bem Sex Role Inventory dependent upon the gender of the judge?* Paper presented at the British Psychological Society Annual Conference, Blackpool, UK.

Hamilton, C. J., & Wolsey, L. (2001). *Individual differences in executive development.* Paper presented at the BPS Cognitive Conference/ESCOP, University of Edinburgh, Edinburgh, Scotland.

Hampson, E. (1995). Spatial Cognition in Humans – Possible Modulation by Androgens and Estrogens. *Journal of Psychiatry & Neuroscience, 20*(5), 397–404.

Hampson, E., & Kimura, D. (1988). Reciprocal Effects of Hormonal Fluctuations on Human Motor and Perceptual-Spatial Skills. *Behavioral Neuroscience, 102*(3), 456–9.

Hampson, E., & Moffat, S. D. (1994). Is Testosterone Related to Spatial Cognition and Hand Preference in Humans. *Brain and Cognition, 26*(2), 255–66.

Hanley, J. R., Young, A. W., & Pearson, N. A. (1991). Impairment of the Visuospatial Sketch Pad. *Quarterly Journal of Experimental Psychology Section a-Human Experimental Psychology, 43*(1), 101–25.

Happé, F. G. E., Winner, E., & Brownell, H. (1998). The getting of wisdom: Theory of mind in old age. *Developmental Psychology, 34*(2), 358–62.

Hare-Mustin, R. T., & Marecek, J. (1994). Asking the right questions: feminist psychology and sex differences. *Feminism & Psychology, 4*(4), 531–7.

Hargens, L. L., & Long, J. S. (2002). Demographic inertia and women's representation among faculty in higher education. *Journal of Higher Education, 73*(4), 494–517.

Hargreaves, D. J., Bates, H. M., & Foot, J. M. (1985). Sex-type labelling affects task performance. *British Journal of Social Psychology, 24*(2), 153–5.

Hargreaves, D. J., & Colley, A. M. (Eds). (1986). *The pyschology of sex roles*. London: Harper and Row Ltd.

Hausmann, M., Becker, C., Gather, U., & Güntürkün, O. (2002). Functional cerebral asymmetries during the menstrual cycle: a cross-sectional and longtitudinal analysis. *Neuropsychologia, 40*(7), 808–16.

Hausmann, M., & Güntürkün, O. (2000). Steroid fluctuations modify functional cerebral asymmetries: the hypothesis of progesterone-mediated interhemispheric decoupling. *Neuropsychologia, 38*(10), 1362–74.

Haxby, J. V., Hoffman, E. A., & Gobbini, M. I. (2002). Human neural systems for face recognition and social communication. *Biological Psychiatry, 51*(1), 59–67.

Hecht, H., & Proffitt, D. R. (1995). The Price of Expertise – Effects of Experience on the Water-Level Task. *Psychological Science, 6*(2), 90–5.

Hecht, S. A., & Shackelford, T. K. (2001). Pure short-term memory capacity has implications for understanding individual differences in math skills. *Behavioral and Brain Sciences, 24*(1), 124–5.

Heister, G., Landis, T., Regard, M., & Schroederheister, P. (1989). Shift of Functional Cerebral Asymmetry During the Menstrual-Cycle. *Neuropsychologia, 27*(6), 871–80.

Hellige, J. B., & Cumberland, N. (2001). Categorical and coordinate spatial processing: More on contributions of the transient/magnocellular visual system. *Brain and Cognition, 45*(2), 155–63.

Hepper, P. (2005). Unravelling our beginnings. *Psychologist, 18*(8), 474–7.

Herlitz, A., Airaksinen, E., & Nordstrom, E. (1999). Sex differences in episodic memory: The impact of verbal and visuospatial ability. *Neuropsychology, 13*(4), 590–7.

Herlitz, A., Nilsson, L. G., & Backman, L. (1997). Gender differences in episodic memory. *Memory & Cognition, 25*(6), 801–11.

Herlitz, A., & Yonker, J. E. (2002). Sex differences in episodic memory: The influence of intelligence. *Journal of Clinical and Experimental Neuropsychology, 24*(1), 107–14.

Hess, T. M., Auman, C., Colcombe, S. J., & Rahhal, T. A. (2003). The impact of stereotype threat on age differences in memory performance. *Journals of Gerontology Series B – Psychological Sciences and Social Sciences, 58*(1), 3–11.

Heywood, S., & Chessell, K. (1977). Expanding angles? *Perception, 6*(5), 571–82.

Higher Education Statistics Agency (1995) HESA Staff Record 1995 (Data file). Available from Higher Education Statistics Agency web site, retrieved June 28, 2006 from http://www.hesa.ac.uk

Higher Education Statistics Agency (2001) HESA Individualized Staff Record 2000/01 (Data file). Available from Higher Education Statistics Agency web site, retrieved June 28, 2006 from http://www.hesa.ac.uk

Higher Education Statistics Agency (2004) HESA SFR 70 (Data file). Available from Higher Education Statistics Agency web site, retrieved June 8, 2006 from http://www.hesa.ac.uk

Hines, M., Golombok, S., Rust, J., Johnston, K. J., & Golding, J. (2002). Testosterone during pregnancy and gender role behavior of preschool children: A longitudinal, population study. *Child Development, 73*(6), 1678–87.

Hirschy, A. J., & Morris, J. R. (2002). Individual differences in attributional style: the relational influence of self-efficacy, self-esteem, and sex role identity. *Personality and Individual Differences, 32*(2), 183–96.

Ho, H. Z., Gilger, J. W., & Brink, T. M. (1986). Effects of Menstrual-Cycle on Spatial Information-Processes. *Perceptual and Motor Skills, 63*(2), 743–51.

Holloway, W. (1994). Beyond sex differences: A project for feminist psychology. *Feminism & Psychology, 4*(4), 538–46.

Holt, C. L., & Ellis, J. B. (1998). Assessing the current validity of the Bem Sex-Role Inventory. *Sex Roles, 39*(11–12), 929–41.

Hooven, C. K., Chabris, C. F., Ellison, P. T., & Kosslyn, S. M. (2004). The relationship of male testosterone to components of mental rotation. *Neuropsychologia, 42*(6), 782–90.

Hopko, D. R., Ashcraft, M. H., Gute, J., Ruggiero, K. J., & Lewis, C. (1998). Mathematics anxiety and working memory: Support for the existence of deficient inhibition mechanism. *Journal of Anxiety Disorders, 12*(4), 343–55.

Horgan, T. G., Mast, M. S., Hall, J. A., & Carter, J. D. (2004). Gender differences in memory for the appearance of others. *Personality and Social Psychology Bulletin, 30*(2), 185–96.

Horney, K. (1924). On the genesis of the castration complex in women. *International Journal of Psychoanalysis, 5*(1), 50–65.

Hubel, D. H., & Wiesel, T. N. (1970). Cells Sensitive to Binocular Depth in Area-18 of Macaque Monkey Cortex. *Nature, 225*(5227), 41–2.

Hutchinson, S., Lee, L. H. L., Gaab, N., & Schlaug, G. (2003). Cerebellar volume of musicians. *Cerebral Cortex, 13*(9), 943–9.

Huttenlocher, P. R. (1979). Synaptic density in human frontal cortex. Developmental changes and the effect of aging. *Brain research, 163*(2), 195–205.

Hutton, U. M. Z., & Towse, J. N. (2001). Short-term memory and working memory as indices of children's cognitive skills. *Memory, 9*(4–6), 383–94.

Hyde, J. S. (1996). *Half the human experience: The psychology of women.* Massachusetts: D.C. Heath and Company.

Hyde, J. S. (2005). The gender similarities hypothesis. *American Psychologist, 60*(6), 581–92.

Hyde, J. S., Fennema, E., & Lamon, S. J. (1990). Gender Differences in Mathematics Performance: A Meta-Analysis. *Psychological Bulletin, 107*(2), 139–55.

Hyde, J. S., Fennema, E., Ryan, M., Frost, L. A., & Hopp, C. (1990). Gender Comparisons of Mathematics Attitudes and Affect – a Metaanalysis. *Psychology of Women Quarterly, 14*(3), 299–324.

Hyde, J. S., & Kling, K. C. (2001). Women, motivation, and achievement. *Psychology of Women Quarterly, 25*(4), 364–78.

Hyde, J. S., & Linn, M. C. (1988). Gender Differences in Verbal Ability: A Meta Analysis. *Psychological Bulletin, 104*(1), 53–69.

Isaacs, E. B., & Vargha-Khadem, F. (1989). Differential course of development of spatial and verbal memory span: A Normative study. *British Journal of Developmental Psychology, 7*(4), 377–80.

Ishigaki, H., & Miyao, M. (1994). Implications for Dynamic Visual-Acuity with Changes in Age and Sex. *Perceptual and Motor Skills, 78*(2), 363–69.

James, T. W., & Kimura, D. (1997). Sex Differences in Remembering the Locations of Objects in an Array: Location-Shifts Versus Location-Exchanges. *Evolution and Human Behavior, 18*(3), 155–63.

James, W. (1890). *The Principles of Pyschology.* New York: Dover.

Janowsky, J. S., Chavez, B., & Orwoll, E. (2000). Sex steroids modify working memory. *Journal of Cognitive Neuroscience, 12*(3), 407–14.

Johnson, B. W., McKenzie, K. J., & Hamm, J. R. (2002). Cerebral asymmetry for mental rotation: effects of response hand, handedness and gender. *Neuroreport, 13*(15), 1929–32.

Johnson, J. S., & Newport, E. L. (1989). Critical Period Effects in 2nd Language-Learning – the Influence of Maturational State on the Acquisition of English as a 2nd Language. *Cognitive Psychology, 21*(1), 60–99.

Johnson, M. (2000). Functional Brain Development in Infants: Elements of an Interactive Specialization Framework. *Child Development, 71*(1), 75–81.

Johnson, M. H., & Morton, J. (1991). *Biology and cognitive development: The case of face recognition.* Oxford: Blackwell.

Johnston, T. D., & Edwards, L. (2002). Genes, interactions, and the development of behavior. *Psychological Review, 109*(1), 26–34.

Jordan, K., Wurstenberg, T., Heinze, H. J., Peters, M., & Jancke, L. (2002). Women and men exhibit different cortical activation patterns during mental rotation tasks. *Neuropsychologia, 40*(13), 2397–408.

Josephs, R. A., Newman, M. L., Brown, R. P., & Beer, J. M. (2003). Status, testosterone, and human intellectual performance: Stereotype threat as status concern. *Psychological Science, 14*(2), 158–63.

Joshi, M. S., MacLean, M., & Carter, W. (1999). Children's journey to school: Spatial skills, knowledge and perceptions of the environment. *British Journal of Developmental Psychology, 17*(1), 125–39.

Judd, C. M., & Park, B. (1993). Definition and Assessment of Accuracy in Social Stereotypes. *Psychological Review, 100*(1), 109–28.

Just, M. A., & Carpenter, P. A. (1985). Cognitive Coordinate Systems – Accounts of Mental Rotation and Individual-Differences in Spatial Ability. *Psychological Review, 92*(2), 137–72.

Just, M. A., Carpenter, P. A., Maguire, M., Diwadkar, V., & McMains, S. (2001). Mental rotation of objects retrieved from memory: A functional MRI study of spatial processing. *Journal of Experimental Psychology-General, 130*(3), 493–504.

Kail, R. (1997). Processing time, imagery, and spatial memory. *Journal of Experimental Child Psychology, 64*(1), 67–78.

Kail, R., & Salthouse, T. A. (1994). Processing Speed as a Mental-Capacity. *Acta Psychologica, 86*(2–3), 199–225.

Kane, M. J., Bleckley, M. K., & Conway, A. R. A. (2001). A Controlled-Attention View of Working-Memory Capacity. *Journal of Experimental Psychology: General, 130*(2), 169–83.

Kane, M. J., & Engle, R. W. (2002). The role of prefrontal cortex in working-memory capacity, executive attention, and general fluid intelligence: An individual-differences perspective. *Psychonomic Bulletin & Review, 9*(4), 637–71.

Kane, M. J., Hambrick, D. Z., Tuholski, S. W., Wilhelm, O., Payne, T. W., & Engle, R. W. (2004). The generality of working memory capacity: A latent-variable approach to verbal and visuospatial memory span and reasoning. *Journal of Experimental Psychology-General, 133*(2), 189–217.

Katsurada, E., & Sugihara, Y. (1999). A Preliminary validation of the Bem Sex Role Inventory in Japanese culture. *Journal of Cross-Cultural Psychology, 30*(5), 641–5.

Keehner, M. M., Tendick, F., Meng, M. V., Anwar, H. P., Hegarty, M., Stoller, M. L., et al. (2004). Spatial ability, experience, and skill in laparoscopic surgery. *American Journal of Surgery, 188*(1), 71–75.

Keller, J. (2002). Blatant stereotype threat and women's math performance: Self-handicapping as a strategic means to cope with obtrusive negative performance expectations. *Sex Roles, 47*(3–4), 193–8.

Kerkman, D. D., Wise, J. C., & Harwood, E. A. (2000). Impossible "mental rotation" problems. A mismeasure of women's spatial abilities. *Learning and Individual Differences, 12*(3), 253–69.

Kessels, R. P. C., Kappelle, L. J., De Haan, E. H. F., & Postma, A. (2002). Lateralization of spatial-memory processes: evidence on spatial span, maze learning, and memory for object locations. *Neuropsychologia, 40*(8), 1465–73.

Kim, H.-B., Fisher, D. L., & Fraser, B. J. (2000). Classroom environment and teacher interpersonal behaviour in secondary science classes in Korea. *Evaluation and Research in Education, 14*(1), 3–22.

Kimura, D. (1992). Sex differences in the brain. *Scientific American, 267*(3), 119–25.

Kimura, D. (1999). *Sex and Cognition.* Cambridge, MA: The MIT Press.

Kiruma, D. (2002). Sex Hormones Influence Human Cognitive Pattern. *Neuroendocrinology Letters, 23*(4), 67–77.

Kimura, D., & Clarke, P. G. (2002). Women's advantage on verbal memory is not restricted to concrete words. *Psychological Reports, 91*(3), 1137–42.

Kitzinger, C. (1994). Should psychologists study sex differences? *Feminism & Psychology, 4*(4), 501–6.

Klein, R. M. (2000). Inhibition of return. *Trends in Cognitive Sciences, 4*(4), 138–47.

Klein, R. M., & MacInnes, W. J. (1999). Inhibition of return is a foraging facilitator in visual search. *Psychological Science, 10*(4), 346–52.

Klenberg, L., Korkman, M., & Lahti-Nuuttila, P. (2001). Differential development of attention and executive functions in 3-to 12-year-old Finnish children. *Developmental Neuropsychology, 20*(1), 407–28.

Kline, P. (1991). *Intelligence: the pyschometric View.* London: Routledge.

Knickmeyer, R., Baron-Cohen, S., Raggatt, P., & Taylor, K. (2005). Foetal testosterone, social relationships, and restricted interests in children. *Journal of Child Psychology and Psychiatry, 46*(2), 198–210.

Knickmeyer, R. C., Wheelwright, S., Taylor, K., Raggatt, P., Hackett, G., & Baron-Cohen, S. (2005). Gender-typed play and amniotic testosterone. *Developmental Psychology, 41*(3), 517–28.

Kohlberg, L. (1966). A cognitive-developmental analysis of children's sex-role concepts and attitudes. In E. E. Maccoby (Ed.), *The development of sex differences.* Stanford: Stanford University Press.

Kolb, B., Forgie, M., Gibb, R., Gorny, G., & Rowntree, S. (1998). Age, experience and the changing brain. *Neuroscience and Biobehavioral Reviews, 22*(2), 143–59.

Konrad, A. M., & Harris, C. (2002). Desirability of the Bem Sex-Role Inventory Items for Women and Men: A Comparison Between African Americans and European Americans. *Sex Roles, 47*(5/6), 259–71.

Koshino, H., Boese, G. A., & Ferraro, F. R. (2000). The relationship between cognitive ability and positive and negative priming in identity and spatial priming tasks. *Journal of General Psychology, 127*(4), 372–82.

Kosmidis, M. H., Vlahou, C. H., Panagiotaki, P., & Kiosseoglou, G. (2004). The verbal fluency task in the Greek population: Normative data, and clustering and switching strategies. *Journal of the International Neuropsychological Society, 10*(2), 164–72.

Kosslyn, S. M. (1980). *Image and Mind.* Cambridge: Harvard University Press.

Kosslyn, S. M. (1994). *Image and Brain: The resolution of the imagery debate.* Massachusetts: The MIT Press.

Kovacs, I. (2000). Human development of perceptual organization. *Vision Research, 40*(10–12), 1301–10.

Kramer, J. H., Yaffe, K., Lengenfelder, J., & Delis, D. C. (2003). Age and gender interactions on verbal memory performance. *Journal of the International Neuropsychological Society, 9*(1), 97–102.

Kuhl, P. K., Williams, K. A., Lacerda, F., Stevens, K. N., & Lindblom, B. (1992). Linguistic Experience Alters Phonetic Perception in Infants by 6 Months of Age. *Science, 255*(5044), 606–8.

Kuklinski, R. S., & Weinstein, R. S. (2001). Classroom and Developmental Differences in a Path Model of Teacher Expectancy Effects. *Child Development, 72*(5), 1554–78.

Kumari, V., Gray, J. A., Gupta, P., Luscher, S., & Sharma, T. (2003). Sex differences in prepulse inhibition of the acoustic startle response. *Personality and Individual Differences, 35*(4), 733–42.

Laflamme, D., Pomerleau, A., & Malcuit, G. (2002). A comparison of fathers' and mothers' involvement in childcare and stimulation behaviors during free-play with their infants at 9 and 15 months. *Sex Roles, 47*(11–12), 507–18.

Larrson, M., Lovden, M., & Nilsson, L. G. (2003). Sex differences in recollective experience for olfactory and verbal information. *Acta Psychologica, 112*(1), 89–103.

Lau, W.-C., & Lynn, R. (2001). Gender Differences on the Scholastic Aptitude Test, the American College Test and College Grades. *Educational Psychology, 21*(2), 133–6.

Law, D. J., Morrin, K. A., & Pellegrino, J. W. (1995). Training Effects and Working-Memory Contributions to Skill Acquisition in a Complex Coordination Task. *Learning and Individual Differences, 7*(3), 207–34.

Lawton, C. A., & Kallai, J. (2002). Gender differences in wayfinding strategies and anxiety about wayfinding: A cross-cultural comparison. *Sex Roles, 47*(9–10), 389–401.

Lawton, C. A., & Morrin, K. A. (1999). Gender differences in pointing accuracy in computer-simulated 3D mazes. *Sex Roles, 40*(1), 73–83.

Lebrun, C. E. I., van der Schouw, Y. T., de Jong, F. H., Pols, H. A. P., Grobbee, D. E., & Lamberts, S. W. J. (2005). Endogenous oestrogens are related to cognition in healthy elderly women. *Clinical Endocrinology, 63*(1), 50–5.

Lee, K. M., & Kang, S. Y. (2002). Arithmetic operation and working memory: differential suppression in dual tasks. *Cognition, 83*(3), B63–B68.

Lehnung, M., Leplow, B., Haaland, V. O., Mehdorn, M., & Ferstl, R. (2003). Pointing accuracy in children is dependent on age, sex and experience. *Journal of Environmental Psychology, 23*(4), 419–25.

Lessov-Schlaggar, C. N., Reed, T., Swan, G. E., Krasnow, R. E., DeCarli, C., Marcus, R., *et al.* (2005). Association of sex steroid hormones with brain morphology and cognition in healthy elderly men. *Neurology, 65*(10), 1591–96.

Levine, S. C., Huttenlocher, J., Taylor, A., & Langrock, A. (1999). Early Sex Differences in Spatial Skill. *Developmental Psychology, 35*(4), 940–9.

Lewin, C., & Herlitz, A. (2002). Sex differences in face recognition – Women's faces make the difference. *Brain and Cognition, 50*(1), 121–8.

Li, S. C. (2003). Biocultural orchestration of developmental plasticity across levels: The interplay of biology and culture in shaping the mind and behavior across the life span. *Psychological Bulletin, 129*(2), 171–94.

Ling, J., Hamilton, C., & Heffernan, T. (2006). Sex differences in the Poggendorff illusion: identifying the locus of the effect. *Perceptual and Motor Skills, 102*(1), 142–46.

Linn, M. C., & Petersen, A. C. (1985). Emergence and Characterization of Sex-Differences in Spatial Ability – a Meta-Analysis. *Child Development, 56*(6), 1479–98.

Lips, H. M. (1993). *Sex and Gender: An introduction.* Mountain View: Mayfield Publishing company.

Livesey, D. J., & Inyili, D. (1996). A Gender Difference in Visual-Spatial Ability in 4-Year-Old Children: Effects on Performance of a Kinesthetic Acuity Task. *Journal of Experimental Child Psychology, 63*(2), 436–46.

Logie, R. H. (1995). *Visuo-Spatial Working Memory.* Hove: Lawrence Earlbaum Associates, Publishers.

Logie, R. H., Venneri, A., Della Sala, S., Redpath, T. W., & Marshall, I. (2003). Brain activation and the phonological loop: The impact of rehearsal. *Brain and Cognition, 53*(2), 293–6.

Loring-Meier, S., & Halpern, D. F. (1999). Sex differences in visuospatial working memory: Components of cognitive processing. *Psychonomic Bulletin & Review, 6*(3), 464–71.

Luciana, M., & Nelson, C. A. (1998). The functional emergence of prefrontally-guided working memory systems in four- to eight-year-old children. *Neuropsychologia, 36*(3), 273–93.

Lynn, R., Allik, J., Pullmann, H., & Laidra, K. (2004a). Sex differences on the progressive matrices among adolescents: some data from Estonia. *Personality and Individual Differences, 36*(6), 1249–55.

Lynn, R., Backhoff, E., & Contreras-Nino, L. A. (2004b). Sex differences on g, reasoning and visualisation tested by the progressive matrices among 7–10 year olds: some normative data for Mexico. *Personality and Individual Differences, 36*(4), 779–87.

Lynn, R., Fergusson, D. M., & Horwood, L. J. (2005). Sex differences on the WISC-R in New Zealand. *Personality and Individual Differences, 39*(1), 103–14.

Lynn, R., & Irwing, P. (2002). Sex differences in general knowledge, semantic memory and reasoning ability. *British Journal of Psychology, 93*(4), 545–56.

Lynn, R., & Mau, W. C. (2001). Ethnic and sex differences in the predictive validity of the scholastic achievement test for college grades. *Psychological Reports, 88*(3), 1099–104.

Lynn, R., & Tse-Chan, P. W. (2003). Sex differences on the progressive matrices: Some data from Hong Kong. *Journal of Biosocial Science, 35*(1), 145–50.

Lytton, H. (2000). Toward a model of family-environmental and child-biological influences on development. *Developmental Review, 20*(1), 150–79.

McCafferty, L. E., & Hamilton, C. J. (2005). *Visuo-spatial working memory competencies in individuals with Prader-Willi Syndrome.* Paper presented at the Xth European Conference in Imagery and Cognition, St Andrews University, Scotland.

Mackintosh, N. J., & Bennett, E. S. (2003). The fractionation of working memory maps onto different components of intelligence. *Intelligence, 31*(6), 519–31.

MacPherson, A. C., Klein, R. M., & Moore, C. (2003). Inhibition of return in children and adolescents. *Journal of Experimental Child Psychology, 85*(4), 337–51.

MacPherson, S. E., Phillips, L. H., & Della Sala, S. (2002). Age, executive function, and social decision making: A dorsolateral prefrontal theory of cognitive aging. *Psychology and Aging, 17*(4), 598–609.

Maeder, P. P., Meuli, R. A., Adriani, M., Bellmann, A., Fornari, E., Thiran, J. P., *et al.* (2001). Distinct pathways involved in sound recognition and localization: A human fMRI study. *Neuroimage, 14*(4), 802–16.

Magnotta, V. A., Andreasen, N. C., Schultz, S. K., Harris, G., Cizadlo, T., Heckel, D., *et al.* (1999). Quantitative In Vivo Measurement of Gyrification in the Human Brain: Changes Associated with Aging. *Cerebral Cortex, 9*(2), 151–60.

Majeres, R. L. (1999). Sex differences in phonological processes: Speed matching and word reading. *Memory and Cognition, 27*(2), 246–53.

Maki, P. M. (2005). Estrogen effects on the hippocampus and frontal lobes. *International Journal of Fertility and Womens Medicine, 50*(2), 67–71.

Manger, T., & Eikeland, O.-J. (1998). The effects of spatial visualisation and students' sex on mathematical achievement. *British Journal of Psychology, 89*(1), 17–26.

Manning, J. T., Baron-Cohen, S., Wheelwright, S., & Sanders, G. (2001). The 2nd to 4th digit ratio and autism. *Developmental Medicine and Child Neurology, 43*(3), 160–4.

Manning, J. T., Bundred, P. E., Newton, D. J., & Flanagan, B. F. (2003). The second to fourth digit ratio and variation in the androgen receptor gene. *Evolution and Human Behavior, 24*(6), 399–405.

Manning, J. T., Martin, S., Trivers, R. L., & Soler, M. (2002). 2nd to 4th digit ratio and offspring sex ratio. *Journal of Theoretical Biology, 217*(1), 93–5.

Manning, J. T., Scutt, D., Wilson, J., & Lewis-Jones, D. I. (1998). The ratio of 2nd to 4th digit length: a predictor of sperm numbers and concentrations of testosterone, luteinizing hormone and oestrogen. *Human Reproduction,* *13*(11), 3000–4.

Manning, J. T., & Taylor, R. P. (2001). Second to fourth digit ratio and male ability in sport: implications for sexual selection in humans. *Evolution and Human Behavior, 22*(1), 61–9.

Marks, D. F. (1973). Visual Imagery Differences in Recall of Pictures. *British Journal of Psychology, 64*(Feb), 17–24.

Markus, H., Crane, M., Bernstein, S., & Siladi, M. (1982). Self-Schemas and Gender. *Journal of Personality and Social Psychology, 42*(1), 38–50.

Martin, C. L. (1993). New Directions for Investigating Childrens Gender Knowledge. *Developmental Review, 13*(2), 184–204.

Martin, C. L., & Halverson, C. F. (1983). Gender Constancy – a Methodological and Theoretical-Analysis. *Sex Roles, 9*(7), 775–90.

Martin, C. L., Ruble, D. N., & Szkrybalo, J. (2002). Cognitive theories of early gender development. *Psychological Bulletin, 128*(6), 903–33.

Marx, D. M., & Roman, J. S. (2002). Female role models: Protecting women's math test performance. *Personality and Social Psychology Bulletin, 28*(9), 1183–93.

Massa, L. J., Mayer, R. E., & Bohon, L. M. (2005). Individual differences in gender role beliefs influence spatial ability test performance. *Learning and Individual Differences, 15*(2), 99–111.

Masters, M. S. (1998). The gender difference on the Mental Rotations test is not due to performance factors. *Memory & Cognition, 26*(3), 444–8.

Mateer, C. A., Polen, S. B., & Ojemann, G. A. (1982). Sexual Variation in Cortical Localization of Naming as Determined by Stimulation Mapping. *Behavioral and Brain Sciences, 5*(2), 310–11.

Maylor, E. A., Allison, S., & Wing, A. M. (2001). Effects of spatial and nonspatial cognitive activity on postural stability. *British Journal of Psychology, 92*(2), 319–38.

Maylor, E. A., Moulson, J. M., Muncer, A. M., & Taylor, L. A. (2002). Does performance on theory of mind tasks decline in old age? *British Journal of Psychology, 93*(4), 465–85.

McBurney, D. H., Gaulin, S. J. C., Devineni, T., & Adams, C. (1997). Superior spatial memory of women: Stronger evidence for the gathering hypothesis. *Evolution and Human Behavior, 18*(3), 165–74.

McCarthy, M. M., & Konkle, A. T. M. (2005). When is a sex difference not a sex difference? *Frontiers in Neuroendocrinology, 26*(2), 85–102.

McGee, M. G. (1979). Human spatial abilities: Psychometric studies and environmental, genetic, hormonal and neurogenic influences. *Psychologial Bulletin, 86*, 889–918.

McGivern, R. F., Huston, J. P., Byrd, D., King, T., Siegle, G. J., & Reilly, J. (1997). Sex differences in visual recognition memory: Support for a sex-related difference in attention in adults and children. *Brain and Cognition, 34*(3), 323–36.

McGowan, J. F., & Duka, T. (2000). Hemispheric lateralisation in a manual-verbal task combination: the role of modality and gender. *Neuropsychologia, 38*(7), 1018–27.

McGuinness, D. (1985). *When children don't learn.* New York: Basic Books, Inc.

McGuinness, D., & Morley, C. (1991). Sex differences in the development of visuo-spatial ability in pre-school children. *Journal of Mental Imagery, 15*(3–4), 143 –50.

McIntyre, R. B., Paulson, R. M., & Lord, C. G. (2003). Alleviating women's mathematics stereotype threat through salience of group achievements. *Journal of Experimental Social Psychology, 39*(1), 89–90.

McKeever, W. F. (1986). The Influences of Handedness, Sex, Familial Sinistrality and Androgyny on Language Laterality, Verbal-Ability, and Spatial Ability. *Cortex, 22*(4), 521–37.

McKeever, W. F., Cerone, L. J., & Chase-Carmichael, C. (2000). Developmental instability and right shift theory hypotheses concerning correlates of familial sinistrality: Negative findings. *Laterality, 5*(2), 97–110.

McKeever, W. F., & Deyo, R. A. (1990). Testosterone, Dihydrotestosterone, and Spatial Task Performances of Males. *Bulletin of the Psychonomic Society, 28*(4), 305–8.

McKeever, W. F., Rich, D. A., Murray, M. G., & Seitz, K. S. (1988). Handedness and Spatial Ability. *Bulletin of the Psychonomic Society, 26*(6), 522–3.

McManus, I. C. (1984). Genetics of handedness in relation to language disorder. *Advances in Neurology, 42*, 125–38.

McWilliams, W., Hamilton, C. J., & Muncer, S. J. (1997). On mental rotation in three dimensions. *Perceptual and Motor Skills, 85*(1), 297–8.

Medland, S. E., Geffen, G., & McFarland, K. (2002). Lateralization of speech production using verbal/manual dual tasks: meta-analysis of sex differences and practice effects. *Neuropsychologia, 40*(8), 1233–9.

Mehta, Z., & Newcombe, F. (1991). A Role for the Left-Hemisphere in Spatial Processing. *Cortex, 27*(2), 153–67.

Mellanby, J., Martin, M., & O'Doherty, J. (2003). The 'gender gap' in final examination results at Oxford University. *British Journal of Psychology, 91*(3), 377–90.

Metsala, J. L. (1999). Young Children's Phonological Awareness and Nonword Repetition as a Function of Vocabulary Development. *Journal of Educational Psychology, 91*(1), 1–3.

Meyers-Levy, J. (1989). Gender differences in information processing: A selectivity interpretation. In P. Cafferata & A. M. Tybout (Eds), *Cognitive and affective responses to advertising.* (pp. 219–60). Lexington, MA: Lexington Books.

Miller, R. J. (2001). Gender differences in Ilusion Response: The influence of spatial strategy and sex ratio. *Sex Roles, 44*(3/4), 209–25.

Miller, H., & Bichsel, J. (2004). Anxiety, working memory, gender, and math performance. *Personality and Individual Differences, 37*(3), 591–606.

Millslagle, D. G. (2000). Visual activity and coincidence anticipation timing by experienced and inexperienced womenplayers of fast pitch softball. *Perceptual and Motor Skills, 90*(2), 498–504.

Milner, A. D., & Goodale, M. A. (1995). *The visual brain in action*. Oxford: Oxford University Press.

Milner, B. (1971). Interhemispheric Differences in Localization of Psychological Processes in Man. *British Medical Bulletin, 27*(3), 272–7.

Miyake, A., Friedman, N. P., Emerson, M. J., Witzki, A. H., Howerter, A., & Wager, T. D. (2000). The Unity and Diversity of Executive Functions and Their Contributions to Complex "Frontal Lobe" Tasks: A Latent variable Analysis. *Cognitive Psychology, 41*(1), 49–100.

Miyake, A., Friedman, N. P., Rettinger, D. A., Shah, P., & Hegarty, P. (2001a). How are visuospatial working memory, executive functioning, and spatial abilities related? A latent-variable analysis. *Journal of Experimental Psychology-General, 130*(4), 621–40.

Miyake, A., Witzki, A. H., & Emerson, M. J. (2001b). Field dependence-independence from a working memory perspective: A dual-task investigation of the Hidden Figures Test. *Memory, 9*(4–6), 445–57.

Moffat, S. D., & Hampson, E. (1996). A curvilinear relationship between testosterone and spatial cognition in humans: Possible influence of hand preference. *Psychoneuroendocrinology, 21*(3), 323–37.

Mondloch, C. J., Le Grand, R., & Maurer, D. (2002). Configural face processing develops more slowly than featural face processing. *Perception, 31*(5), 553–66.

Montello, D. R., Lovelace, K. L., Golledge, R. G., & Self, C. M. (1999). Sex-related differences and similarities in geographic and environmental spatial abilities. *Annals of the Association of American Geographers, 89*(3), 515–34.

Morra, S. (1994). Issues in Working memory Measurement: Testing for M Capacity. *International Journal of Behavioral Development, 17*(1), 143–59.

Morton, J., & Johnson, M. H. (1991). CONSPEC and CONLERN: a two-process theory of infant face recognition. *Psychological Review, 98*(2), 164–81.

Morton, N., & Morris, R. G. (1995). Image Transformation Dissociated from Visuospatial Working-Memory. *Cognitive Neuropsychology, 12*(7), 767–91.

Mullis, I. V. S., Martin, M. O., Gonzales, E. J., Gregory, E. J., Garden, R. A., O'Connor, A. M., *et al.* (1999). *Findings from IEA's Repeat of the Third International Mathematics and Science Study at the Eighth Grade*. Boston: International Study Center.

Murphy, J. M., & Gilligan, C. (1980). Moral Development in Late Adolescence and Adulthood – a Critique and Reconstruction of Kohlberg Theory. *Human Development, 23*(2), 77–104.

Nash, S. C. (1979). Sex Role as a Mediator of Intellectual Functioning. In M. A. Wittig & A. C. Petersen (Eds), *Sex-Related Differences in Cognitive Functioning*. (pp. 263–302). New York: Academic Press.

National Center for Education Statistics (2002) Historical Summary of Faculty, students, degrees, and finances in degree-granting institutions: 1869–1870 to 2000-01 (Data file). Available from National Center for Education Statistics web site, retrieved June 22, 2006 from http://www.nces.ed.gov

National Center for Education Statistics (2004) Digest of Education Statistics 2004 (Data file). Available from National Center for Education Statistics web site, retrieved June 20, 2006 from http://www.nces.ed.gov

Neale, J. M., & Liebert, R. M. (1986). *Science and Behavior: An Introduction to Methods of Research*. London: Prentice-Hall.

Neave, N., Hamilton, C., Hutton, L., Tildesley, N., & Pickering, A. T. (2005). Some evidence of a female advantage in object location memory using ecologically valid stimuli. *Human nature, 16*(2), 146–63.

Neave, N., Menaged, M., & Weightman, D. R. (1999). Sex differences in cognition: The role of testosterone and sexual orientation. *Brain and Cognition, 41*(3), 245–62.

Necka, E. (1992). Cognitive Analysis of Intelligence – the Significance of Working Memory Processes. *Personality and Individual Differences, 13*(9), 1031–46.

Nelson, C. A. (1995). The Ontogeny of Human-Memory – a Cognitive Neuroscience Perspective. *Developmental Psychology, 31*(5), 723–8.

Nelson, C. A. (2001). The Development and Neural Bases of Face Recognition. *Infant and Child Development, 10*(1–2), 3–18.

Neubauer, A. C., & Fink, A. (2003). Fluid intelligence and neural efficiency: effects of task complexity and sex. *Personality and Individual Differences, 35*(4), 811–27.

Newcombe, N., Bandura, M. M., & Taylor, D. G. (1983). Sex-Differences in Spatial Ability and Spatial Activities. *Sex Roles, 9*(3), 377–86.

Newcombe, N., & Dubas, J. S. (1992). A Longitudinal Study of Predictors of Spatial Ability in Adolescence Females. *Child Development, 63*(1), 37–46.

Nopoulos, P., Flaum, M., O'Leary, D., & Andreasen, N. C. (2000). Sexual dimorphism in the human brain: evaluation of tissue volume, tissue composition and surface anatomy using magnetic resonance imaging. *Psychiatry Research-Neuroimaging, 98*(1), 1–13.

Norman, J. F., Ross, H. E., Hawkes, L. M., & Long, J. R. (2003). Aging and the perception of speed. *Perception, 32*(1), 85–96.

Nowell, A., & Hedges, L. V. (1998). Trends in Gender Differences in Academic Achievement from 1960 to 1994: An analysis of Differences in Mean, Variance and Extreme Scores. *Sex Roles, 39*(1/2), 21–43.

Nyberg, L., Habib, R., & Herlitz, A. (2000). Brain activation during episodic memory retrieval: Sex differences. *Acta Psychologica, 105*(2–3), 181–94.

Nyborg, H. (1988). Mathematics, Animosity, and Sex-Hormones. *Behavioral and Brain Sciences, 11*(2), 206–7.

Nyborg, H. (1990). Sex hormones, brain development and spatio-perceptual strategies in Turner syndrome. In D. B. Berch & B. G. Bender (Eds), *Sex chromosome abnormalities and human behavior* (pp. 100–28). Washington: American Association for the Advancement of Science.

Oberg, C., Larsson, M., & Backman, L. (2002). Differential sex effects in olfactory functioning: The role of verbal processing. *Journal of the International Neuropsychological Society, 8*(5), 691–8.

O'Brien, L. T., & Crandall, C. S. (2003). Stereotype threat and arousal: Effects on women's math performance. *Personality and Social Psychology Bulletin, 29*(6), 782–9.

O'Laughlin, E. M., & Brubaker, B. S. (1998). Use of landmarks in cognitive mapping: Gender differences in self report versus performance. *Personality and Individual Differences, 24*(5), 595–601.

Oldfield, R. C. (1971). The assessment and analysis of handedness: the Edinburgh inventory. *Neuropsychologia, 9*(1), 97–113.

Orlofsky, J. L., & O'Heron, C. A. (1987). Development of a Short-Form Sex Role Behavior Scale. *Journal of Personality Assessment, 51*(2), 267–77.

Orsini, A., Grossi, D., Capitani, E., Laiacona, M., Papagno, C., & Vallar, G. (1987). Verbal and Spatial Immediate Memory Span – Normative Data from 1355 Adults and 1112 Children. *Italian Journal of Neurological Sciences, 8*(6), 539–48.

Osborne, J. W. (2001). Testing stereotype threat: Does anxiety explain race and sex differences in achievement? *Contemporary Educational Psychology, 26*(3), 291–310.

Palladino, P., Cornoldi, C., De Beni, R., & Pazzaglia, F. (2001). Working memory and updating processes in reading comprehension. *Memory & Cognition, 29*(2), 344–54.

Palmer, D. L., & Folds-Bennett, T. (1998). Performance on two attention tasks as a function of sex and competition. *Perceptual and Motor Skills, 86*(2), 363–70.

Parkin, A. J., & Java, R. I. (2000). Determinants of age-related memory loss. In T. J. Perfect E. A. Maylor (Eds), *Models of Cognitive Aging* (pp. 188–203). Oxford: Oxford University Press.

Parsons, T. D., Larson, P., Kratz, K., Thiebaux, M., Bluestein, B., Buckwalter, J. G., *et al.* (2004). Sex differences in mental rotation and spatial rotation in a virtual environment. *Neuropsychologia, 42*(4), 555–62.

Passolunghi, M. C., & Siegel, L. S. (2001). Short-term memory, working memory, and inhibitory control in children with difficulties in arithmetic problem solving. *Journal of Experimental Child Psychology, 80*(1), 44–57.

Pastells, A. A. I., & Roca, D. S. (2003). A comparative analysis of the phonological loop versus the visuo-spatial sketchpad in mental arithmetic tasks in 7–8 y.o. children. *Psicothema, 15*(2), 241–6.

Pattison, P., & Grieve, N. (1984). Do Spatial Skills Contribute to Sex Differences in Different Types of Mathematical Problems? *Journal of Educational Psychology, 76*(4), 678–89.

Paus, T., Collins, D. L., Evans, A. C., Leonard, G., Pike, B., & Zijdenbos, A. (2001). Maturation of white matter in the human brain: A review of magnetic resonance studies. *Brain Research Studies, 54*(3), 255–66.

Pazzaglia, F., & De Beni, R. (2001). Strategies of processing spatial information in survey and landmark-centred individuals. *European Journal of Cognitive Psychology, 13*(4), 493–508.

Pedhazur, E. J., & Tetenbaum, T. J. (1979). Bem Sex Role Inventory: A Theoretical and Methodological Critique. *Journal of Personality and Social Psychology, 37*(6), 996–1016.

Peters, M. (1997). Gender differences in intercepting a moving target by using a throw or button press. *Journal of Motor Behavior, 29*(4), 290–6.

Peters, M., & Campagnaro, P. (1996). Do women really excel over men in manual dexterity? *Journal of Experimental Psychology-Human Perception and Performance, 22*(5), 1107–12.

Peters, M., Jancke, L., Staiger, J. F., Schlaug, G., Huang, Y., & Steinmetz, H. (1998). Unsolved Problems in Comparing Brain Sizes in Homo Sapiens. *Brain and Cognition, 37*(2), 254–85.

Petrides, K. V., Chamorro-Premuzic, T., Frederickson, N., & Furnham, A. (2005). Explaining individual differences in scholastic behaviour and achievement. *British Journal of Educational Psychology, 75*(2), 239–55.

Pezaris, E., & Casey, M. B. (1991). Girls Who Use "Masculine" Problem Solving Strategies on a Spatial task: Proposed Genetic and Environmental Factors. *Brain and Cognition, 17*(1), 1–22.

Phillips, K., & Silverman, I. (1997). Differences in the relationship of menstrual cycle phase to spatial performance on two- and three-dimensional tasks. *Hormones and Behavior, 32*(3), 167–75.

Phillips, L. H., & Della Sala, S. D. (1998). Aging, Intelligence, And Anatomical Segregation In The Frontal Lobes. *Learning and Individual Differences, 10*(3), 217–43.

Phillips, L. H., & Hamilton, C. (2001). The working memory model in adult aging research. In J. Andrade (Ed.), *Working Memory in Perspective* (pp. 101–25). Hove: Psychology Press.

Phillips, L. H., MacPherson, S. E., & Della Sala, S. (2002). Age, cognition and emotion: the role of anatomical segregation in the frontal lobes. In J. Grafman (Ed.), *Handbook of Neuropsychology* (2nd ed., pp. 73–97). Amsterdam: Elsevier Science B.V.

Phillips, W. A., & Christie, D. F. M. (1977). Components of Visual Memory. *Quarterly Journal of Experimental Psychology, 29*(February), 117–33.

Piaget, J. (1967). *The child's conception of the world.* Totowa: Littlefield, Adams.

Piazza, M., & Dehaene, S. (2004). From Number Neurons to Mental Arithmetic: The Cognitive Neuroscience of Number sense. In M. S. Gazzaniga (Ed.), *The Cognitive Neurosciences* (pp. 865–76). Cambridge, Mass: MIT Press.

Pinkerton, J. V., & Henderson, V. W. (2005). Estrogen and cognition, with a focus on Alzheimer's disease. *Seminars in Reproductive Medicine, 23*(2), 172–9.

Podzebenko, K., Egan, G. F., & Watson, J. D. G. (2002). Widespread dorsal stream activation during a parametric mental rotation task, revealed with functional magnetic resonance imaging. *Neuroimage, 15*(3), 547–58.

Pomerleau, A., Bolduc, D., Malcuit, G., & Cossette, L. (1990). Pink or Blue – environmental gender stereotypes in the first two years of life. *Sex Roles, 22*(5–6), 359–67.

Porac, C. (1994). Anomalous Dominance, Incidence Rate Studies, and Other Methodological Issues. *Brain and Cognition, 26*(2), 206–10.

Porac, C., Coren, S., Girgus, J. S., & Verde, M. (1979). Visual geometric illusions: Unisex phenomena. *Perception, 8*(4), 401–12.

Postma, A., & De Haan, E. H. F. (1996). What Was Where? Memory for Object Locations. *The Quarterly Journal of Experimental Psychology, 49A*(1), 178–99.

Postma, A., Izendoorn, R., & De Haan, E. H. F. (1998). Sex differences in object location memory. *Brain and Cognition, 36*(3), 334–45.

Postma, A., Jager, G., Kessels, R. P. C., Koppeschaar, H. P. F., & van Honk, J. (2004). Sex differences for selective forms of spatial memory. *Brain and Cognition, 54*(1), 24–34.

Postma, A., Meyer, G., Tuiten, A., van Honk, J., Kessels, R. P. C., & Thijssen, J. (2000). Effects of testosterone administration on selective aspects of object-location memory in healthy young women. *Psychoneuroendocrinology, 25*(6), 563–75.

Postma, A., Winkel, J., Tuiten, A., & van Honk, J. (1999). Sex differences and menstrual cycle effects in human spatial memory. *Psychoneuroendocrinology, 24*(2), 175–92.

Poulin, M., O'Connell, R. L., & Freeman, L. M. (2004). Picture recall skills correlate with 2D : 4D ratio in women but not men. *Evolution and Human Behavior, 25*(3), 174–81.

Prieto, G., & Delgado, A. R. (1999). The role of instructions in the variability of sex-related differences in multiple-choice tests. *Personality and Individual Differences, 27*(6), 1067–77.

Prinzel, L. J., & Freeman, F. G. (1997). Task-specific sex differences in vigilance performance: Subjective workload and boredom. *Perceptual and Motor Skills, 85*(3), 1195–1202.

Pritchard, V. E., & Neumann, E. (2004). Negative Priming Effects in Children Engaged in Nonspatial Tasks: Evidence for early Development of an Intact Inhibitory Mechanism. *Developmental Psychology, 40*(2), 191–203.

Pryzgoda, J., & Chrisler, J. C. (2000). Definitions of gender and sex: The subtleties of meaning. *Sex Roles, 43*(7–8), 553–69.

Pugh, K. R., Shaywitz, B. A., Shaywitz, S. E., Shankweiler, D. P., Katz, L., Fletcher, J. M., *et al.* (1997). Predicting reading performance from neuroimaging profiles: The cerebral basis of phonological effects in printed word identification. *Journal of Experimental Psychology-Human Perception and Performance, 23*(2), 299–318.

Pulos, S. (1997). Explicit knowledge of gravity and the water-level task. *Learning and Individual Differences, 9*(3), 233–47.

Putz, D. A., Gaulin, S. J. C., Sporter, R. J., & McBurney, D. H. (2004). Sex hormones and finger length – What does 2D : 4D indicate? *Evolution and Human Behavior, 25*(3), 182–99.

Quaiser-Pohl, C., & Lehmann, W. (2002). Girls' spatial abilities: Charting the contributions of experiences and attitudes in different academic groups. *British Journal of Educational Psychology, 72*(2), 245–60.

Quartz, S. R. (1999). The constructivist brain. *Trends in Cognitive Sciences, 3*(2), 48–57.

Quartz, S. R., & Sejnowski, T. J. (1997). The neural basis of cognitive development: A constructivist manifesto. *Behavioral and Brain Sciences, 20*(4), 537–56.

Qubeck, W. J. (1997). Mean differences among subcomponents of Vandenberg's Mental Rotation Test. *Perceptual and Motor Skills, 85*(1), 323–32.

Radecki, C. M., & Jaccard, J. (1996). Gender-role differences in decision-making orientations and decision-making skills. *Journal of Applied Social Psychology, 26*(1), 76–94.

Rakover, S. S. (2002). Featural vs. configurational information in faces: A conceptual and empirical analysis. *British Journal of Psychology, 93*, 1–30.

Ragland, J. D., Coleman, A. R., Gur, R. C., Glahn, D. C., & Gur, R. E. (2000). Sex differences in brain-behavior relationships between verbal episodic memory and resting regional cerebral blood flow. *Neuropsychologia, 38*(4), 451–61.

Rammstedt, B., & Rammsayer, T. H. (2002). Gender differences in self-estimated intelligence and their relation to gender role orientation. *European Journal of Personality, 16*(5), 369–82.

Rammstedt, B., & Rammsayer, T. H. (2002). Self-estimated intelligence – Gender differences, relationship to psychometric intelligence and moderating effects of level of education. *European Psychologist, 7*(4), 275–84.

Raz, N., Gunning-Dixon, F., Head, D., Rodrigue, K. M., Williamson, A., & Acker, J. D. (2004). Aging, sexual dimorphism, and hemispheric asymmetry of the cerebral cortex: replicability of regional differences in volume. *Neurobiology of Aging, 25*(3), 377–96.

Reed, T. E., Vernon, P. A., & Johnson, A. M. (2004). Sex difference in brain nerve conduction velocity in normal humans. *Neuropsychologia, 42*(12), 1709–14.

Regan, B. C., Julliot, C., Simmen, B., Vienot, F., Charles-Dominique, P., & Mollon, J. D. (2001). Fruits, foliage and the evolution of primate colour vision. *Philosophical Transactions of the Royal Society of London Series B-Biological Sciences, 356* (1407), 229–83.

Reimers, S., & Maylor, E. A. (2005). Task switching across the life span: Effects of age on general and specific switch costs. *Developmental Psychology, 41*(4), 661–71.

Reio Jr, T. G., Czarnolewski, M., & Eliot, J. (2004). Handedness and spatial ability: Differential patterns of relationships. *Laterality, 9*(3), 339–58.

Rensink, R. A. (2002). Change detection. *Annual Review of Psychology, 53*, 245–77.

Resnick, S. M., & Maki, P. M. (2001). Effects of hormone replacement therapy on cognitive and brain aging. In *Selective Estrogen Receptor Modulators (Serms)* (Vol. 949, pp. 203–14).

Richardson, J. T. E. (1999). *Imagery*. Hove: Psychology Press.

Richardson, J. T. E., & Woodley, A. (2003). Another look at the role of age, gender and subject as predictors of academic attainment in higher education. *Studies in Higher Education, 28*(4), 475–93.

Ritter, D. (2004). Gender role orientation and performance on stereotypically feminine and masculine cognitive tasks. *Sex Roles, 50* (7–8), 583–91.

Robert, M., & Berthiaume, F. (2002). A chronometric analysis of water-level performance in boys and girls knowing about the involved physical invariance or not. *Annee Psychologique, 102*(4), 657–92.

Robert, M., & Chevrier, E. (2003). Does men's advantage in mental rotation persist when real three-dimensional objects are either felt or seen? *Memory & Cognition, 31*(7), 1136–45.

Robert, M., & Heroux, G. (2004). Visuo-spatial play experience: Forerunner of visuo-spatial achievement in preadolescent and adolescent boys and girls? *Infant and Child Development, 13*(1), 49–78.

Roberts, J. E., & Bell, M. A. (2000). Sex differences on a computerized mental rotation task disappear with computer familiarization. *Perceptual and Motor Skills, 91*(3), 1027–34.

Roberts, J. E., & Bell, M. A. (2003). Two- and three-dimensional mental rotation tasks lead to different parietal laterality for men and women. *International Journal of Psychophysiology, 50*(3), 235–46.

Robinson, S. J., & Manning, J. T. (2000). The ratio of 2nd to 4th digit length and male homosexuality. *Evolution and Human Behavior, 21*(5), 333–45.

Rode, C., Wagner, M., & Gunturkun, O. (1995). Menstrual-Cycle Affects Functional Cerebral Asymmetries. *Neuropsychologia, 33*(7), 855–65.

Rosenthal, R. (1991). *Meta-analytic procedures for social research*. London: Sage Publications.

Rouxel, G. (2000). Cognitive-affective determinants of performance in mathematics and verbal domains – Gender differences. *Learning and Individual Differences, 12*(3), 287–310.

Rushton, J. P., & Ankney, C. D. (1996). Brain size and cognitive ability: Correlations with age, sex, social class, and race. *Psychonomic Bulletin and Review, 3*(1), 21–36.

Rushton, J. P., & Ankney, C. D. (2000). Size matters: a review and new analyses of racial differences in cranial capacity and intelligence that refute Kamin and Omari. *Personality and Individual Differences., 29*(4), 591–620.

Rushton, J. P., & Rushton, E. W. (2003). Brain size, IQ, and racial-group differences: Evidence from musculoskeletal traits. *Intelligence, 31*(2), 139–55.

Rustemeyer, R. (1999). Teacher's expectations of gender-specific performance in mathematics and the corresponding (self-)evaluation of school- girls and boys. *Psychologie in Erziehung Und Unterricht, 46*(3), 187–200.

Rutter, M. (2002). Nature, nurture, and development: From evangelism through science toward policy and practice. *Child Development, 73*(1), 1–21.

Sadato, N., Ibanez, V., Deiber, M. P., & Hallett, M. (2000). Gender difference in premotor activity during active tactile discrimination. *Neuroimage, 11*(5), 532–40.

Salthouse, T. A. (2000). Steps towards the explanation of adult differences in cognition. In T. J. Perfect & E. A. Maylor (Eds), *Models of Cognitive Aging* (pp. 19–49). Oxford: Oxford University Press.

Salway, A. F. S., & Logie, R. H. (1995). Visuospatial Working-Memory, Movement Control and Executive Demands. *British Journal of Psychology, 86*(2), 253–69.

Sanders, G., & Waters, F. (2001). Fingerprint asymmetry predicts within sex differences in the performance of sexually dimorphic tasks. *Personality and Individual Differences, 31*(7), 1181–91.

Sandstrom, N. J., Kaufman, J., & Huettel, S. A. (1998). Males and females use different distal cues in a virtual environment navigation task. *Cognitive Brain Research, 6*(4), 351–60.

Saucier, D., Bowman, M., & Elias, L. (2003). Sex differences in the effect of articulatory or spatial dual- task interference during navigation. *Brain and Cognition, 53*(2), 346–50.

Saucier, D. M., & Elias, L. J. (2002). Laterality of phonological working memory: Dependence on type of stimulus, memory load, and sex. *Brain and Cognition, 48*(2–3), 526–31.

Saucier, D. M., McCreary, D. R., & Saxberg, J. K. J. (2004). Does gender role socialization mediate sex differences in mental rotations. *Personality and Individual Differences, 32*(6), 1101–11.

Scali, R. M., Brownlow, S., & Hicks, J. L. (2000). Gender differences in spatial task performance as a function of speed or accuracy orientation. *Sex Roles, 43*(5–6), 359–76.

Schirmer, A., & Kotz, S. A. (2003). ERP evidence for a sex-specific Stroop effect in emotional speech. *Journal of Cognitive Neuroscience, 15*(8), 1135–48.

Schmader, T. (2002). Gender identification moderates stereotype threat effects on women's math performance. *Journal of Experimental Social Psychology, 38*(2), 194–201.

Schmader, T., & Johns, M. (2003). Converging evidence that stereotype threat reduces working memory capacity. *Journal of Personality and Social Psychology, 85*(3), 440–52.

Schmader, T., Johns, M., & Barquissa, M. (2004). The Costs of Accepting Gender Differences: The Role of Stereotype Endorsement in Women's Experience in the Math Domain. *Sex Roles, 50*(11/12), 835–50.

Schroeder, D. H., & Salthouse, T. A. (2004). Age-related effects on cognition between 20 and 50 years of age. *Personality and Individual Differences, 36*(2), 393–404.

Scottish Qualification Authority (2001) Scottish Examination Board 'Annual Statistical Report 2001' (Data file). Available from Scottish Qualification Authority web site, retrieved June 30, 2006 from http://www.sqa.org.uk

Sekuler, R., & Sekuler, A. B. (2000). Vision and aging. In A. Kazdin (Ed.), *Encyclopedia of Psychology.* Oxford: Oxford University Press.

Shah, P., & Miyake, A. (1996). The Separability of Working Memory Resources for Spatial Thinking and Language Processing: An Individual Differences Approach. *Journal of Experimental Psychology: General, 125*(1), 4–27.

Sharps, M. J., Price, J. L., & Williams, J. K. (1994). Instructional and Stimulus Influences on Mental Image Rotation Performance. *Psychology of Women Quarterly, 18*(3), 413–25.

Sharps, M. J., Welton, A. L., & Price, J. L. (1993). Gender and Task in the Determination of Spatial Cognitive Performance. *Psychology of Women Quarterly, 17*(1), 71–83.

Shepard, R. N., & Metzler, J. (1971). Mental rotation of three-dimensional objects. *Science, 171*(3972), 701–3.

Sherry, D. F., & Hampson, E. (1997). Evolution and the hormonal control of sexually-dimorphic spatial abilities in humans. *Trends in Cognitive Sciences, 1*(2), 50–5.

Sherwin, B. B. (2005). Estrogen and memory in women: how can we reconcile the findings? *Hormones and Behavior, 47*(3), 371–5.

Signorella, M. L., & Jamison, W. (1986). Masculinity, Femininity, Androgyny, and Cognitive Performance: A Meta-Analysis. *Psychological Bulletin, 100*(2), 207–28.

Signorella, M. L., Jamison, W., & Krupa, M. H. (1989). Predicting Spatial Performance From Gender Stereotyping in Activity Preferences and in Self-Concept. *Developmental Psychology, 25*(1), 89–95.

Silverman, I., & Eals, M. (1992). Sex differences in spatial abilities: Evolutionary theory and data. In L. C. J.M. Barkow, & J.Tooby (Eds), *The adapted mind: Evolutionary psychology and the generation of culture.* (pp. 533–49). New York: Oxford University Press.

Simcock, G., & Hayne, H. (2003). Age-Related Changes in Verbal and Nonverbal Memory During Early Childhood. *Developmental Psychology, 39*(5), 805–14.

Siok, W. T., Jin, Z., Fletcher, P., & Tan, L. H. (2003). Distinct brain regions associated with syllable and phoneme. *Human Brain Mapping, 18*(3), 201–7.

Skelton, C. (2001). *Schooling The Boys: Masculinities and primary education.* Buckingham: Open University Press.

Sluming, V. A., & Manning, J. T. (2000). Second to fourth digit ratio in elite musicians: Evidence for musical ability as an honest signal of male fitness. *Evolution and Human Behavior, 21*(1), 1–9.

Smith, C. A., McCleary, C. A., Murdock, G. A., Wilshire, T. W., Buckwalter, D. K., Bretsky, P., *et al.* (1999). Lifelong estrogen exposure and cognitive performance in elderly women. *Brain and Cognition, 39*(3), 203–18.

Smith, E. S., & Jonides, J. (1997). Working Memory: A View from Neuroimaging. *Cognitive Psychology, 33*(1), 5–42.

Smith, J. L., & White, P. H. (2002). An examination of Implicitly Activated, Explicitly Activated, and Nullified Stereotypes on Mathematical Performance: It's Not Just a Woman's Issue. *Sex Roles, 47*(3/4), 179.

Solberg, J. L., & Brown, J. M. (2002). No sex differences in contrast sensitivity and reaction time to spatial frequency. *Perceptual and Motor Skills, 94*(3), 1053–55.

Spence, J. T. (1985). Gender identity and its implications for the concepts of masculinity and femininity. In *Psychology and Gender: Nebraska Symposium on Motivation* (Vol. 32, pp. 59–95). Lincoln: University of Nebraska Press.

Spence, J. T. (1991). Do the BSRI and PAQ Measure the Same or Different Concepts. *Psychology of Women Quarterly, 15*(1), 141–65.

Spence, J. T., & Helmreich, R. (1978). *Masculinity and Femininity: Their psychological Dimensions, Correlates and Antecedents.* Austin: University of Texas Press.

Spence, J. T., Helmreich, R., & Stapp, J. (1974). The Personal Attributes questionnaire: a measure of sex role stereotypes and masculinity-femininity. *JSAS Catalog of Selected Documents in Psychology, 4,* 43.

Spence, J. T., & Helmreich, R. L. (1981). Androgyny Versus Gender Schema – Comment. *Psychological Review, 88*(4), 365–8.

Spencer, S. J., Steele, C. M., & Quinn, D. M. (1999). Stereotype threat and women's math performance. *Journal of Experimental Social Psychology, 35*(1), 4–28.

Streri, A., & Gentaz, E. (2004). Cross-modal recognition of shape from hand to eyes and handedness in human newborns. *Neuropschologia, 42*(10), 1365–9.

Stroop, J. R. (1935). Studies in serial-verbal reaction. *Journal of Experimental Psychology, 18,* 643–62.

Stumpf, H., & Haldimann, M. (1997). Spatial ability and academic success of sixth grade students at international schools. *School Psychology International, 18*(3), 245–59.

Stuss, D. T., & Anderson, V. (2004). The frontal lobes and theory of mind: Developmental concepts from adult focal lesion research. *Brain and Cognition, 55*(1), 69–83.

Sugihara, Y., & Katsurada, E. (2000). Gender-role personality traits in Japanese culture. *Psychology of Women Quarterly, 24*(4), 309–18.

Susskind, J. E. (2003). Children's perception of gender-based illusory correlations: Enhancing preexisting relationships between gender and behavior. *Sex Roles, 48*(11–12), 483–94.

Swanson, H. L. (1999). Reading comprehension and working memory in learning-disabled readers: Is the phonological loop more important than the executive system? *Journal of Experimental Child Psychology, 72*(1), 1–31.

Swanson, H. L., & Berninger, V. W. (1996a). Individual differences in children's working memory and writing skill. *Journal of Experimental Child Psychology, 63*(2), 358–85.

Swanson, H. L., & Berninger, V. W. (1996b). Individual differences in children's writing: A function of working memory or reading or both processes? *Reading and Writing, 8*(4), 357–83.

Swim, J. K. (1994). Perceived Versus Metaanalytic Effect Sizes – an Assessment of the Accuracy of Gender Stereotypes. *Journal of Personality and Social Psychology, 66*(1), 21–36.

Tagaris, G. A., Kim, S. G., Strupp, J. P., Andersen, P., Ugurbil, K., & Georgopoulos, A. P. (1997). Mental rotation studied by functional magnetic resonance imaging at high field (4 Tesla): Performance and cortical activation. *Journal of Cognitive Neuroscience, 9*(4), 419–32.

Tagaris, G. A., Richter, W., Kim, S. G., Pellizzer, G., Andersen, P., Ugurbil, K., et al. (1998). Functional magnetic resonance imaging of mental rotation and memory scanning: A multidimensional scaling analysis of brain activation patterns. *Brain Research Reviews, 26*(2–3), 106–12.

Tenenbaum, H. R., & Leaper, C. (2003). Parent-child conversations about science: The socialization of gender inequities? *Developmental Psychology, 39*(1), 34–47.

Terlecki, M. S., & Newcombe, N. S. (2005). How important is the digital divide? The relation of computer and videogame usage to gender differences in mental rotation ability. *Sex Roles, 53*(5–6), 433–41.

Thomas, H., & Kail, R. (1991). Sex-Differences in Speed of Mental Rotation and the X-Linked Genetic Hypothesis. *Intelligence, 15*(1), 17–32.

Thomas, K. M., Drevets, W. C., Whalen, P. J., Eccard, C. H., Dahl, R. E., Ryan, N. D., et al. (2001). Amygdala response to facial expressions in children and adults. *Biological Psychiatry, 49*(4), 309–16.

Tinbergen, N. (1963). On aims and methods of ethology. *Zeitschrift fur Tierpsychologie, 20*, 410–33.

Tinklin, T. (2003). Gender differences and High Attainment. *British Educational Research Journal, 29*(3), 307–25.

Tottenham, L. S., Saucier, D., Elias, L., & Gutwin, C. (2003). Female advantage for spatial location memory in both static and dynamic environments. *Brain and Cognition, 53*(2), 381–3.

Tracy, D. M. (1987). Toys, Spatial Ability, and Science and Mathematics Achievement: Are They Related? *Sex Roles, 17*(3/4), 115–138.

Trbovich, P. L., & LeFevre, J. A. (2003). Phonological and visual working memory in mental addition. *Memory & Cognition, 31*(5), 738–45.

Tuholski, S. W., Engle, R. W., & Baylis, G. C. (2001). Individual differences in working memory capacity and enumeration. *Memory & Cognition, 29*(3), 484–92.

Tunnell, G. (1981). Sex-Role and Cognitive Schemata – Person Perception in Feminine and Androgynous Women. *Journal of Personality and Social Psychology, 40*(6), 1126–36.

Unger, R. K. (1979). Toward a Redefinition of Sex and Gender. *American Psychologist, 34*(11), 1085–94.

Universities and Colleges Admissions Services (2003) 'Annual data, 2003 entry' (Data file). Available from Universities and Colleges Admissions Services web site, retrieved June 25, 2006 from http://www.ucas.com

van der Sluis, S., de Jong, P. F., & van der Leij, A. (2004). Inhibition and shifting in children with learning deficits in arithmetic and reading. *Journal of Experimental Child Psychology, 87*(3), 239–66.

Van Houtte, M. (2004). Why boys achieve less at school than girls: the difference between boys' and girls' academic culture. *Educational Studies, 30*(2), 159–73.

Van Petten, C. (2004). Relationship between hippocampal volume and memory ability in healthy individuals across the lefespan: review and meta-analysis. *Neuropschologia, 42*(10), 1394–1413.

Van Petten, C., Plante, E., Davidson, P. S. R., Kuo, T. Y., Bajuscak, L., & Glisky, E. L. (2004). Memory and executive function in older adults: relationships with temporal and prefrontal gray matter volumes and white matter hyperintensities. *Neuropschologia, 42*(10), 1313–35.

Vandierendonck, A., Kemps, E., Fastame, M. C., & Szmalec, A. (2004). Working memory components of the Corsi blocks task. *British Journal of Psychology, 95*(1), 57–79.

Vasta, R., Rosenberg, D., Knott, J. A., & Gaze, C. E. (1997). Experience and the water-level task revisited: Does expertise exact a price? *Psychological Science, 8*(4), 336–9.

Vecchi, T., & Girelli, L. (1998). Gender differences in visuo-spatial processing: The importance of distinguishing between passive storage and active manipulation. *Acta Psychologica, 99*(1), 1–16.

Vecchi, T., & Richardson, J. T. E. (2001). Measures of visuospatial short-term memory: The Knox Cube Imitation Test and the Corsi Blocks Test compared. *Brain and Cognition, 46*(1–2), 291–5.

Velle, W. (1987). Sex differences in sensory functions. *Perspectives in Biology and Medicine, 30*(4), 490–522.

Venneri, A., Cornoldi, C., & Garuti, M. (2003). Arithmetic difficulties in children with Visuospatial Learning Disability (VLD). *Child Neuropsychology, 9*(3), 175–83.

Vingerhoets, G., Santens, P., Van Laere, K., Lahorte, P., Dierckx, R. A., & De Reuck, J. (2001). Regional brain activity during different paradigms of mental rotation in healthy volunteers: A positron emission tomography study. *Neuroimage, 13*(2), 381–91.

Voyer, D. (1996). On the magnitude of laterality effects and sex differences in functional brain asymmetries. *Laterality, 1*(1), 51–83.

Voyer, D. (1997). Scoring procedure, performance factors, and magnitude of sex differences in spatial performance. *American Journal of Psychology, 110*(2), 259–76.

Voyer, D., Nolan, C., & Voyer, S. (2000). The relation between experience and spatial performance in men and women. *Sex Roles, 43*(11–12), 891–915.

Voyer, D., Rodgers, M. A., & McCormick, P. A. (2004). Timing conditions and the magnitude of gender differences on the Mental Rotations Test. *Memory & Cognition, 32*(1), 72–82.

Voyer, D., Voyer, S., & Bryden, M. P. (1995). Magnitude of Sex-Differences in Spatial Abilities – a Metaanalysis and Consideration of Critical Variables. *Psychological Bulletin, 117*(2), 250–70.

Vygotsky, L. S. (1962). *Thought and Language.* Massachusetts: MIT Press.

Waiter, G. D., Williams, J. H. G., Murray, A. D., Gilchrist, A., Perrett, D. I., & Whiten, A. (2004). A voxel-based investigation of brain structure in male adolescents with autistic spectrum disorder. *Neuroimage, 22*(2), 619–25.

Want, S. C., Pascalis, O., Coleman, M., & Blades, M. (2003). Recognizing people from the inner or outer parts of their faces: Developmental data concerning 'unfamiliar' faces. *British Journal of Developmental Psychology, 21*(1), 125–35.

Warrick, P. D., & Naglieri, J. A. (1993). Gender Differences in Planning, Attention, Simultaneous, and Successive (Pass) Cognitive-Processes. *Journal of Educational Psychology, 85*(4), 693–701.

Watson, N. V., & Kimura, D. (1989). Right-Hand Superiority for Throwing but Not for Intercepting. *Neuropsychologia, 27*(11–12), 1399–414.

Watson, N. V., & Kimura, D. (1991). Nontrivial Sex-Differences in Throwing and Intercepting – Relation to Psychometrically-Defined Spatial Functions. *Personality and Individual Differences, 12*(5), 375–85.

Weber-Fox, C., Spencer, R., Cuadrado, E., & Smith, A. (2003). Development of neural processes mediating rhyme judgments: Phonological and orthographic interactions. *Developmental Psychobiology, 43*(2), 128–45.

Weiss, E., Siedentopf, C. M., Hofer, A., Deisenhammer, E. A., Hoptman, M. J., Kremser, C., *et al.* (2003). Sex differences in brain activation pattern during a visuospatial cognitive task: a functional magnetic resonance imaging study in healthy volunteers. *Neuroscience Letters, 344*(3), 169–72.

Weiss, E. M., Kemmler, G., Deisenhammer, E. A., Fleishhacker, W. W., & Delazer, M. (2003). Sex differences in cognitive functions. *Personality and Individual Differences, 35*(4), 863–75.

Wendt, P. E., & Risberg, J. (1994). Cortical Activation During Visual-Spatial Processing – Relation between Hemispheric-Asymmetry of Blood-Flow and Performance. *Brain and Cognition, 24*(1), 87–103.

Westergaard, G. C., Liv, C., Haynie, M. K., & Suomi, S. J. (2000). A comparative study of aimed throwing by monkeys and humans. *Neuropsychologia, 38*(11), 1511–17.

Wilson, C., & Francis, L. J. (1997). Beyond Gender Stereotyping: Examing the Validity Of The Bem Sex-Role Inventory among 16–19 Year Old Females in England. *Personality and Individual Differences, 23*(1), 9–13.

Witelson, S. F. (1991). Neural Sexual Mosaicsm: Sexual Differentiation of the Human Tempero-Parietal Region for Functional Asymmetry. *Psychoneuroendocrinology, 16*(1–3), 131–53.

Witelson, S. F., Kigar, D. L., & Harvey, T. (1999a). Albert Einstein's brain – Reply. *Lancet, 354*(9192), 1822ff.

Witelson, S. F., Kigar, D. L., & Harvey, T. (1999b). The exceptional brain of Albert Einstein. *Lancet, 353*(9170), 2149–53.

Witkin, H. A., Oltman, P. K., Raskin, E., & Karp, S. A. (1971). *A manual for the Embedded Figures Tests*. Palo Alto: Consulting Psychology Press, Inc.

Wood, E., Desmarais, S., & Gugula, S. (2002). The impact of Parenting experience on gender stereotyped toy play of children. *Sex Roles, 47*(1–2), 39–49.

Wright, D. B., & Sladden, B. (2003). An own gender bias and the importance of hair in face recognition. *Acta Psychologica, 114*(1), 101–14.

Wynn, T. G., Tierson, F. D., & Palmer, C. T. (1996). Evolution of Sex Differences in Spatial Cognition. *Yearbook of Physical Anthropology, 39*, 11–42.

Yang, M., & Woodhouse, G. (2001). Progress from GCSE to A and AS Level: institutional and gender differences, and trends over time. *British Educational Research Journal, 27*(3), 245–67.

Yonker, J. E., Eriksson, E., Nilsson, L. G., & Herlitz, A. (2003). Sex differences in episodic memory: Minimal influence of estradiol. *Brain and Cognition, 52*(2), 231–8.

Young, D. J., & Fraser, B. J. (1994). Gender Differences in Science Achievement – Do School Effects Make a Difference. *Journal of Research in Science Teaching, 31*(8), 857–71.

Zacks, J. A., Gilliam, F., & Ojemann, J. G. (2003). Selective disturbance of mental rotation by cortical stimulation. *Neuropsychologia, 41*(12), 1659–67.

Zhang, J., Norvilitis, J. M., & Jin, S. H. (2001). Measuring gender orientation with the Bem Sex Role Inventory in Chinese Culture. *Sex Roles, 44*(3–4), 237–51.

Zilles, K., Schleicher, A., Langermann, C., Amunts, K., Morosan, H., Palomero-Gallagher, N., *et al.* (1997). Quantitative Analysis of Sulci in the Human Cerebral cortex, Regional Heterogeneity, Gender Difference, Asymmetry, Intersubject Variability and Cortical Architecture. *Human Brain Mapping, 5*(218–21).

Zimmer, H. D., Speiser, H. R., & Seidler, B. (2003). Spatio-temporal working memory and short-term object location tasks use different memory mechanisms. *Acta Psychologica, 114*(1), 41–65.

Author Index

Subject Index